HANDBOOK OF
Cognitive Therapy
Techniques

By the Same Author

Cognitive-Behavior Therapy: A Restructuring Approach
(with T. Giles)

Straight Talk to Parents: Cognitive Restructuring for Families
(with I. Assafi and S. Chapman)

Talk Sense to Yourself: A Guide to Cognitive Restructuring Therapy
(with B. Casey)

A NORTON PROFESSIONAL BOOK

HANDBOOK OF
Cognitive Therapy
Techniques

Rian E. Mc Mullin, Ph.D.

W · W · NORTON & COMPANY · *NEW YORK · LONDON*

CREDITS

Hidden Christ, drawn by Dorothy Archbold and published in Porter, American Journal of Psychology, 1954, 67, 550–551.
Circle Limit IV, M. C. Escher. © M. C. Escher Heirs c/o Cordon Art-Baarn-Holland.

Man-Woman Figures, drawn by Gerald Fisher and published in *Ambiguity of form: Old and new*, Perception and Psychophysics, 1968, 4, 189–192.

Concealed Cow, drawn by Leo Portishman and published in Dallenbach, American Journal of Psychology, 1951, 64, 431–433.

Geometric Figures, drawn by Julius Sprinker, copied by Gottschaldt, K., and published in Ellis, W. *A source book of gestalt psychology*, New York: Harcourt, Brace, and Co., 1939, 109–122. All rights controlled by Routledge and Kegan Paul Ltd.

Published simultaneously in Canada by Penguin Books Canada Ltd., 2801 John Street, Markham, Ontario L3R 1B4.
Printed in the United States of America.

Library of Congress Cataloging-in-Publication Data

Mc Mullin, Rian E.
  Handbook of cognitive therapy techniques.

  "A Norton professional book"—P. facing t.p.
  Bibliography: p.
  Includes index.
  1. Cognitive therapy. I. Title. [DNLM: 1. Behavior
Therapy—methods—handbooks. 2. Cognition—handbooks.
WM 39 M478h]
RC489.C63M36 1986   616.89′142   86-12824

ISBN 0-393-70035-6

W. W. Norton & Company, Inc., 500 Fifth Avenue, New York, N. Y. 10110
W. W. Norton & Company Ltd., 37 Great Russell Street, London WC1B 3NU

    4 5 6 7 8 9 0

In honor of the life and work of my father,
Thomas Edward Mc Mullin (1898–1978).

Foreword

Rian Mc Mullin's *Handbook of Cognitive Therapy Techniques* is a unique book that in several significant respects goes beyond and effectively supplements the many other volumes on rational-emotive therapy (RET), cognitive-behavioral therapy (CBT), and Mc Mullin's cognitive restructuring therapy (CRT) that have been published since I wrote *Reason and Emotion in Psychotherapy* in 1962.

How so?

First, this handbook includes more specific methods of cognitive intervention than does any other work that I know about. It is unusually comprehensive and systematic regarding a great number of methods of disputing and replacing irrational beliefs that contribute to emotional and behavioral disturbance.

Second, it takes an integrative approach to therapy by including cognitive methods that are implicit in several experiential, behavioral, psychodynamic, and other schools. In fact, it nicely implements the point I made in "Cognitive Aspects of Abreactive Therapy" (*Voices*, 1974, *10*(1), 48–56. Reprinted: New York: Institute for Rational-Emotive Therapy) by creatively defining and emphasizing the cognitive elements in many "noncognitive" techniques and by showing how they can be specifically used in RET, CRT, and CBT. It is especially good to read, in this respect, Mc Mullin's section on cognitive focusing, which adapts Eugene Gendlin's focusing technique to cognitive restructuring therapy.

Third, this handbook is unusually clear and precise in explaining what each cognitive technique is, what basic principles underlie it, how it can be specifically used, what is a distinct example of its use, with what kind of clients it can best be employed, and where further information about it can be obtained.

In addition, Mc Mullin's *Handbook of Cognitive Therapy Techniques* is often original and brilliant and is well organized and thoroughgoing. Virtually all therapists who carefully read and think about its teachings will be able to derive considerable help from it. And so will their clients!

Albert Ellis, Ph.D.
Institute for Rational-Emotive Therapy
New York City

Contents

ix

Preface

Cognitive restructuring therapy (CRT) is one of the newest approaches to counseling being used by psychologists, psychiatric social workers, psychiatrists and other mental health professionals today. There is something about this modern, sophisticated, technological era in which we live that makes it hard to imagine that there are still frontiers to be explored, but in this case there *is* something new under the sun.

I got involved in this new therapy about 16 years ago, while working in the counseling center of a small, eastern, liberal arts college. Periodically, I would meet with other therapists from college counseling centers throughout the region in order to exchange ideas and discuss common problems in our respective case loads. It was during these deliberations that we became aware of a particular type of client that we were encountering in increasing numbers in all of our centers.

The typical profile for this client was that he or she was from a upper-middle-class background, well-educated, and a very high achiever. Nevertheless, the client suffered from what we then referred to as "free-floating anxiety." Victims of this condition would appear to be in every way "healthy" in their daily behaviors, except that at some point they would suddenly and inexplicably succumb to panic attacks. They would become visibly agitated, perspire excessively, and become inarticulate and nervous to the extreme, as though their very lives had suddenly been put in jeopardy by some unseen threat. They would immediately seek out a counselor for help, and, at least initially, the counselor would treat them as crisis cases. However, even after the crisis had passed, it was not at all clear what had provoked it, or why.

It was the inability to identify a particular stimulus for this recurring condition that led us to designate it as "free-floating," but the condition has since been labeled a panic disorder leading to agoraphobia.

We tried to treat this then-mysterious disorder with the techniques that we had learned in our graduate training. Some of us were behaviorists; others were psychodynamic, client-centered, humanistic or existential therapists. But we were all equally unsuccessful with these clients. As it became clear that some new treatment strategy would be necessary, we began to experiment with a combination of semantic and behavioral techniques. The rudiments of cognitive restructuring therapy evolved out of this experimentation.

But the real power of the concept derived from its applicability with a much broader range of clients. The fundamental postulates of cognitive restructuring therapy were clarified during those early years of trial and error, and crystallized with the help of Bill Casey while I was working with the typical clients seen in a large urban mental health center. They can best be described using the following ABC analogy à la Albert Ellis.

A	B	C
Trigger event, or stimulus	How the event is perceived, and evaluated, which is a function of client's core beliefs	Response, or how the client reacts to the stimulus

The stimulus-response dimensions of this analogy are familiar to every mental health professional, but in most therapeutic approaches the "B" is either neglected entirely or greatly underemphasized in importance. The key point here is that people often react more to what a stimulus prompts them to *think about* than to the stimulus itself. Hence, a man afraid of failing because he had been taught to overachieve may recoil at the prospect of any endeavor which is not guaranteed to succeed.

A harsh word from a spouse prompts different reactions in two different people, primarily because of their differing underlying belief structures, which color how they perceive the criticism. The person who is firmly convinced of his or her personal inferiority accepts the criticism as another confirmation of the validity of that belief, and might experience severe emotional discomforts in this and other aspects of life. The person who is confident may see the criticism as a reflection of the spouse's unhappiness and frustration.

In the case of the agoraphobic who suddenly finds herself crossing the expanse of an uncrowded college campus alone, or even staring out of her window across an open field, the trigger to her panic reaction is often a belief that she would lose control and go insane if she were left alone.

One of the clearest indications that the source of a client's discomfort is a core belief and not an environmental stimulus is a reaction disproportionate to what can reasonably be expected from the stimulus alone. For instance, the man who experiences a panic reaction when getting a promotion is clearly reacting to more than the promotion.

While we were developing cognitive restructing therapy, many other therapists and researchers in major universities in this country and others were coming to the same realizations that we had, with the result that other brands of cognitive therapy have evolved. There are some variations in different brands of cognitive therapy, reflecting different experiences and emphases of the various practitioners, such as Ellis (1985), Mahoney and Thoresen (1974), Meichenbaum (1977) and Beck (1976). Nevertheless, the essence of this approach is fundamentally the same wherever it is practiced, and consists of three basic steps:

1. Therapists begin by helping their clients to find the thoughts, beliefs or schemata that are causing their negative emotions and behaviors. This is not a casual process, for the cognitive therapist uses a systematic method to discover and list these damaging cognitions. Because it has previously been described in detail by others and in my former work (Mc Mullin and Giles, 1981), this handbook does not cover this procedure in depth.
2. Therapists then help their clients to analyze their thoughts and beliefs, in an effort to assess their validity and usefulness. Although in several other cognitive approaches the therapist makes judgments about the validity of these beliefs, in cognitive restructuring therapy the clients themselves are taught to do their own analysis and to draw their own logical conclusions. In this way, the client *owns* a final judgment that a particular thought is irrational, and is more likely to accept and abide by that judgment. This book describes some of the methods in Chapter 5; a more comprehensive description of the procedures is provided in previous works (see Casey and Mc Mullin, 1976; Mc Mullin and Casey, 1975; Mc Mullin and Giles, 1981; Mc Mullin et al. 1978.)
3. Finally, the therapist helps clients to change their irrational beliefs, to "shift" their perceptions from those that are unrealistic and harmful to those that are more rational and useful. This is the main emphasis of this particular handbook. From the client's point of view, this is the crucial step in counseling, because only by changing thoughts to the emotions elicited by those thoughts also change. Previous works have hinted at some methods for accomplishing these "shifts," but none has listed a comprehensive description of the techniques.

The techniques presented in this book are designed primarily for clinicians in connection with step #3. This is a "how-to" reference for therapists and counselors who render service in a variety of settings (public and private clinics, schools, hospitals, corporate health centers, etc.), and who want to improve their ability to more effectively treat clients who need to restructure their cognitions in order to function optimally. It is not a book on theory or research, although some theoretical postulates and experimental references are provided.

I take full responsibility for the techniques described in this book. They were developed over 20 years of therapy experience, and are based upon the research methodologies summarized in part in the appendix to this book. However, these techniques, like all psychotherapeutic procedures, have developed from the common pool of published journal reports and books and from discussions among colleagues. I have attempted to give credit for a technique, or an aspect of a technique, where I could identify its origins, but after years of practice it is not always possible to pinpoint an exact source in a free flow of creative thought. Hence, if I have slighted someone in my references, it is unintentional, and I apologize for the oversight.

The techniques are supported not only by many years of research and practice, but also by the generally accepted tenets of such noted semantic therapists as Albert Ellis and behaviorists such as B. F. Skinner. The astute researcher can consider these techniques as useful grist for his or her experimentation. Research concerning techniques which the clinician can use, and with a population that the therapist generally sees, is useful indeed. Such research might isolate the active elements in the techniques and remove the tangential aspects of the procedures, enabling us to improve the effectiveness of our clinical interventions.

Not all the techniques developed by all of the therapists who call themselves cognitive therapists are included here. Other therapists have written excellent books and research articles about their techniques, and there is no need to repeat them here. If the reader finds one of his or her favorite techniques not included, it is simply because we did not find it that useful, or arbitrarily used another approach, or simply were unaware of their preferred approach.

All the examples are from real clients seen in therapy during the last 16 years. The transcripts are accurate descriptions or summaries of the therapeutic sessions. Certain identifying information has been changed and spurious first names are used to protect client confidentially.

A conservative estimate would be that *millions* of individuals, from all walks of life, suffer in some magnitude from cognitive disorders. Often the client bears the brunt of this anguish alone, but it can reach such a level of severity that it has a serious impact on his or her family, friends, and associates, and it can be life-threatening, since its victims are sometimes driven to utter desperation and can do harm to themselves or others.

Cognitive therapy is a tool for modern times. It is not the only tool that you will ever need in promoting the mental and physical well-being of your clients, but it is an important addition to every professional's helping skills.

ACKNOWLEDGMENTS

There are many people I wish to thank for their contributions to this book. For editing of the manuscript I wish to thank William J. Hilton. For help in the early development of some techniques, I thank Bill Casey. I thank Stephen Chapman for his help in organizing the material, and Gail Brown for her proofreading of the final manuscript. For her guidance and encouragement during the two years of preparation of this material, I thank Janice Prince. And, last and most important, my thanks to my daughters, Michele and Linda, for their support and tolerance while I was writing this book.

HANDBOOK OF
Cognitive Therapy Techniques

1
Countering Techniques

A single theory underlies all cognitive restructuring techniques that employ countering. This theory states that *when a client argues against an irrational thought, and does so repeatedly, the irrational thought becomes progressively weaker.*

The theory does not assume that countering one thought with another can magically change an emotional-physiological state. Rather, it assumes that the counterthought might elicit affective conditions, which in turn reduce the negative emotion or remove the stimulus triggering this emotion.

The roots of countering are more in the realm of philosophy than psychology. Disputing, challenging and arguing all are ancient methods, at least as old as Plato's dialogues. Today these techniques are used by virtually everyone, in all kinds of situations—from barroom arguments about religion to lofty presidential debates.

The present chapter can be subdivided into two sections: *types of counters,* such as anti-catastrophic reappraisals, coping statements, rational beliefs, and nonpathological thinking; and *ways to counter,* such as guided countering, roleplaying, RET, diary research, and counterattacking.

COMPONENTS OF IDEAL COUNTERS

Principles

Counters are thoughts that go against an irrational thought. A counter can be one word ("Nonsense!") a phrase ("Not true!"), a sentence ("Nobody at this party cares if I'm not good at charades"), or an elegant philosophy ("My purpose in life is not to be as popular as I can, but to develop my own potentials, even if others disapprove.").

The ideal counter is a philosophy that pulls in a hierarchy of client values, perceptions, and experiences, drowning the thought in powerful currents flowing in the opposite direction. Short phrases or slogans also can be useful when they are tied to a counter philosophy—not because they have the strength to overcome the irrationality, but because they are quick reminders of the philosophy itself. The therapist should help the client form counters which are grounded in such a client philosophy.

Components

1. Help the client identify counters for each irrational thought. Make sure the counters oppose the irrational thought forcefully. For example, "It is impossible to succeed in everything you do" is a better counter than, "It is often quite difficult to succeed in everything you do."
2. Have the client develop as many counters as possible; 20 counters are twice as good as 10.
3. Make sure the counters are realistic and logical. Cognitive restructuring therapy does not subscribe to the power of positive thinking, in which people often tell themselves positive lies. Instead we stress the power of truthful, realistic thinking, asking clients to say true things to themselves, not just things that sound nice. Although it may feel good to think, for example, that "life gets easier with each passing day," this may not be true. Some days are still rough sailing.
4. Instruct the client to dispute irrational thoughts over and over again. In some cases, months or years are needed for this technique to be effective, and many clients balk at this investment of time. Sometimes, when

countering is first introduced, clients will object that they've already tried the technique, but to no avail. After exploring what they mean by countering, the therapist usually discovers that most clients mean arguing with themselves for an hour or two some Sunday afternoon. Usually they don't understand that it may take arguing an hour a day for a year or more to overcome a lifelong core belief.

5. Ensure that each counter is in the same mode as the irrational thought. Pair visual irrationalities with counter visualizations, linguistical mistakes with linguistical counters, angry beliefs with compassionate ones, passive thoughts with assertive ones, proprioceptive irrationalities with proprioceptive realisms, etc. For example, a client who fears tall buildings because she pictures them falling over will be better helped by a counter visualization of a building constructed on the rock of Gibraltar, rather than the linguistical argument that buildings don't fall over. When the counter is of the same modality and logical type as the irrational thought, it is more likely to have a disruptive impact on this thought.

Comment

In our years of clinical practice, we have explored virtually all methods of making counters effective—e.g., through the use of relaxation, counters with popular appeal, and insight into the origins of a counter. The above rules were the ones our experience proved to be most important.

———

PROBING FOR COUNTERS

Principles

Some years ago, we used to give clients a list of 20 or more standard counters for each type of irrational thought. Although some clients found these lists useful, overall they were only moderately effective. Often the clients would memorize the counters and use them when they got upset. But the counters lacked power, and clients would frequently end up repeating them mechanically, without any firm emotional conviction.

Far more effective was to have clients develop their own counters. Apparently, self-created counters worked because clients already had them in their repertoire of beliefs, so all they had to do was to form new associations with their irrational thoughts.

Helping clients develop their own counters requires more interpersonal skill than simply giving them arguments. The therapist must be more of a guide and less of an instructor, gradually probing into clients' thoughts until a core counter emerges. Probing questions encourage clients to think about the meaning of their statements until they recognize the illogic implicit in irrational thoughts. Since the therapist is unsure of the answers the client will give, the therapeutic sessions take on the atmosphere of a shared inquiry in which client and counselor mutually search for effective counters.

Method

1. Develop a list of the client's basic irrational thoughts.
2. Before each session, review the list for the core distortions in the client's thinking.
3. As you go over the list, write down all possible probes that occur to you. These questions should explore both logical and practical contradictions in the client's irrational beliefs.
4. Develop six types of questions.

   a. *Basic questions* isolate the client's overriding irrational thoughts. These core beliefs, the "metaphysical hard-core" (Guidano and Liotti, 1983), are present in a variety of roles the client may have played as a parent, employee, spouse, and friend, as well as throughout the client's history; the client may have thought this way as a child, adolescent, young adult, and mature adult. ("Why have you always thought you are you basically less worthwhile than others?")

   b. *Cluster questions* ask about the core belief directly. ("How are you basically less worthwhile as a father, employee, boss, husband, son?" and "Why did you feel inferior as a young boy? An adolescent? A young father?")

   c. *Association questions* connect two beliefs, situations or emotions. ("How is your fear of airplanes similar to your fear of parties?")

   d. *Historical questions* connect present and past beliefs. ("How is your fear of going crazy in a supermarket similar to your fear of being alone when you were young?")

   e. *Contradiction questions* point out the ways in which the client responds differently in similar situations. ("What did you say to yourself on Tuesday, when you wanted to take a ride in the mountains, that you didn't say to yourself on Saturday, when you refused to go?")

   f. *Follow-up questions* take the client's answers and reframe them into further probes to help the client continue his or her own analysis. ("You say you were too tired to go to the mountains on Saturday. What might you have been thinking on Saturday that could have made you feel tired?")

5. Probing sessions can be conducted in person and taped so that no counters are lost. Alternatively, the therapist may wish to write probing questions for the client to take home as homework. Clients should spend several weeks thinking about the answers.

6. Continue the above method of questioning until the client discovers a key answer which can be later used as a counter against the belief.

Example

This is an excerpt from a counseling session with Marianne, a 22-year-old woman who had seen me for 10 sessions because she was having trouble becoming independent from her parents. She had already learned the basic elements of cognitive therapy.

During the first part of the session she stated that she was having chest pains and at times had trouble breathing. After extensive medical examination with several doctors, she was told that her heart and lungs were perfect. However, she still feared she might have heart disease or lung cancer.

She first started to experience these fears about three months earlier at her job as a sales clerk in a small department store. She was tired much of the time and had to deal with a lot of obnoxious customers. To cope with the situation, she drank excessive amounts of coffee and smoked up to two packs of cigarettes during the morning. One day when she took her lunch break she suddenly started to feel dizzy and to have chest pains and difficulty breathing. She believed she was having a heart attack and went to the nearest emergency room. The doctors did a complete examination, but found nothing wrong.

Since that time, however, she had continued to have chest pains, and despite repeated examinations and doctors' reassurances, still feared getting a heart attack.

THERAPIST: You are familiar with my cognitive approach. I believe that the key to what you are feeling can be found in what you are saying to yourself and what you have been believing for the last three months. But today, instead of me just guessing about these things, I'd like to ask some other

questions. Your answers may give us the clues as to what may be causing your symptoms. OK?

CLIENT: Whatever you say.

THERAPIST: Do you think there is any connection between your belief that
you have a heart problem and the situation that happened at work?

CLIENT: Well, yes! That's when I first noticed the chest pains.

THERAPIST: How could this situation have given you a heart problem?

CLIENT: Well, I've been under a lot of strain recently and maybe the strain
that day was the last straw for my heart.

THERAPIST: If you do have a heart problem, why have scores of doctors been
unable to find anything wrong?

CLIENT: I don't know. Maybe the whole thing is just my imagination, but
I really feel the pain in my chest. I know I'm not just imagining it.

THERAPIST: I don't doubt for one moment that you really have a pain in your
chest. What we are trying to find out is why you have it. Can you think
of any other explanation of your chest pains besides having a heart attack?

CLIENT: No.

THERAPIST: Have you noticed any connection between your chest pains and
anxiety?

CLIENT: Well, yes. The more chest pains I have, the more anxious I am.

THERAPIST: How about the more anxious you are, the more chest pains you
have?

CLIENT: Are you saying the whole thing is caused by my anxiety?

THERAPIST: I am asking you, not telling you. Granted, I have some ideas
about what's going on with you, but I want you to find the fallacies in
your own thinking. What strikes me most about your situation is you say
your heart problem spontaneously developed three months ago. It was
at work and a very stressful day. You are only 22, have no history of heart
problems in your family, and scores of doctors haven't found a scintilla
of evidence that there is anything wrong with your heart. So how can we
determine whether your chest pains are due to a heart problem or
something else?

CLIENT: Well, I know I don't have any real evidence for believing it's my
heart. But every time I have the chest pain I get scared.

THERAPIST: Sure, but what are you saying to yourself every time you have
chest pains?

CLIENT: (Client pauses for 30 seconds.) That I am having a heart attack.
(Another pause) Yeah! I see what you mean. Maybe I'm scared because
I am telling myself it's my heart.

THERAPIST: Maybe. For the sake of argument let assume that's true; you are
scared because you have called one of the symptoms of your anxiety a

serious heart problem. But can you remember what you think right before you feel chest pains that might cause them? How could the same thought — that you have a heart problem — cause the chest pains which would in turn cause you to conclude you have a heart problem?

CLIENT: I don't understand.

THERAPIST: How could thinking you had a heart problem cause your chest pains?

CLIENT: (Client is silent for about a minute.) Oh yes, I see it now. It might make me pay close attention to anything going on in my chest, looking for any possible sign that something is wrong. I think I have probably done that. I worry so much about my heart that I get tense, the tension causes chest pains, and then I worry that my chest pain means I have a bad heart.

THERAPIST: Yes, I think that is a real possibility. And it would explain why you have been worried about your heart since that day in the store. But we still need an explanation as to why you got so tense that day. What happened that day in particular that caused your anxiety?

CLIENT: I don't know.

THERAPIST: Do you think there could be any relationship between your chest pains and having to put up with a score of obnoxious customers?

CLIENT: I don't know, I have had bad customers before.

THERAPIST: Can you pick a specific time?

CLIENT: Well . . . yes. Yesterday, for example.

THERAPIST: OK. Write down on a piece of paper what you thought, what you felt, and how you acted yesterday, and then on the other side what you felt, thought and acted that day three months ago.

THERAPIST: (Pause while she writes) OK. Now compare the two lists. What is different about the two situations?

CLIENT: (Pause) Well, three months ago I was tired, drank five cups of coffee and smoked two packs of cigarettes that morning. (Pause) Yeah! I get it. I really worked myself up with all that caffeine and nicotine.

THERAPIST: Looks that way. But we still don't know why you worked yourself up that way. But we do know you have the core belief that you are fragile and inadequate and still need your parents to protect you. Is there any possibility that something happened three months ago that activated that belief?

(The client thought for some time and we explored some related questions.)

CLIENT: I remember now. I was tired that day because the night before I had had another argument with my mom about moving out.

THERAPIST: How did that activate the core belief?

CLIENT: I got worried about being alone and unprotected.

THERAPIST: Good! That fear is the main reason you came to see me and we will continue to work on it. But in the meantime, let's look again at your more immediate fear of getting a heart attack or having lung cancer. You have come up with some other interpretations of this thinking. I think it would be useful to write them down, so that you can use the counters against the thought of having a heart problem.

With my help, the client discovered the following counters:

1. My chest pains mean that I'm tense, not that I'm having a heart attack.
2. I'm tense because three months ago I had an anxiety attack after drinking five cups of coffee and smoking two packs of cigarettes.
3. I misread the cause of my tension and mistakenly called it a heart problem.
4. Since that time I have been hypersensitive to my chest, causing me to feel more tense, causing my chest to hurt more, causing me to get even tenser, and so on, until I am constantly worried about my heart.
5. My tension, then and now, comes from the same golden oldie belief that I can't take care of myself without my parents.
6. When I get scared again, I'll work on my core fear and try not to sidetrack myself into thinking I have heart problems.

Comment

Probing questions should not be open-ended, but should progressively close in towards a core counter. These questions should be as specific as possible, guiding clients to uncover the meaning behind their emotions and behaviors. You can reflect your own opinions in the questions, as shown in the preceding example, but be sure to identify these inferences as opinions, not facts. The questions should primarily be interpretive, not just requests for factual information. They should be so directed that they challenge clients' self-schema, requiring them to reframe and re-assimilate contradictory data.

Further Information

Specifically prepared probes are used in many therapeutic orientations. See Binder, Binder, and Rimland (1976). Therapeutic probes and other counselor leads are discussed by Miller (1962). The shared method of inquiry is used by many disciplines besides psychology. See Dennis and Moldof (1977, 1978) for how it is used to analyze stories and novels.

ALTERNATIVE INTERPRETATION

Principles

The client's first interpretation of an event is usually not the best. Many clients impulsively intuit the meaning of a given situation, then stick to this initial interpretation, assuming it must be correct. Later judgments, often more rational, only rarely seem to implant themselves as solidly as the first. Thus, some people continue to believe, for example, that anxiety causes psychosis, or that tension in the pectoral muscles indicates a heart attack, simply because they had these thoughts first. Once implanted, these ideas can be very difficult to change.

Unfortunately, the earliest interpretation of a scene is often the worst, and clients with misguided ideas need to be taught this concept. They must learn to suspend their initial judgment until they can obtain more information and perceive situations more objectively.

Method

1. Have the client keep a written record of the worst emotions experienced during a one-week period, noting, in a sentence or two, the activating event (situation), and the first interpretation of this event (belief).
2. For the next week, have the client continue with the same exercise, finding at least four more interpretations for each event. Each interpretation should be different from the first, but equally plausible.
3. At the next session, help the client decide which of the four interpretations has the most evidence objectively supporting it. Be sure to use logic rather than subjective impressions.
4. Instruct the client to continue to find alternative interpretations, put first judgment in abeyance, and make a decision about the correct belief only when time and distance lend the necessary objectivity. Continue this procedure for at least a month, until the client can do it automatically.

Example

Situation 1

A single 25-year-old woman just broke up with her boyfriend.

First Interpretation

There is something wrong with me. I am inadequate, and I'll probably never develop a lasting relationship with a man.

Alternative Interpretations

1. I haven't met the right man.
2. I don't want to give up my freedom right now.
3. My boyfriend and I didn't have the right chemistry together.
4. My boyfriend was afraid to commit to me or to the relationship.

Situation 2

After a year of taking tranquilizers the client discontinues them. The next day he feels a little anxious.

First Interpretation

See, I knew it. I needed the pills to keep me from getting anxious; without them I'll crack up.

Alternative Interpretations

1. I'm anxious because I don't have my crutch anymore. My rabbit's foot has been taken away.
2. I was anxious before I stopped taking the pills, so something else is probably causing the tension.
3. I have been anxious a thousand times with or without the pills. It only lasts for an hour or so, then goes away. So will this.
4. Not having the chemicals in my body makes me feel different—not worse, not better, but different. I have been calling this different feeling "anxiety," because I interpret all different feelings as something scary, but I could just as well call this feeling "unfamiliar." It is not really dangerous.

Situation 3
A client's husband said she had fat legs.

First Interpretation
My legs are grotesque. I'm deformed. I feel like I shouldn't wear shorts or pants because everyone will see them. Nature gave me a raw deal.

Alternative Interpretations

1. He's an idiot!
2. He was angry at me for not having dinner ready. He knows I'm sensitive about my weight and was trying to hurt me back.
3. He is going through his midlife crisis and wants me to look like an 18-year-old, so he'll feel younger.
4. He has fat legs and he's projecting.

———

Situation 4
The client developed agoraphobia six years ago. She still has panic attacks despite four months of counseling with two therapists.

First Interpretation
I'm crazy! I'll always be afraid to go out, and if two professional therapists can't help me, no one can.

Alternative Interpretations

1. My therapists were no good.
2. The techniques they used weren't appropriate for my problem.
3. I didn't give the therapy enough time.
4. It takes more than four months to get over agoraphobia.
5. I didn't work at it.

———

Situation 5
As a client sat in the cafeteria at work, she noticed two colleagues talking in whispers, occasionally glancing in her direction.

First Interpretation

They're saying rotten things about me. Why am I so unpopular? Nobody ever likes me.

Alternative Interpretations

1. They aren't talking about me at all.
2. They're discussing something personal and are afraid people will overhear.
3. They're talking about sex.
4. They're planning a surprise party for me.

Comment

For this technique to be effective, the accuracy of the alternative interpretations is not crucial. What is essential is for the client to realize that alternative interpretations are possible, and that first explanations are not magically true simply because they're first. Having alternative ways of analyzing events helps clients weaken the certainty of the first interpretation, making it likely they will consider others and ultimately arrive at one less damaging to their self-esteem.

Further Information

Numerous studies in social psychology support the importance of primacy of subjects' beliefs. See Fishbein and Ajzen (1975), Hovland and Janis (1959), Miller and Campbell (1959), and Petty and Cacioppo (1981).

ANTI-CATASTROPHIC REAPPRAISALS

Principles

Most people are consistent in their thinking. Hence, in different situations and at different times they distort reality in the same way. The most common type of distortion is "castastrophizing," or the extreme exaggeration of impending doom. Many clients observe a minor threat in the environment and believe the worst conceivable danger is imminent. After years of practice, their exaggerations become habitual, causing chronic anxiety and a constant dread of the environment.

What these clients fail to recognize is that the word catastrophe implies a *great* calamity, misfortune, or disaster. Although clients may accurately perceive some danger in a given situation, in catastrophizing they grossly exaggerate the degree of danger, along with its potential for damage. Their brains expand pain into torture, embarrassment into disgrace, an unpleasant experience into an intolerable one.

The best counters to catastrophic beliefs are narrow, in that they specifically attack active elements in the irrational thought, which usually amounts to a gross overgeneralization. The therapist can attack this element by telling the client to think of the best conceivable outcome, overstating the best outcome instead of the worst. This new interpretation overcorrects the negative emotion caused by the catastrophizing, improving the probability that the final affective response will approximate reality.

Method

1. List the situations the client catastrophizes.
2. Record the damage the client anticipates for each situation.
3. On a continuum from 1 to 10, record the extent of the anticipated damage.
4. After discussing counter-catastrophizing with clients, record the best possible thing that could happen in each of the situations. Again, mark the extent of the damage for this outcome.
5. Have the client decide, based on past experience, whether the catastrophic or best possible outcome is most likely to occur.
6. Where appropriate, have the client use the continuum to predict danger in upcoming situations which are feared. After the event actually occurs, have the client check the scale to see whether the anticipated level of damage occurred.
7. Clients should practice counter-catastrophizing regularly until they can more realistically assess anticipated damage.

Example

Dean, a top businessman, was referred to me by his private physician. He was unusually successful, having presented his expert advice to major corporations worldwide for many years. Despite this, he suffered from chronic anxiety and had panic attacks before each presentation. A year and a half of chlordiazepoxide treatment brought no reduction in his anxiety.

As is typical in this type of anxiety, the client thought the same core belief before each presentation. He imagined that his head would start shaking because he was nervous, whereupon all the corporate executives would discover he wasn't the cool, calm professional he pretended to be. He imagined this tick would destroy his facade, and everyone in the audience would see his "cowardice."

This man's deeply rooted core belief was that he was basically inferior and needed to hide behind a competent facade. Letting others see behind the facade would mean complete and instantaneous rejection. The damage would be beyond repair. It would be the worst possible thing that could ever happen to him.

The client's core attitude can be broken down into specific sub-beliefs, as follows:

1. Everyone in the audience would ignore what he was saying the minute they saw his head shake.
2. They would know he was a total fake and would never believe in him again.
3. Because they would see him as a sissy and not a real man, they would never associate with him again.
4. Since these top level executives wouldn't want to be around such a wimp, he would never be able to give his lectures again, he would lose all his male friends, women would hate his weakness, and he would be poor, alone, and destitute.

For each one of these thoughts, we made a catastrophe scale, as shown below. The "X" on each scale indicates the extent of the predicted damage, were the event to occur.

How catastrophic would it be if . . .

everyone saw my tick?

```
                                        X
    1    2    3    4    5    6    7    8    9    10
```

the audience concentrated on it?

```
                                   X
    1    2    3    4    5    6    7    8    9    10
```

the audience thought I was a total fake?

									X
1	2	3	4	5	6	7	8	9	10

the audience knew I was a sissy?

								X	
1	2	3	4	5	6	7	8	9	10

I lost all my income, and all my male and female friends?

						X			
1	2	3	4	5	6	7	8	9	10

Next we listed the best possible things that could happen and marked the anticipated damage from these outcomes on the same scale. The outcomes were that few people would see his tick, and those who did wouldn't concentrate on it. No one would think he was a fake or sissy, and he would lose no income or friends. The client rated all of these outcomes around a zero damage level.

By comparing the ratings for the worst and best possible outcomes, it became apparent that the client was catastrophizing by a factor of eight.

We then made a whole series of other continua taken from past predictions. By comparing what had happened in prior situations to what the client had predicted would happen, we found that very little damage had actually occurred and that the best possible outcomes were consistently closer to reality than the worst. In fact, the client could not think of a single time, out of hundreds of situations, when anything remotely similar to his worst predictions had eventuated.

For the next six weeks, this man predicted the best and worst possible outcome of each presentation he was about to make, along with the estimated damage. The next day he went back to his scale and determined which prediction was most accurate. Without exception, the "best possible outcome" occurred.

Comment

The use of the continuum isn't essential to this method, but it generally helps clarify the client's level of catastrophizing.

The client often asks, "What if the worst thing imaginable *does* happen, even though it's highly unlikely? Shouldn't I worry about that?" In this situation, you can point out to clients that if they feared all low probability events, they would have to hide in caves to avoid meteors, avoid crossing streets to keep from getting hit by trucks, and stop eating food to keep from being poisoned. Even though these things can and do happen, we can still be happy. Our job is to avoid probable dangers, not every conceivable catastrophe.

Further Information

Catastrophic thinking is discussed in detail by the rational emotive therapists. See Ellis (1962, 1973), Ellis and Grieger (1977), and Maultsby (1984).

COPING STATEMENTS

Principles

Many clients expect to fail miserably. Bandura (1977b) and others have described this expectation as "low self-efficacy," the belief that one cannot execute the behaviors required to produce positive outcomes. Clients exhibiting this expectation consistently underestimate their ability to cope with various situations. They believe they will fail at their jobs, be rejected by their lovers, or flunk out of school. After a while these expectations tend to become self-fulfilling. However, coping statements can avert this pattern, helping improve client self-efficacy.

Coping may be distinguished from mastery: In mastery, the clients imagine doing a task perfectly; in coping, they anticipate various problems with the task, but also picture dealing with these problems. Coping statements are superior to mastery imagery because they sensitize the clients to possible mistakes and prepare them to recover from errors they may make in real situations.

Method

1. Create a hierarchy of situations in which the client is depressed or anxious.
2. With the client's help, prepare a self-talk dialogue to be used during the stressful situation. The dialogue should realistically anticipate mistakes,

errors, and negative emotions, and include step-by-step instructions on how to overcome these problems. It should cover the time before, during, and after the anxious situation.

3. Rehearse the dialogue out loud with the client for each item on the hierarchy. For best results, use a modeling procedure (Meichenbaum, 1977), in which the therapist says the dialogue and the client first repeats it and then imagines it. Monitor the client throughout the rehearsal and correct any mistakes.

4. Encourage clients to practice their coping techniques, using whatever method seems most effective. For instance, some clients find it beneficial to listen passively to a cassette tape of the therapist reading the dialogues. Others prefer a tape that describes each situation on the hierarchy in detail, allowing them to practice the dialogues covertly. Still others carry the dialogues on index cards and read them *in vivo*. In most cases, clients need to practice their scripts for at least six weeks.

Example

Paula, who was referred to me by another psychologist, had been agoraphobic for two years. One of the highest fears on her hierarchy was shopping alone in a large supermarket; whenever she tried to shop, her anxiety would overwhelm her and she would leave. By the time I first saw her, she hadn't been to a store for a year and a half.

We practiced the following dialogue for several sessions. Initially, we recorded it and she listened to the recording three times a week for five weeks. She then practiced the script *in vivo* six times, during actual agoraphobic situations. This and other cognitive techniques finally eliminated her phobia.

Coping Dialogue

"This morning I'm going to the supermarket. I'll probably be tense in the beginning, but only because I have stayed away from stores for some time—not because stores are really something to fear. Stores are NOT dangerous. Even little children, and very old people go to grocery stores. If stores were dangerous, they'd have a big warning sign in the front which said 'WARNING, THE SURGEON GENERAL HAS DETERMINED THAT SUPERMARKETS ARE DANGEROUS TO YOUR HEALTH.'"

(Client imagines entering store.) "Here I am, looking around! It's just like every other store. There's lots of produce, and canned goods and meats. No one in the history of the world has ever been attacked by a can of peas. Still, I feel a little nervous inside. Since stores don't have the power to create fear, it must be something I am telling myself. Let's see what superstitious notion I'm buying into. Ah, yes! It's that same old idiotic thought—that I'm going to lose control and embarrass myself in front of all these people. Golden oldie bullshit! I have been saying that nonsense to myself for two years, I have never lost control and I never will. It's just a stupid game I play with myself, like pretending if I put my finger in my ear, my nose will fall off. These people have more things to do in this store than to watch me to see if I show the tiniest sign of tension. They are more interested in finding a ripe tomato. Besides, I don't have to control this tension. All I have to do is buy my can of succotash and leave—big deal! It doesn't matter how tense I get. My job isn't to shop without tension; it's only to shop. And I'm going to shop no matter how I feel. Even if I have to crawl through the checkout line on my hands and knees, I'm going to stay. My life has been ruled by a silly superstition long enough."

(Client completes shopping, leaves store.) "There, I did it! That's the only thing that counts. What I do in life is far more important than how I feel when doing it. I'll keep doing this until I get rid of my superstitions and the fear they produce."

Comment

While most clients benefit a great deal from practicing coping statements through imagery, these statements ultimately must be practiced *in vivo*. Otherwise, the client can sabotage the technique, saying, for example, "It's very nice to think this way, but I still haven't gone to the store."

We don't believe, however, that you should pressure clients to practice their scripts in the environment until they have rehearsed them extensively and covertly. To do so would only create more anxiety, increasing the probability of failure.

Further Information

For more information on coping statements see Cautela (1971b), Goldfried (1971), and Suinn and Richardson (1971). A more thorough investigation of the theory behind this technique is provided by Lazarus et al. (1980), Mahoney & Thoresen (1974) and Meichenbaum (1975, 1977).

There is also an extensive body of literature on self-efficacy. See Bandura (1977a, 1977b, 1978, and 1982), Bandura and Schunk (1981), Bandura et al. (1980), and Teasdale (1978).

More information about coping vs. mastery imagery can be found in Mahoney and Arnkoff (1978), Richardson (1969), and Singer (1974).

COUNTERATTACKING

Principles

The intensity of emotion the client invests in a counterattack can be the key to its success. Without question, disputing is most effective when the client attacks a thought with emotion, in a high state of assertive arousal. The expression of emotion virtually eliminates the repetitious, mechanical parroting which so often renders counters ineffectual.

Often it is helpful, before the counterattack is initiated, to encourage the client to be angry. After all, irrational beliefs caused all the client's emotional pain—so why should they be treated tenderly? Frequently only an aggressive attack can elicit a strong enough emotional level to overturn an irrational thought.

An analogy explains why emotions are important to changing beliefs. I call it the "Melted Wax Theory" and tell clients:

> Consider, for a moment, that thoughts are like wax impressions in our brains. They are often formed when we have a strong emotion like fear or anger. These emotions act on our thoughts like heat, causing them to liquefy and reform into new beliefs.
>
> When the heat of high emotional arousal has dissipated, the thought is solidified. To change the belief one has to either chip away at the wax impression, which takes a long time, or reheat the wax so the thought can be remolded. If a person gets angry and assertive with irrational thoughts, it is like heating them up so that they can be poured into a new mold.

Method

1. Develop a list of counters.
2. Help the client counter forcefully. The client should practice the counterattack technique in front of you, modeling your behavior until a comparable level of intensity is achieved. Gradually shape the client's responses towards a dramatic attack with intensity and energy.
3. The therapist can strengthen the counterattack by encouraging clients to

use physical exertion, progressively contracting their muscles. Initially, clients counterattack while their muscles are limp, then slightly tensed, then strongly contracted. Frequently the client's emotional arousal parallels physical arousal.

4. Clients also strengthen their counterattacks through voice modulation, gradually sharpening their voices and increasing the volume. The counterstatement can at first be said nasally and softly, then normally through the mouth, then moderately loud while filling the upper part of the lungs, then loudly, with the lungs filled with air. As with physical exertion, the voice becomes an analogy for the client's level of anger.

Example 1

Phillip, a young man, entered counseling after attending an assertiveness training class I had given. Despite being an accomplished football player, sturdy and 6'5", he was extremely shy with women. The assertiveness had helped him generally, but he still couldn't ask a woman for a date. However, he had no difficulty being assertive with men and handled male confrontation appropriately. After a complete cognitive analysis, we isolated one central belief: He thought women were weak, fragile creatures, who must be protected by males. He viewed himself as a complete lummox, a Baby Huey who could step on the sensitive toes of these delicate people.

The client's personal history indicated that his father had taught him this belief. Apparently, the father feared that his son's large size would make him too aggressive—a problem the father had had when growing up. As a result, he taught his son to be extremely careful not to hurt women. The lesson took such good hold that the client hadn't dated for two years and was so nervous around women that he said practically nothing in their presence, for fear of bruising their delicate feelings. Women, of course, rejected him out of hand as an extremely dumb, if attractive, jock.

As we went through the usual cognitive preliminaries, the client developed a long and accurate list of counterarguments against his core thought. However, when he tried to use them he would counter so passively that his arguments were ineffective. It was at this point that we decided to use counterattacking.

I introduced the technique as follows:

> I am your boxing coach but I can't get into the ring with you because the ring is inside your head. Your present opponent is the core belief that women are extremely fragile. This belief has been beating you up for years, making you inordinately shy around women and preventing

you from developing normal relationships. Now the trouble is that even though you know the belief is false, you haven't been convincing yourself. You haven't been fighting. On those rare occasions when you do fight, you do it so weakly that the belief easily overpowers you. It keeps giving you a black eye, and you hardly fight back at all.

You must start defending yourself whenever this belief enters your head. You can't appease it. It's like dealing with any other bully: the more you give in, the more—and more ferociously—it comes back to beat on you. You must start attacking the belief as hard as you can.

Initially the thought is stronger than you and will win the fight. But if you persist, you will gradually become stronger and stronger as it becomes weaker. After a while you will begin to win some of the time, then most of the time, until finally it won't come back anymore. Let's get started with your first boxing lesson.

Example 2

The following example demonstrates a method you can use to introduce physical exertion into a client's counterattack.

I would like you to do something that will help you understand how to counter with emotional energy. Let's pick one of your thoughts that has caused you some problems. You have said that you are afraid that if you get anxious you will faint. Now what would be a good counter for that thought? (In this case, the client chose the counter, "I never have fainted from anxiety.") Very good, a good counter. But it's not enough simply to have a good counter. How you say it is also very important.

Now just for practice I would like you to say the counter, but say it through your nose. I know it seems silly and feels a little bit embarrassing, but please go ahead, say your counter nasally. (Pause.) Very good. Now I would like you to say the same counter, but this time say it with your mouth. (Pause.) Now fill the upper part of your lungs and say it with more force. (Pause.) That's fine. Now this time make it as powerful as you can. Fill all your lungs with air, make your body rigid, and say the counter with as much force as you can. (Pause.)

Excellent! That last one was a counter. All the others were not. The words were right, but there was no force behind them. In the future when I speak of countering, I mean the last type. Whenever you counter, do it as hard as you can. ·

Comment

This technique is useful in helping passive clients, and is the treatment of choice for many depressed patients. However, it must be used carefully, as it may backfire with especially anxious clients. Since the technique accelerates clients' emotional level, it sometimes causes the anxious client to become even more fearful. For this client a soft, relaxed countering may be more appropriate.

It is crucial, too, that clients attack their beliefs, not themselves. Tell your clients:

> It can be helpful if you call your irrational thoughts silly, stupid, or ridiculous, but don't say you are stupid for believing them. You believe them because you have been taught them; anyone with your background and experiences would believe as you do.

Although most countering techniques take a long time to weaken irrational beliefs, counterattacking occasionally produces dramatic reversals. I have seen several clients quickly remove beliefs they held for years, because they got really angry at these beliefs.

One client, for example, kept quitting her job whenever she had an anxiety attack. This woman had been through years and years of long-term therapy, but nothing seemed to help—until she got thoroughly fed up with her situation. One afternoon, after she quit a job, her third that year, something unusual happened; she changed what she said to herself. Here's how she described her self-talk:

> I'm really getting tired of this. Here I am again in the same place for the same reason. I'm upset because I'm afraid I'll go crazy and I think quitting work will safeguard my sanity. It's really stupid! I'm messing up my life, spending a lot of money, worrying people who care about me. It would probably be better if I just went crazy. Then I could spend my whole life running away like a chicken with it's head cut off. This stinks! If I get scared again, I get scared. So what, big deal! I'm tired of running. I won't run anymore! If I go insane, the hell with it!

The next week she got another job—the best she could find. That was 15 years ago. She never left because of anxiety again.

Further Information

The connection between emotions and beliefs is researched and discussed by Arnold (1960) and Plutchik (1980) and in the classic studies by Schachter (1966) and Schachter and Singer (1962).

———

LABEL SHIFTING

Principles

For some people, a single misused label can create intense anxiety. These labels, or "intervening cognitions," include not only thoughts, nonverbalized sentences, and philosophical perspectives, but also single words and phrases. Each of these vehicles acts as a symbol that collects emotional responses through operant, classical, or cognitive conditioning. Once the symbol and affective response have been paired, the symbol has the capacity to elicit the emotion directly.

Symbols are by definition arbitrary, indicating only a consensus about what something means; usually one symbol can substitute for another quite easily. The exception to this generalization is found in words. Though words may easily enough be substituted by other words, different words often carry totally divergent emotional connotations. Thus, as the astute therapist knows, many clients consistently choose words with negative connotations when they could just as well select neutral or positive labels.

Label shifting helps clients identify their negative labels and shift them to more objective, positive, emotional associations. They learn in this process that the only difference between one word and another is the emotional valence.

Method

1. Make a list of the specific events or situations (referents) the client associates with negative words. For instance, what referents does the client visualize when using the words "inferior," "sick," and "weak"?

2. Describe these referents in objective, nonevaluative terms. What would a motion picture camera record of the event or situation? What would an objective third party overhear?
3. List the major negative labels the client uses to describe the situations.
4. Help the client list the neutral and positive labels that could be used to interpret the referents. Explain how these new labels are just as valid as previous labels, but elicit more positive emotions.
5. Have the client practice using new labels every day, recording the situation, finding the negative label for it, and substituting a more positive word.

Example

A person who . . .	Could be called . . .	Or could be called . . .
changes one's mind a lot	wishy-washy	flexible
expresses one's opinion	egotistical	honest, assertive
is emotionally sensitive	sick, fragile	alive, caring, open
is selective in choosing a mate	afraid to commit	patient, careful, discriminating
gets depressed sometimes	neurotic	normal human being
isn't good at a game	stupid, inferior	hasn't practiced
isn't orderly	sloppy, piggish	spontaneous, carefree
pleases others	social phobic	likable
believes what others say	gullible	trusting
loves another strongly	dependent	loving
gets anxious	weak, cowardly	learned to, was taught
is nontraditional	malcontent, heretical, immoral	independent, uninhibited, free
is helped by another	manipulated	cared for
is not working hard on a task	lazy	relaxed
is sure of something	conceited	self-confident
stands up for personal rights	argumentative	gutsy

thinks before making decision	indecisive	careful
takes risks	harebrained	brave
sticks to projects	compulsive	determined
gets excited	hysterical	exuberant

Comment

Some clients may argue that a negative word is more logically correct than a positive word; for example, one client suggested that wishy-washy people change their minds far more than flexible people; therefore, wishy-washy is a more accurate descriptor. Although there may be some concrete differences among synonyms, many of the differences are purely reflective of our value systems. We call people wishy-washy only because we think they change their minds too much, or more than we think they should—not because there is some objective standard of how much people are permitted to switch their opinions and still be called flexible.

Label switching is rarely used alone. Most frequently it is an adjunct to other cognitive restructuring approaches.

Further Information

The "Rumplestiltskin effect" describes the dramatic changes that can take place by switching the words clients use to describe their problems. See Torrey (1972).

———

NONPATHOLOGICAL THINKING

Principles

Cognitive restructuring therapy, like cognitive behavioral therapy, bases its techniques on the experiments and assumptions of learning theory. In all its many variations, learning theory avoids the use of the medical model to describe clients' problems. Many clients, however, subscribe wholeheartedly to this model.

These clients view strong emotions as signs of an unpleasant, if nebulous, condition they call "sick." Because they use this word, they are more likely to display the emotions and behaviors which the "sick" label elicits. Initially, they simply think they are emotionally crippled, unbalanced, diseased, or in some way deranged for feeling strong emotions. Then they start to play the part, acting out the role of the patient with all the accompanying behavioral and cognitive manifestations, such as passivity, helplessness, and expecting the doctor to cure them.

Because of the damaging effects of the "sick" concept, this thought should be one of the first the client attacks.

Method

1. Develop a master list of core beliefs connected to the client's negative emotions.
2. Go over each belief with the client and identify any sign that the client is implying a psychological sickness.
3. Explain in detail the inappropriateness of the disease label and substitute components of the learning theory model for each belief.
4. Throughout all your therapy sessions, help the client change any thought or word that implies sickness. Listen for words like "deranged," "mentally unsound," "crazy," "unbalanced," "falling to pieces," "nervous breakdown," "freaking out," "ill," "sick," "unhealthy," "disturbed," etc.
5. Substitute a social learning model for a medical model. Treat clients as students under your tutelage, not as patients under your care. Expect clients to do the homework you assign, to study your principles, and to challenge you if they disagree. Make it clear that you consider counseling to be a joint project, 50/50. You instruct; they study.

Before clients enter into therapy with me, I give them a sheet which describes the kind of therapy I do, what they can expect from me and what I expect from them. Here are some excerpts:

My Services

As you know, I practice a particular type of counseling. You and I must decide whether my therapy is the best type for you. If not, I will help you get the right kind. Remember, a recent survey found that there are over 250 different types of therapy (Corsini, 1981).

My Philosophy

I don't view our relationship as doctor-patient, friend-confidant, leader-follower, or guru-novitiate; I view it as teacher-student. It is my job to give you, as clearly as I can, the tools to solve your own problems. It is your job to use the tools. We are equal partners in your growth.

Openness

Since we are partners in your growth, you have a right to know what I am doing, why I am doing it, how long it will take and what I think are the causes and solutions to your problems. I am not a witch doctor who uses secret, mystical methods to cure people. I want you to know what I think, so always feel free to ask me about what I am doing, and why.

General

I will do everything I can to help you by using standard techniques and developing new ones if the old ones haven't worked. If, despite our mutual effort, the counseling doesn't help you, I'll do my best to refer you to someone else who can help you more.

Example

For two years, Beth had severe generalized anxiety attacks, during which she was completely immobilized. By the time she came to me for treatment she had been in analysis for six years, three times per week. Originally she had entered analysis to work out her grief and anger over the early loss of her parents, after which she had been sent, during adolescence, to live with her aunt and uncle, whom she described as rigid and rejecting. She believed analysis had helped her cope with grief and anger, and was puzzled when, after four years of therapy, her anxiety attacks began. During her last two years of analysis, they had become progressively worse.

The first step in this client's therapy was to persuade her that a more directive, cognitive approach to therapy would reduce her anxiety, though the style would differ significantly from the analysis she had undergone. Secondly, we explored the cognitive triggers for her anxiety, which seemed to be an offshoot of her analytic therapy. During one session with her analyst, she had misunderstood what he had said about the "id," which in turn caused her to believe that deep down inside her unconscious she was a very sick and potentially crazy person. As she said, "It's like an evil force inside of me could take me over at any time. I have to constantly guard against these unconscious impulses so that they don't take me over."

This thought would occur whenever she felt emotions like anger, fear, or sadness. She would immediately label these feelings as sick, unconscious, and dangerous, then have an anxiety attack because she feared losing control. In most cases, her emotions were perfectly normal and could be understood in the context in which they occurred. However, she had a great deal of difficulty seeing this, insisting, instead, that her feelings were a sign that her unconscious was about to erupt.

This client's anxiety was eliminated after nine weeks of practice using index cards, listening to audiotapes, and mentally rehearsing beliefs which didn't make her out as sick. Following are some of the situations she initially misread and later reinterpreted.

Situation 1

She got anxious during piano recitals in front of a lot of people.

Pathological Thought

I am anxious and scared because of something sick going on in my unconscious.

Rational Belief

I am anxious about messing up in front of my friends.

Situation 2

She got angry after her boyfriend canceled his date the third weekend in a row.

Pathological Thought

I must guard against my unconscious anger because it may erupt and make me go crazy.

Rational Belief

I am angry because he isn't considering my feelings and I haven't been assertive enough to tell him.

Situation 3

She had an anxiety attack after reading a novel about someone having a nervous breakdown.

Pathological Belief

Deep down inside I am sick and unstable, possessed by overpowering forces.

Rational Belief

I am afraid because I think I may be unstable—not because I am. There is nothing deep down inside me, other than the usual blood, bones and tissues—like anyone else. These masses of cells don't have the quality of psychological sickness and they have no mystical power of possessing the rest of me. Reading the book reminded me of my superstitious fears—fears which have nothing to do with an abstraction called the unconscious. I have created this abstraction in my mind, called it sick and abnormal, then told myself it's going to take over the rest of me. My fear comes directly from what I say to myself, not from some mystical part of me my imagination has created.

Comment

This technique is not appropriate for use with psychotics or clients who have severe medical problems.

When removing the sick label, the therapist should be careful not to implant the concept of guilt. Some clients mistakenly think that if they aren't sick then they must be bad (i.e., "If you're not deranged, you have only yourself to blame for having problems.").

Further Information

Many authors argue against the use of the term "sickness" for psychological problems. See Korchin (1976), Rabkin (1974), Skinner (1953, 1972, 1974), Szasz (1960, 1970a, 1970b, 1978), and Ullmann and Krasner (1975).

RATIONAL BELIEFS

Principles

Like many therapeutic methods, countering irrational beliefs creates one problem while solving another. Successful countering weakens an irrational thought, but it forces the client to focus on the thought initially. Once focused on, the irrational thought produces the negative emotion. So countering, in effect, works backwards to remove a negative emotion that the process of countering has just created. Countering must work against both the thought and the emotion it elicits. This requires an especially strong counter, as negative emotions tend to strengthen irrational beliefs.

Both in theory and practice, a more useful type of countering is to have the client avoid thinking the irrational thought, thus eluding the need to work against the negative emotion. The rational belief technique does just this. The client imagines the realistic belief immediately after being exposed to the environmental triggers. With this approach, the client doesn't argue against an irrational thought, but concentrates on thinking rationally.

Method

1. Make a list of the situations in which the client has gotten upset. They can be specific situations, from the past or present, or general life situations the client is likely to face.
2. Prepare rational beliefs, or self-statements, the client can use in these situations. These beliefs should exaggerate neither the positive nor negative features of the situations, but should be founded on an objective view of what is occurring. Spend some time finding the most sensible interpretation of the situation.
3. Record the trigger to each situation on one side of a 5″ by 7″ index card. On the other side write a complete description of the rational perception the client is trying to achieve.
4. Several times a day, for at least six weeks, the client should imagine being in the situation until it is clearly in mind.
5. When this visualization becomes clear, the client should picture thinking the rational belief, until it too becomes clear.
6. Clients should practice the exercise until they reflexively perceive the rational belief whenever they picture the event.
7. If intervening irrational thoughts enter the clients' thinking, they should immediate use "thought stopping" (Wolpe, 1969) and try once again to use the rational belief.

Example

Situation	*Rational Belief*
afraid of meeting strangers	I have an opportunity of meeting new and interesting people.
guilty about sexual dreams	Sexual dreams can be fun.
makes a mistake	Now I have a chance to learn something new.

rejected by friend	That's unfortunate.
treated unfairly	I could insist on fair treatment in this situation.
fear of public speaking	I have an opportunity to tell others what I think.
anxious	Anxiety is unpleasant, but not dangerous.
feels inferior	In some things, I am; In others, I'm not.
scared	Fear is just chemicals my body creates.
criticized by others	If they are right, I have learned something; if wrong, I can ignore it.

Comment

Rational beliefs are not simply the most positive perceptions of situations. They should be the most realistic. In most cases the therapist needs to investigate the situations meticulously to determine the most rational coign of vantage.

Further Information

Many social psychological research studies support the view that attitude change is more likely to occur if subjects haven't committed themselves to a prior belief. See Brehm, 1966, and Brehm et al., 1966.

––––––––

UTILITARIAN COUNTERS

Principles

Counters typically attack the validity of the client's beliefs by assailing their unreasonableness. However, there is a kind of counter which quietly disputes beliefs on the premise that they are not useful. This pragmatic approach to countering can significantly help the client who thinks rational, but useless, thoughts. For example, it is logically true that one will die, but it is not useful to think this thought 50 times a day. Thus, utilitarian counters help clients examine the pragmatism of beliefs, not simply their validity.

Method

1. Prepare a list of the client's irrational thoughts.
2. Prepare a list of situations in which the thoughts typically occur.
3. Help the client select a specific behavioral goal to achieve in each situation. "What do I want to accomplish, now?" For example, you might develop goals for the client to respond assertively to unfair criticism, or to admit openly to mistakes, etc.
4. Have the client ask, for each thought, "Does this thought help me reach my goal or not?"
5. Ignoring whether the thought is true or not, help clients find self-statements which will be more useful in helping them reach their goals.
6. Tell the client to substitute the pragmatic belief for the impractical one each time the opportunity arises.
7. Help the client work through an entire hierarchy of situations, substituting useful thoughts for impractical ones.

Example

Impractical Belief
    She rejected me because I am basically an inferior male.

Goal
    To be less likely to be rejected in the future.

Useful Belief
    She rejected me because I behaved in ways she viewed as negative. Since other women also have rejected these behaviors, I'll do what I can to change them.

———

Impractical Belief
    I must control all my feelings to be happy.

Goal
    To be happy.

Useful Belief

Overcontrol causes unhappiness. My energy is better spent trying to control my environment than myself. When I feel bad, I'll try to understand the causes of the emotion and change them if I can, but I don't have to exorcise them.

———

Impractical Belief

I should be constantly on guard about any potential danger that may attack me.

Goal

To protect myself and be safe.

Useful Belief

Worrying does nothing to protect me. If I am faced with a danger, I will first determine whether it is truly dangerous. If it is, I will do something practical to reduce it, and if there's nothing I can do, I'll try to accept it. Once I make these decisions, I'll go on with other aspects of my life, since further thinking about it would be useless. (Ellis & Harper, 1961).

———

Impractical Belief

I must be the best in everything I try.

Goal

Desire for excellence.

Useful Belief

The best way to achieve excellence is to concentrate my time and energy on those tasks I consider important and spend little effort on less fulfilling activities. Trying to be the best in everything wastes my energies on low priority tasks and significantly reduces my chances of reaching my goals.

Comment

A word of warning is needed on utilitarian counters. Attacking the utility of a statement does nothing to counter an irrational belief, and may in fact reinforce it. For example, it may be better to argue against the belief that, "I could go crazy," rather than suggest that there are better ways to protect oneself from going crazy besides scaring oneself.

Further Information

Developing a pragmatic perspective is one of the important concepts in communication theory. See Lin (1973) and Watzlawick, Bavelas and Jackson (1967).

Pragmatism has been associated with psychology since its inception, particularly in the works of William James (1890, 1907). See also the functionalist school of psychology (Angell, 1904; Carr, 1925; Dewey, 1886; Woodworth, 1958).

HUMOROUS COUNTERS

Principles

Many clients have a tendency to express their concerns with profound seriousness. And many inexperienced therapists unknowingly reinforce this tendency. Like the country doctor a century and a half ago, who had little knowledge of what caused patient ills and often used superstitious treatments, therapists traditionally have compensated for a lack of knowledge with the appearance of great and serious concern. This no doubt has pleased many clients. However, it was as if both participants in therapy had an unspoken agreement that the client would play the role of a Job-like, pathetic soul in the throes of an uncontrollable neurosis, while the crusading doctor would try mightily to free the client from torment. This approach allowed both actors to chase away the petty boredom of living in what can be a very dull, mundane world; in therapy, at least, they could pretend they were engaged in a serious, Titanic struggle between the forces of neurotic evil and healthy good.

Today, most clients still take their myriad of problems with deadly seriousness, considering each as extremely important, requiring absolute attention and concentration. And the therapist is expected—or more often required—to go along with this charade.

Unfortunately, this approach tends to backfire on client and therapist alike. The more serious the drama, the more likely the client is to begin to believe it. And when this happens, the client's make-believe terror sometimes turns into the real thing.

To prevent this situation from evolving, the therapist should make every attempt to get clients to laugh at their own irrationalities. Humor can serve as an excellent counter to clients' gravity, counteracting negative emotions.

The antidote to client seriousness, then, is counselor humor. Humor conveys the ultimate counter to the idea that life is a tragedy, letting clients know that they don't need to be actors in a Greek drama. Instead they can choose to see themselves less gravely. A life without fun and laughter is not much of a life.

Method

1. Make a list of client beliefs.
2. With the client's help, search for the humorous element behind each irrational thought. This may be a joke, a witty sarcasm, an internal contradiction, an incongruity, or a humorous quotation.
3. Since humor must be paired with thoughts consistently to form new associations, the client should practice laughing at irrational thoughts for many weeks.

Example

Thought
  "I feel guilty about some of the things I have done in life."

Quotation
  "As fur as *I* can see, a conscience is put in you just to *object* to whatever you *do* do, don't make no difference what it *is*. . . . So I reckoned I wouldn't bother no more *about* it, but do *whichever* come *handiest at the time.*" (*Huckleberry Finn*, Mark Twain)

———

Thought
  "I am afraid of getting old."

Quotation
  "I think all this talk about age is foolish. Every time I'm one year older, everyone else is, too." (Gloria Swanson)

———

Thought
  "I need other people to respect me."

Quotation
  "Do not worry about what people are thinking about you—for they are not thinking about you. They are wondering what you are thinking about them." (Anonymous)

––––––––

Thought
  "There is one true love."

Quotation
  "Love is a gross exaggeration of the difference between one person and everybody else." (George Bernard Shaw)

––––––––

Thought
  "I should be able to help everybody who needs it."

Quotation
  "No one can feel as helpless as the owner of a sick goldfish." (Kin Hubbard)

––––––––

Thought
  "I have had nothing in life but bad breaks."

Quotation
  "If there is no wind, row." (Polish proverb)

––––––––

Thought
  "I guess I must be just basically lazy."

Quotation
  "The symptoms of laziness and fatigue are practically identical." (Frederick Lewis Allen)

––––––––

Thought
  "I don't think my teenager will ever become responsible."

Quotation
  "A boy gets to be a man when a man is needed." (John Steinbeck)

Thought
  "I need to be successful."

Quotation
  "One of the weaknesses of our age is our apparent inability to distinguish our needs from our greeds." (Don Robinson)
"It is a funny thing about life—if you refuse to accept anything but the best you very often get it." (Somerset Maugham)

Thought
  "One should strive for perfection at all times."

Quotation
  "(A perfectionist is) one who takes infinite pains, and often gives them to other people." (Kenneth L. Krichbaum)

Thought
  "Truth is mighty and will prevail."

Quotation
  "(This is) . . . the most majestic compound fracture of fact which any of woman born has yet achieved. For the history of our race, and each individual's experience, are sown thick with evidences that a truth is not hard to kill, and that a lie well told is immortal." (Mark Twain)

Thought
  "It's terrible to make mistakes."

Quotation
  "Babe Ruth's record of 714 home runs will never be forgotten. But how

many of us know that the Babe struck out 1330 times, a record unapproached by any other player in the history of baseball?" (Harold Helfer)

———

Thought
   "There is an ideal answer to my concerns."

Quotation
   "There is always an easy solution to every human problem—neat, plausible, and wrong." (H. L. Mencken)

———

Thought
   "Other people are smarter than I."

Quotation
   "Everybody is ignorant, only on different subjects." (Will Rogers)

———

Thought
   "I need to make a lot of money to be respectable."

Quotation
   "The real measure of our wealth is how much we should be worth if we lost our money." (J. H. Jowett)

———

Thought
   "I forget the insights I have discovered about myself."

Quotation
   "Men occasionally stumble over the truth, but most of them pick themselves up and hurry off as if nothing had happened." (Winston Churchill)

———

Thought
   "It's important not to trust people too much or they will take advantage of you."

Quotation

Suspicion is " . . . like feeding a dog on his own tail. It wouldn't fatten the dog." (Mark Twain)

Comment

Keep in mind, as you use this technique, that even with humor, you can use too much of a good thing. Be careful not to laugh at clients, but only with clients; the object of humorous counters is to get clients to laugh at their irrational thoughts. For humorous counters to be effective the laughter must flow naturally during the counseling session; strained humor, in counseling and elsewhere, is not funny.

Further Information

See Ellis and Abrahms (1978), Chapman and Foot (1976, 1977), and Haley (1973) for more detailed discussion of humor in therapy.

OBJECTIVE COUNTERING

Principles

Many countering techniques employ high levels of emotional arousal to shift irrational beliefs. However, sometimes a cool, non-emotional style is more effective in changing thoughts. This is because an objective, impersonal consideration of the client's irrationalities can defuse negative emotions, while an intense attack cannot.

The objective countering technique requires the therapist to present a logical, non-emotional argument, then persuade the client to model the therapist's style. Both client and counselor analyze the client's beliefs coldly and impersonally, as if they were using a mathematical formula.

Objective countering states that the client's beliefs can be changed if the therapist helps accumulate more logic against a thought than the client has in support of it; when the logical evidence tips the scales, the belief will shift. This view contrasts with the opinion that the emotional intensity or habitual strength of a counter is more essential than the logic behind it. But no matter which view ultimately prevails, this technique paves the way for the use of countering approaches using more emotional procedures.

Method

1. Have the client identify the major core beliefs underlying negative emotions.
2. Help the client dissect each belief into its basic logical components. Scrupulously avoid subjective judgments about the belief and its component parts.
3. With the client's help, examine each belief in terms of the principles of inductive and deductive logic. Decide, with the client, whether or not the belief is logical.
4. If the client judges a belief to be false, have the client write down all the logical reasons for the rejection.
5. Tell the client to recall these reasons for rejection whenever the false belief recurs, until it no longer reappears.

Example of Introduction
   The following instructions are given to clients to introduce objective countering.

> We are surrounded by what is real. It impinges on all our senses, our emotions, and our brain. We are born in it, live in it, and die in it. Some of what is real produces pain, some sadness, some danger, but much of the real produces joy, happiness, and contentment.
>
> Most of us see the real when we are very young, when it is clear and sharp. But as we get older we start to lose the clarity of our perceptions, and the world starts looking murky. We get more and more distant from the real and our brains start developing imaginary systems which block our views and distort our natural perceptions. Others' views also start impinging and distorting our view of the real. Some of us lose this view all together.
>
> Where once only real pain could cause us unhappiness, now abstractions and cognitive fantasies cause pain. Where once a stubbed toe could cause us to cry, now hurt feelings can bring tears. Where once the pain would be removed the minute the stimulus was taken away, now the pain continues for weeks, months or even years after the stimulus has disappeared. Where once we would seek our greatest joy in the real, now we throw away tangible joy and pleasure for metaphysical abstrac-

tions. The abstractions give us no substance, no warmth, no closeness, for they are empty illusions, counterfeit pleasures. We often ignore the priceless wealth of the real, for worthless notions of the unreal.

Our only chance for true happiness is to return again to the real. And the only way we can do this is by evaporating all illusions and seeing clearly again. So let's take a look at your thoughts and see what is real and what is make-believe.

Example of Analysis

The idea that there are different classes of people is one core belief which is not founded in the real and can therefore be weakened by objective discussion.

Class consciousness causes some clients to feel depressed and anxious if they believe their parents were low class. Despite their own achievements (many are highly successful), these clients still believe, almost existentially, that at their core they lack a basic worth because they come from a poor background.

These clients constantly fear being exposed. They judge their obvious talents and successes as part of a facade they hold up to fool society, guarding against situations where others will see though their masks and uncover them.

Other clients worry about their class, but in a different way. These clients come from upper-class families, but believe they lack certain admired characteristics evident among lower-class individuals. They may believe, for instance, that lower-class people have an energy or life force that makes them strong and better able to handle the pragmatic problems of living. Male clients in particular often feel they lack the masculine power and courage of lower-class men, thinking of themselves as wimps or dandies.

After the client is shown how to view thoughts objectively, the abstraction causing a particular problem is identified and analyzed. In the following schema, the abstraction of class is dissected.

Definitions of Class

Synonyms: breed, blood, character, genus, level, stratum, position, rank, ancestry, lineage, stock, pedigree, descent, birth, aristocracy/commoner/royalty.

Assumptions Which Logically Underlie the Client's Concept

1. Each individual possesses a nonphysical class imprint.
2. This imprint is somehow passed on through our genes.
3. It is immutable.

4. Different qualities of worth (high, medium, low) intrinsically bind themselves to this nonphysical hereditary aspect called class.
5. This quality of worth is also immutable.
6. People know their class and their quality intuitively.
7. Everyone is of the same class as their parents, grandparents, and great-grandparents, ad infinitum.
8. Your children, grandchildren, etc., are of the same class and quality as you are.
9. If you appear to be of a different class or quality than your lineage, this is a façade. You are a fake, fooling society, and others will find you out sooner or later. When people who pretend to be a higher class are put to the test, they will always show their true class.

Evaluation of Concept

As a sociological concept, class can be a useful abstraction (Davis and Moore, 1945; Warner et al., 1949). But the term is bankrupt when people apply it to their own worthiness. When applied to a person, the word is a meaningless; it describes a quality that doesn't exist. Class "thingness" is the concept that each person has an basic inherited ranking of worth, independent of accomplishments, which can never be changed. It assumes an almost spiritual ranking of one's social soul.

Logical Counters

1. There is no evidence—and no method of finding evidence—for the existence of a nonphysical aspect of a person called class.
2. How can a nonphysical element be inherited?
3. Even if we supposed that such an element existed, there is no method through which an immutable quality of worth would be attached to it. Worth is purely a subjective judgment in the eyes of the beholder, and not intrinsic to what is being observed.
4. What particular physical, mental, psychological, spiritual, or meteorological element inside of people allows them to intuitively know their class?
5. Class is just an arbitrary abstraction imposed on some people by other people. It has no meaning except insofar as it reveals the feelings of one person for another.

Comment

We have found that an objective consideration of problems seems most helpful for the very resistant, defensive client, as this approach is unlikely to trigger strong emotional reactions. However, for other clients, depersonalized objectivity may be damaging. Many clients benefit from the warmth, empathy, and positive caring of the therapist (Rogers, 1951). Depressed clients in particular may need a more emotional approach to energize and empower their counters.

An objective analysis of client concepts is a clean and elegant approach to therapy. However, our experience shows that many clients do not honor logic as much as their therapists. For these clients, other approaches are needed to replace or supplement objective countering.

Further Information

The importance of objective self-appraisal is mentioned by Nisbett and Ross (1980). Objectivity is also one of the major methods used in Abraham Low's will therapy to reduce panic attacks (Low, 1952).

Virtually all cognitive approaches teach clients to observe themselves and their environments more objectively (Bandura, 1977b; Beck et al., 1979; Ellis, 1962; Ellis & Bernard, 1985; Lazarus, 1981; Mahoney and Thoresen, 1974; Meichenbaum, 1977).

METHOD OF DIFFERENCE

Principles

John Stuart Mill wrote about several ways to find the causes of various phenomena (Nagel, 1950). In the first of these methods, the "method of agreement," the researcher looks at all the situations where an effect is present and isolates commonalities, which are then considered as possible causes. In the second method, the "method of difference," the researcher compares those situations where the effect occurs with those situations where it doesn't occur. Any variable present in the first but not in the second could also be a cause.

The latter of these two methods can be used as an effective clinical tool. Applying this method, the therapist examines not only those situations where the client gets upset, but also those where the client doesn't get upset. For example, a client fearful of going to a particular store on Tuesday may have no such fear on Friday. It is useful for the therapist to find out why the client didn't get upset on Friday. What, exactly, is present on Friday that's absent on Tuesday? What did the client tell himself about the situation on Friday that was different from Tuesday?

By examining non-anxious situations in this manner, the therapist often can uncover key counters a client uses to keep calm in tense situations (e.g., "I can handle the store on Friday, since there are no crowds."). Since these counters are already in the client's repertoire, they may be readily transferred to new situations, or used more frequently, with a minimal amount of new learning.

Method

1. Make a list of the situations when the client experienced target emotions such as anxiety, anger, guilt, depression.
2. Make another list of situations, as similar to the first as possible, where the client didn't get upset.
3. Find out what thoughts the client has in the non-anxious situations that he/she doesn't have in the upsetting one, and vice versa.
4. Make a list of these self-statements. You will wish to explore a large number of past and present situations, demonstrating to the client that he/she thinks more realistically at certain times than at others.

Comment

A variation of the method of difference is helpful if you have a client who seems to display a maladaptive response to situations across the board, making it difficult to identify positive responses and the rational self-talk that goes with them. Under these circumstances, it is useful to have the client conduct a survey of people who handle the situations well and find out what they say to themselves that keeps them from getting upset. These surveys can be very enlightening. If the client can learn to say and think what less fearful people think and say, the fear can frequently be eliminated.

Further Information

The method of difference is completely explained in Mill's classic work (Nagel, 1950). His work is more completely discussed in "Finding the Causes" in Chapter 5.

Helping clients with problems by studying people without problems has been championed by a number of humanistic psychologists. See, for example, Coan (1974), Fromm (1973), Jahoda (1958), Jourard and Landsman (1980), Maslow (1971), and Rogers (1959).

PREVENTIVE COUNTERING

Principles

In therapy, as in other human endeavors, preventing problems from occurring is preferable to correcting them. A client may have to spend months or years countering a distorted perception created in a single moment of intense emotional arousal. Preventing these distorted perceptions is one of the most important functions of countering, and one of the least painful.

Method

1. Review the client's history of irrational thinking and anticipate future false beliefs.
2. Prepare preventive measures for each threatening situation the client expects to face or, more generally, for overall client problems.
3. Prepare a master list of situations that most people have to face sometime in their lives, along with irrational thoughts and counters.
4. As with other countering approaches, the client needs to practice counters until they become second nature.

Examples

Following are some key irrational thoughts, ones that cause problems for many clients. Changing these attitudes would reduce the chance of becoming emotionally upset in the future.

Problem
I must find my one true love.

Preventive Counter
Many people perpetuate a very ancient myth. A native tale from the Orient speaks of God having blended male and female into a single human soul, when a demon, jealous and resentful of God's creation, magically split the human spirit. Severing the masculine from the feminine, the demon hurled the divided parts into the north wind, scattering them across the earth.

From that time on all men and women were supposed to spend the rest of their lives searching for their missing halves. If they were fortunate they were promised a life of eternal bliss; if not, they would be lonely and incomplete, forever condemned to a fruitless search.

This superstition is very damaging. Some young people pick the first minimally acceptable partner they find just because they feel it is time to get married. A few even set rigid time limits, such as "I must be married before I'm 30," and marry whoever is standing around when time runs out. Others reject good, decent prospects because they find some flaw, and some abruptly seek divorce after they perceive the faintest blemish, so they can continue their quest for their Romeo or Juliet.

Problem
I am inferior to others.

Preventive Counter
If I compare myself to others, I should use a horizontal rather than a vertical scale. On a vertical scale, people are judged by an overall rating of worth, much as sports writers rate teams; there is a #1 person and a #5,000,000,000 person on this planet. A horizontal scale rejects the notion that one person is in any global sense better than another and recognizes that people have different skills, talents, and abilities. Any overall judgment is like comparing apples and oranges, and therefore false.

The differences among people simply represent the different choices they have made about how to spend their time and energy. Some have chosen to make as much money as they can; others wish to have power. Still others want to acquire a lot of material possessions, while some wish to be brighter than others. If we hold the genetic components constant, people are better at what they have practiced and spent their time doing, worse at what they haven't done. The decisions they have made may prove to be useful or not useful, conducive to happiness or not, but have nothing whatsoever to do with basic worth.

Another way of putting it is that we are all equal, every one of us. We all start out with 100 points: 50 from heredity, 50 from what we practice. Now some people, like a Mozart or Beethoven, invest 80 of their 100 points in becoming a great composer, but since they only have 20 points left for other things such as economic and social success or being a good parent, they aren't very good at these things. Other people spend their 100 points more evenly, devoting 20 on physical health, 20 to developing their minds, 20 to being a good parent, 20 to making money, and 20 to playing a musical instrument, so they become only moderately good at these things.

Which of these two types is better? Obviously the answer depends on the vantage point of the observers. The person who values music more than economic or parental success, for example, might say the first type is better. But objectively both persons are equal. They simply have invested their energies differently.

Despite society's irrational views, the president of a company is not better than the secretary, a husband better than a wife, a professor better than a student, for you can't have one without the other. All component parts must be present for any system to work, be it a corporation, family, or the entire society.

Problem

I should get angry at the way others treat me.

Preventive Counter

My anger is a silly, masturbatory delusion unless four things are true: 1) I did not get what I wanted, 2) I was entitled to get it, 3) It's terrible that I didn't get it, and 4) It's someone else's fault (Ellis, 1985). If these all are true, then my anger is justified and I'll confront the person and try to get what I want. If not, I'll counteract my runaway imagination.

Problem

I have the power to become anything I wish.

Preventive Counter

Throughout history the human race has suffered from the homocentric idea that we have more power over ourselves and our environments then we actually have, when in fact we have little or no control over many of the factors affecting our lives. We have no control, for instance, over our gender, who are parents are, our race, or our nationality, and only a little control over our early environment, our education, and our health. We probably have less than 50% control over encountering a potential mate, becoming rich, or choosing a careers. Yet these factors are among the most important influences in our lives. We are creatures on this planet, not creators of it. Thus, we need to spend our time controlling those things we can rather than feeling guilty about those things we can't.

Problem
To be happy I must be very successful.

Preventive Counter
Societies throughout history have touted a wide diversity of goals defining personal success. Some of them have been to be rich, humble, individualistic, conforming, spontaneous, in control, better than others, meek, strong, fertile, frugal, courageous, cautious, thin, beautiful, obedient, cool and calm, strong and aggressive, competitive, cooperative, holy, practical, seductive, pure, unique, innocent, knowledgeable, certain, shrewd, and good.

"Be rich" cultures worship material goods, like houses, cars, oxen, spears and everything else under the sun. The more materialistic the society, the more likely achievement is to be defined by one's possessions. "Be holier" societies emphasize the spiritual; the man or woman who has gained the sixth level of Nirvana is twice as good as the person who only manages to creep to the third. "Be strong," militaristic societies praise the soldier who is most bellicose, who heaps the most mayhem on the enemy.

Societies perpetuate these illusions to help the culture—not to help the individual. When the culture teaches that a person will be happier when they reach a particular standard of success, what it really means is that the culture will be more viable; these standards are created to make up for what the society lacks to make it politically or economically strong, making personal happiness quite irrelevant. Thus early America, in need of more citizens, honored the woman who held to the traditional values of home and family, but it was doubtful whether the pioneer woman with 10 children was happy with no freedom, no leisure time, no novelty, a minimum of adult interaction and constant health problems. Likewise, young American men emulating the 19th century Horatio Alger type may have found it hard to be happy working 18 hours a day, seven days a week, just to make another million.

Human happiness requires far more than fulfilling some cultural prescription for success. We want safety and a feeling of security; we wish to be cared for and to belong; we seek novelty, change and new stimulation; and perhaps most importantly, we want purpose and meaning. Society's petty success goals, like owning the most expensive car or having the whitest teeth, the biggest biceps, or the silkiest hair, are absurd in comparison. Full human happiness is approached by satisfying all our diverse needs, not simply by surrendering to society's fashionable decrees.

———

Problem
I must get people to like me to be happy. To do this, I must conform.

Preventive Counter

People, like flowers, must be free to grow in their own direction. Nature has created enormous varieties in the members of each species for a reason; if everyone tried to be like everyone else there would be no variety and the species would adapt less easily to change. Variety is necessary so each organism can make its own contribution to the growth of the species. Fortunately, flowers have automatically developed into what nature planned. Equally unfortunately, people try to become what everybody else wants them to be. If there were only one way a person should be, we would only need one person, whom we could then clone into a nation. Our lives have meaning only if we develop our unique individuality. A puppet to society's wishes is of no use to nature.

———

Problem

To be worthwhile, I must be a real man.

Preventive Counter

(A client who was troubled by this thought developed the following counterargument.)

Every culture has created an image of the ideal male, and our society too has its own orthodoxy. Our prototype male is supposed to competently master all aspects of his environment. He should master the physical world by repairing cars, dishwashers, and overrunning toilets with ease, and assembling bikes using only the instruction sheets. He should master the world of finance by driving in expensive cars, affording luxurious houses, and giving his wife fur coats and jewelry. He should master other people by dominating conversations with his quiet grasp of facts and logic. He should be able to defend his mate and offspring from thugs, bullies, and licentious males lusting after the females under his care. He must especially show his power over other males by never being outdone in an argument or humiliated in an athletic contest.

But simple mastery is not enough. The "real man" should accomplish all of this while maintaining an impenetrable exterior and "make my day" élan. Expressing emotions is despicable, so heaven help the man who feels them. Real men have complete control over themselves. These emotions don't even exist for them.

Implicit in these ideal male traits is the misguided notion that they are biologically based; the "real" behind "real man" is chemical necessity. Testosterone drives men to conquer the world and provides them the magnificent composure we all admire so. One can't learn to be a man; one is born that way. And if one isn't master of everything, or if one shows signs of weakness (i.e. emotions), then one's genes and hormones are immediately suspect.

The ideal male concept is immensely damaging. Many men try their entire lives to fit this image. They become perfectionistic, feel guilty and inferior for not having the "right stuff," develop ulcers and become prone to heart attacks. To cope with the increasing pressure, they put in more time on their jobs, become workaholics, and lose their ability to play, relax, or have fun.

Worst of all, men lose their ability to get close to others. They become unable to bond with another man because he has become an enemy or rival. Even more damaging, they lose their ability to get close to women, whom they must constantly dominate, impress, and control. Many men hold up a façade of strength that keeps women from knowing what they really feel; the more intensely the woman wants to know what a man feels, the more he pretends not to feel anything. In this way, many couples grow more and more distant, until the relationship dies of emotional barrenness.

This attitude is patently absurd, as it is impossible for any human to live up to "real man" standards. Humans of either gender don't have the power needed to master everything in their environments. Though strong, a man is physically weaker than any other animal of his size. Though intelligent, he can't solve every scientific social or environmental puzzle. Though stable, he doesn't have full power over his emotions, for in the primitive, subcortical regions of his brain he has the cells that create emotions just like everyone else of the species. Pretending that he doesn't feel these emotions, or berating himself when he does, will only add to his misery.

It is preposterous to assume that the male, by an act of his will or by abundant testosterone, should control the physical, social and emotional variables that the combined efforts of humanity haven't mastered in three and a half million years. The admirable quality of being human of either sex is that we have done well as a species in spite of our weaknesses. It is insulting and degrading to every man and woman to imply that the male somehow should do better and is not a "real man" unless he does.

Comment

Many clients, reluctant to prepare for future problems, wish to work only on the present and then stop counseling the minute they think things have improved. Encourage these clients in particular to do at least some preventive work.

Further Information

The preventive concept of mental health can be explored by reading Caplan (1964). Specific preventive techniques are discussed by Bond and Rosen, (1980), Joffe and Albee (1981), and Kent and Rolf (1979).

COUNTERING PROTECTIVE BELIEFS

Principles

Some irrational thoughts exist because they seem to protect the client. But this security is illusory. Like rabbit's feet or horseshoes, protective thoughts help clients feel safe without providing any real protection.

One of the greatest challenges facing a therapist is to change a core belief surrounded by a protective layer of irrational thoughts. This barrier must be broken down before the therapist can even gain access to the central thought behind it.

Protective beliefs exist for several reasons, as detailed below.

Personal Power

Clients may receive positive or negative reinforcement for believing a certain thought. For example, a thought such as "most people are sniveling incompetents" gives the feeling of greater domination over others. This is one of the most positive rewards a thought can give, making it very difficult for the client to abandon.

Social Support

If a lot of the client's friends, relatives and/or acquaintances believe the thought, the client may feel a lot of social pressure to maintain it. If the client changes the thought, he or she will be at odds with the social support group; holding onto the belief may be essential to maintain social and family ties.

Hierarchy of Values

Irrational thoughts are virtually always attached to a central personal value; to change the belief is to undermine this value. For example, many clients have difficulty countering the thought, "It's always my fault," because they believe their religious convictions require them to feel guilty. "If I start thinking I am not a sinner," the rationalization goes, "then I am committing another sin."

Interpersonal Power

Some clients refuse to dispute their thoughts because they like to be contrary, balking at anything someone else tells them to do. To follow instructions, they feel, is to give in to another person.

Effort

Countering requires effort, and there are many clients who plainly want the positive results of countering, but don't want to make the effort. These clients usually have a history of seeking immediate gratification and are unwilling to wait for countering to take effect.

Anxiety Reduction

Clients may perceive change as dangerous and may maintain a thought to protect them from a greater danger, i.e., "If I get rid of my agoraphobia my husband will leave me."

Method

1. Make a list of all the client's protective beliefs. Note the type of protection each belief furnishes.
2. If you can, locate the exact time the belief was created.
3. Objectively analyze the rationality of each protective belief:

   a. Does the thought truly safeguard the client from some hazard?
   b. Is the danger something the client needs protection from?
   c. Is the cost of shielding oneself from peril greater than the risk itself?
   d. Is there a better way to defend oneself besides thinking this way?
   e. Is the protective thought true, or is it something the client made up just to feel good?

4. With the client's help, develop counter evidence against the protective value of the beliefs.
5. Have the client practice the counters covertly and *in vivo* until the defensive thoughts are weakened.
6. Once the protective beliefs have been removed, use other cognitive restructuring techniques to weaken the core beliefs.

Example

The following is a list of protective beliefs abstracted from the case notes of 20 clients.

1. Home is safe. The farther away from home I travel the greater the danger.
2. If I can't leave a place easily, I'm in jeopardy.
3. Something bad will happen if I think about my problems, so it's best not to reflect about them.
4. Avoiding something or running away safeguards me.
5. I need to have my spouse around at all times.
6. The following things are dangerous and must be avoided at all costs (from clients' case notes): red VW's, gold jewelry, green sweaters, French perfume, the occult, churches, hospitals, going to sleep, drinking wine, medicines, UFO's, dentists, mountains, riding buses, planes, strange places, darkness, afterglow, being relaxed, having an orgasm, feeling anger, riding on a ski lift, elevators, tall buildings, being embarrassed, sitting in the front row of a large meeting, etc. (The list is almost endless. These items were all present when various clients had anxiety attacks, and therefore became associated with the anxiety. The clients mistakenly thought that these things somehow caused the anxiety, and superstitiously avoided them.)
7. Being alone is dangerous.
8. Not concentrating on my fears at all times is risky because it gives them a chance to sneak up on me. (See the discussion of "Harold" in Basic Perceptual Shift of Chapter 2.)
9. Being too happy or too excited or laughing too hard can hurt me because I get out of my emotional "safety zone."
10. If I succeed too well, I could be setting myself up for a huge crash.
11. Feeling any emotion is threatful.
12. I need to be in control of everything around me at all times.
13. I need to master all internal things (thoughts, emotions, physical sensations) immediately, otherwise something terrible will happen to me.
14. I must fit in with everybody else's values and behavior; otherwise I will be totally alone and rejected by everyone.
15. I must not let anyone else know what I really feel or think. If I put down my mask even for an instant, I'll be found out and disgraced.
16. It is grievous to fail in any endeavor.
17. I must try as hard as I can in everything I attempt.
18. Giving up power in any area is always serious.

19. I ought to always be strong.
20. I will be utterly vulnerable if I stop thinking I am a fragile, sick person.
21. I'll be unprotected if I ever get too relaxed.
22. If I don't think women are inferior, all my male and female friends will reject me.
23. I can't be assertive because I don't want to be arrogant and egotistical.
24. It's easier not to fight my thoughts.
25. If I'm not sick others will expect me to be a lot more competent.

Comment

If protective beliefs are not analyzed and changed, the therapist may never gain access to the core problems underlying them. In most cases, the client won't mention a protective belief directly, but will reveal its presence by engaging in subtle sabotage of the therapeutic process—arriving 15 minutes late or missing appointments altogether, not doing homework, and so on. (See "Handling Client Sabotages" in Chapter 6.)

Further Information

Guidano and Liotti (1983) discuss "protective belts" in detail. However, psychoanalytic theorists have done the lion's share of work in examining protective devices. See Freud (1933) on defense mechanisms, as well as Bloom et al. (1977), Holmes (1968, 1972, 1974, 1978, 1981), Houston (1973), and Houston and Holmes (1970).

———

PRACTICING COUNTERS

Principles

Countering is not based entirely on insight; simply recognizing that a thought is irrational is not enough to change it. Many clients enter therapy knowing their thoughts are illogical, but unable to respond rationally when faced with strong environmental triggers.

Repetition is essential to countering. However, most clients have little notion of how long a thought must be disputed before it is changed. If, for example, a client has repeated an irrational thought 100,000 times, disputing it for an hour or so will do little to reduce it. Yet most clients believe they should be able to remove a thought in a day or two, and certainly in no longer than a week. They reason that because they know logically that the thought isn't true, it should be easy to remove. What these clients tend to forget is that thoughts, like any other habits, accrue strength over the years. Just as clients can't learn to speak Spanish or to play a cello in a week, so they can't change their thinking instantaneously.

All the countering techniques described below require a great deal of practice. Just how many repetitions are needed varies from person to person. Following are the most common and most effective methods of countering used today.

Covert Relaxed Countering

High energy countering, particularly when it pulls in the client's anger against irrational beliefs, can be effective for certain types of thoughts (see counterattacking). An aggressive attack against a depressive or passive thought helps change not only the thought, but also the affect it causes.

However, for others types of thoughts—most notably anxious ones—it is often far better to counter in a more relaxed manner. It has been theorized that soft countering reduces the client's state of anxiety, while aggressive countering increases it. In a relaxed state the irrational belief is challenged while the tense emotional response is counteracted by the relaxation, providing two active treatment elements.

Method

1. Initially the client is trained in one of the several methods of alpha-theta relaxation, including standard relaxation, EMG, GSR, pulse rate reduction, white or pink noise, relaxing scripts, nature sounds, and self-hypnosis. (See "Use of Altered States" in Chapter 6)
2. A hierarchy of scenes and accompanying irrational beliefs is prepared.
3. The client then imagines the first scene on the hierarchy. When it is clearly in mind, the client relaxes in full.
4. While relaxing, the client softly and caringly persuades himself that his thinking is wrong and quietly replaces the thought with a rational, realistic perspective.
5. This exercise is repeated until each imagined scene in the hierarchy produces no emotional disturbance.

Example

Here is the script for this countering technique:

(After a relaxed state has been induced) I'd like you to imagine the next scene on your hierarchy as clearly as you can, using all your senses. While imagining this scene, listen to the irrational things you tell yourself about it. Continue until you have both the scene and one key thought clearly in mind. Indicate when you are ready.

(After the client gives the signal) Now relax completely. Let your muscles become loose and limp to the point where they feel warm and heavy. (Repeat whatever relaxation technique was used in the beginning of the session.) Indicate when you are fully relaxed.

Now I'd like you to stay in this relaxed state. If at any time you start to feel tense, stop what you're doing and go back and relax yourself. While you relax, I would like you to talk to yourself silently, in a soft and caring manner. Patiently—but forcefully—convince yourself that your thinking is irrational. Imagine that you are talking to yourself like a loving parent talks to her child who is afraid of imaginary monsters in the bedroom. Gently persuade this child that these thoughts are irrational.

Keep persuading the child until you feel a distinct weakening of your old irrational thinking, and a definite lessening of the unpleasant emotion. Take as long as you want. Indicate when you are done.

This technique is repeated twice more, after which the client again imagines the test scene while the therapist monitors the client's state of relaxation. If the client remains relaxed while imagining the scene, the next item in the hierarchy is presented, and so on, until the client can visualize each scene with minimal anxiety.

Visual Practice

Counters can be memorized in the same way that foreign words are memorized, repeated again and again until they can be used instantaneously. If the client can't remember the counter on the spot, it can't be used.

Memorizing counters speeds up the entire disputing process. Initially, the client won't recall counters until the moment of the irrational thought has come and gone; with practice, however, counters can become second nature, as shown below.

$A \rightarrow B \rightarrow C$ ——————————————————— time ⟶ D

with A = Situation
with B = Irrational Thought or Belief
with C = Emotional Reaction
with D = Disputing or Countering

With practice, the counter moves backward in time, getting closer and closer to interrupting the irrational thought.

$A \rightarrow B \rightarrow C$ ⟶ D
$A \rightarrow B \rightarrow C \rightarrow D$
$A \rightarrow B \rightarrow C \rightarrow D$ (C is now experienced as a flash of fear lasting about 30 seconds.)

When the client learns the counters extremely well, the disputing counters (D's) will automatically occur between the A and B, preventing the negative emotion from arising.

$A \rightarrow D$

Method

1. Have the client make up a set of index cards. On one side have the client write the irrational thought and rate on a 1 to 10 scale how strongly the client believes it.
2. On the other side have the client write down as many counters as possible.
3. Tell the client to read the card every day several times, adding one counter each day. Record any change in belief level on the front of the card.
4. Reading the cards for 6 weeks generally will reduce the strength of the client's belief by at least half.

Auditory Practice

Since most clients report "hearing" their thoughts rather than "seeing" them, auditory memorization is often very effective. This technique has the advantage that it can be practiced while the client is doing other things, such as washing the dishes, cleaning house, etc.

Method

1. Record on a cassette tape a list of the client's irrational thoughts.
2. Leave a blank space after each thought. And instruct the client to counter, or record counters to each thought on the tape.
3. Have the client listen to the tape every day and make up new counters with each listening.

Comment

Be sure to forewarn clients using this technique that the quality of their practice will vary; they'll have some good days, and some bad ones. Like many other procedures, covert countering techniques show improvement of an elliptical nature. Since most clients expect their irrational beliefs to decrease steadily, they must be told to expect bad days to avoid discouragement.

Further Information

The reader will recognize the similarity of some covert countering techniques to Wolpe's desensitization (1958; Wolpe et al., 1964), the difference being the addition of the cognitive component. The Conditioning chapter discusses more of these techniques.

Other practice procedures can be found in the work of Ellis, (1985) and Mahoney and Thoresen (1974).

Further information about the card technique can be found in the work of Beck (1976).

ROLEPLAYING COUNTERS

Principles

One of the most common difficulties with countering is that many clients learn to counter in a mechanical, non-involved fashion. One way to make countering less rote and more realistic is roleplaying. Among other things, acting out counters in a roleplay situation allows the client to develop proprioceptive cues which help tie the counters into the client's personal frame of reference.

Method

1. Make a list of the client's key irrational thoughts.
2. With the client's help, compile a companion list of counters to these thoughts.
3. Roleplay an argument between the rational and irrational thoughts in which the client takes the rational position and you play out the irrational.
4. Variations

   a. Play the role of the person who, at some time in the past, taught the false belief to the client, while the client argues against both the person and the belief.
   b. Using the empty chair technique, have the client play both sides — irrational belief and counters — arguing both for and against the core beliefs.
   c. Help the client to dissect irrational beliefs into component parts; then roleplay each part while the client counters. For example, the thought that, "I could lose control and embarrass myself in front of others," has many components which can be roleplayed. The therapist could roleplay that part of the client which wishes to be in control, the part which would be embarrassed, the client's anxiety, others observing the client's embarrassment, etc., as the client countered each part.
   d. In most cases, it is best for the therapist to model the roleplaying before the client attempts it.

Example

A behavioral therapist sent me Lynn, a client who was so afraid of flying that she hadn't been on a plane for 10 years. The therapist had used traditional desensitization for the aerophobia, and the treatment had been successful in that the client could imagine all the items on her hierarchy without tension. However, she still wouldn't get on a plane. He referred Lynn to me because he hoped a cognitive component would take the client over the last step.

After a few sessions, Lynn had learned the key components of cognitive therapy, but still actively resisted countering her irrational beliefs. Apparently she was willing to learn the intellectual components of cognitive therapy, much as she had learned behavior therapy from the behavior therapist, but was recalcitrant in using this knowledge to help herself. Throughout each session she would argue against any direct suggestion or instruction. Unwilling to accept anyone else's advice, she believed she should be able to solve her problems herself.

I decided that counter roleplaying would put her argumentative nature to good use, enabling her to argue against her own irrational thoughts.

The following is an excerpt from one of my sessions with Lynn.

THERAPIST: I would like to do something a little bit different for this session. Instead of you telling me your irrational belief and me giving your counters, let's reverse it. I'll argue for your beliefs and you argue against them, OK?

CLIENT: I'm not sure I understand what you mean.

THERAPIST: Well, let's get started, and I think you'll get the idea.

CLIENT: OK.

THERAPIST: I think your fear of flying is quite sensible. It's a strange sensation to be in this huge lump of metal 30,000 feet in the sky. And if something goes wrong you can't pull over to the side and get off.

CLIENT: Yeah! It is scary.

THERAPIST: No. I want you to argue against me.

CLIENT: That's hard because I believe what you're saying.

THERAPIST: I know, but try arguing with me anyway.

CLIENT: Well, nothing will happen, probably. It probably won't crash.

THERAPIST: Probably, probably, that's not very reassuring. Who wants to have his guts splattered all over Kansas because you misjudged a probability?

CLIENT: There isn't much of a chance something bad will happen.

THERAPIST: Maybe not. But shouldn't you take every possible precaution?

CLIENT: Like what?

THERAPIST: Like worrying, or not getting on planes or freaking out once you do.

CLIENT: I don't see how worrying would help in the least.

THERAPIST: If you worry, then at least you're prepared for the danger. You wouldn't want something to happen if you weren't ready.

CLIENT: That's silly. Worrying won't keep the plane from crashing.

THERAPIST: Well, I guess that means you have to stay off planes.

CLIENT: Then I'd have to stay in one place all my life.

THERAPIST: Nonsense. You could drive a car, take a bus, or even walk if you had to.

CLIENT: That would take too long.

THERAPIST: Which do you want—to take a long time or get smashed like a pancake?

CLIENT: Aw, come on! I not going to get smashed. Besides, cars and buses have more accidents than planes. And I could break a leg or something if I walked.

THERAPIST: Or get hit by a crashing plane.

CLIENT: (Laughing) Yeah! I'd be safer in a plane. At least I would have metal around me and I wouldn't be caught out in the open.

THERAPIST: Still, planes are a lot scarier than other types of transportation.

CLIENT: So what? Feeling scared isn't going to kill me. But car accidents or bus accidents could.

THERAPIST: Yeah, but you could embarrass yourself on the plane by showing fellow passengers you are scared.

CLIENT: Embarrass myself! Who cares about that? That's nothing compared to being trapped in the same place for the rest of my life. And all because I *couldn't* fly.

THERAPIST: You mean *wouldn't* fly!

CLIENT: (Pause.) Yeah! *Wouldn't!*

Comment

As shown in the above example, this technique is most useful for clients who oppose the counselor's direction, particularly when this behavior seems to be part of their social repertoire. Such clients are highly motivated to win an argument, even if it means giving up irrational thoughts. When roleplaying is used in this way, it is a paradoxical technique (see Chapter 4 for another example of reverse roleplaying). When client and counselor do not switch role, roleplaying is a countering technique because it strengthens the client's ability to dispute unrealistic beliefs.

Further Information

The role playing technique is a cognitive adaptation of some of the procedures developed by Gestalt therapists. The reader may find it useful to refer to some original sources, such as Fagan and Shepherd (1970), Feder and Ronall (1980), Perls (1969a, 1969b, 1973), Polster and Polster (1973).

DISPUTING AND CHALLENGING

Principles

Rational emotive therapy employs a more free-floating style than other countering techniques in this chapter. In RET, the counselor focuses on irrational thoughts as they occur in the client's conversation and client and therapist together dispute and challenge false thinking. The style enables the counselor to stay more fully in touch with the client's immediate concerns, because the therapist follows the client's agenda. In contrast, the standard cognitive restructuring approach is more structured and follows more of the therapist's regimen.

Traditional RET uses a Socratic approach in which the therapist directs the client's attention to a series of logical questions leading to the faults underlying the client's thinking. The counselor freely uses directional probes into key areas of irrationality, reflects and reinforces clients' rational discoveries, and provides factual information.

RET is used in cognitive restructuring therapy as an adjunct rather than as a basic technique. It usually accompanies other, more structured approaches.

Method

1. Keep in mind that, although unstructured, RET does use certain established components at different stages of the therapeutic process.
2. Help the client focus on the central irrational thought causing the anxiety, guilt, anger, or depression.
3. Probe into the evidence against the belief.
4. Dispute the client's catastrophizing (i.e., "It's terrible, horrible, and catastrophic that . . . "), and self-demanding aspects of the client's thinking ("I must, ought to, and should . . . ").
5. In most cases don't give counters directly. Rather, use incisive questions to help the client's discover his own counters.
6. Encourage the client to dispute and challenge irrational thoughts whenever they occur. Some formal practice each day is suggested.

7. You may find it helpful to develop a mental set for the use of RET by listening to a therapeutic session by Albert Ellis or one of his colleagues.

Example

Examples of the RET style are so numerous in the literature that another example would be superfluous. We recommend Ellis' book *Growth Through Reason* (1971) which presents seven verbatim cases in RET. Even better, however, are recordings of RET therapeutic interviews, which can be ordered from the Institute for Rational Emotive Therapy, 45 E. 65th St., New York, NY 10021. These tapes are from the professional tape library and are available only to qualified therapists.

Further Information

The literature on RET is massive. The catalogue from Ellis' Institute for Rational Emotive Therapy lists the major publications. If the reader is not familiar with RET, the following sources provide a good introduction: Ellis (1962, 1973, 1985), Ellis and Bernard (1985), Ellis and Grieger (1977), and Ellis and Harper (1971, 1975). For RET methods with more specialized client populations, see Hauck (1967) and Ellis, Wolfe, and Moseley (1966)—children; Ellis and Harper (1971)—marital; Ellis (1975)—sex therapy.

DIARY RESEARCH

Principles

All the countering techniques in this section share a major problem—the therapist does not know for certain that the procedures are going to work. Generally, it is not bad to assume their efficacy, for they have been tested on thousands of clients at clinics throughout the country. But every new client entering therapy presents a unique challenge, and we cannot be certain a specific technique will be effective just because it has helped others.

It's best to discover what works for a particular client in a particular situation through experimentation, rather than following a favorite technique or two. The easiest, or most logical, or cleverest counter may have helped hundreds of clients, and may even have had scores of books written about it — but what good is it if it doesn't help the client sitting in front of you?

The purpose of diary research is to help clients find their most effective counters by experimentation.

Method

1. Have clients keep a record of all the counters they find effective in reducing anxiety or other negative emotions.
2. For each counter have clients record, on a series of 10-point scales, (a) the strength of the emotion before countering, (b) the strength of the countering, (c) how long the counter was used, and (d) the strength of the emotion after countering.
3. The best counters are those which remove a negative emotion when it is quite strong. Clients should be especially careful to keep accurate records on these counters that remove or reduce anxiety attacks or severe depressive episodes.
4. After a sufficient number of workable counters has been gathered, have clients pick those which produced the greatest reductions in negative emotions. Next, instruct clients to develop a whole new series of counters emphasizing the key points in previously successful counters.
5. Have clients continue to refine these counters, based on trial and error. Eventually clients will develop some very powerful, effective disputes.
6. In many cases it is also useful to have clients recall all the counters they used throughout their lives when disputing the same or similar thoughts. Often the disputes which worked especially well in the past will continue to work well in the future.

Example

Following are some excerpts from the counter diary of a client we will call David, a 31-year-old professional who had weekly anxiety attacks for several years. The trigger for these attacks was always the thought that he would go insane.

The attacks had started after a relative of David's was institutionalized for severe emotional difficulties. Although David had absolutely no symptoms of psychosis, he lived in mortal terror of becoming schizophrenic. He would be stricken with anxiety whenever he was exposed to people, movies, or conversations which depicted or mentioned insanity or abnormal behavior of any kind. One year of psychoanalytic therapy and six months of behavioral desensitization had not reduced his anxiety.

David was unable to attend therapy on a regular basis, so we decided he should use the counter diary technique, which can be done at home. He reported to me periodically by phone.

For one year he keep a careful record of all the counters that were effective in reducing the severity of his anxiety attacks. Once a month he would rate the effectiveness of each counter based on the formula:

CE = the sum of (X – Y) divided by N
where:

      CE   = counter effectiveness

      X – Y = the difference between the anxiety before countering (X), and the anxiety after countering (Y), measured in subjective units of discrimination (SUDs).

      N   = the number of times the client used the counter when anxious.

Based on his research, this client was able to develop increasingly effective disputes, significantly reducing the frequency and intensity of his anxiety attacks in one year's time. He continued the counter diary after therapy terminated. Three years later, he was entirely free of anxiety attacks.

Excerpts from David's Counter Diary

    No. 145. Look at your anxiety like this—it's just catastrophizing. Consider the troubles that others have, and how upset they deserve to be. Your problems are considerably less than theirs, but you catastrophize considerably more. (The client rated the effectiveness of this counter at 2.4 on a scale of 10.)

    No. 146. The fear you have now is the same feeling you had years ago. The only difference is that now you're calling this feeling crazy. (3.4)

    No. 147. Look around at the reality. Ignore your emotions. (2.9)

    No. 148. The flaw in me is a flaw in life. (1.9)

    No. 149. Remember and retrace your history of castastrophizing. You are doing it right now. Stop it! (5.7)

    No. 150. Don't try so hard to get rid of your emotions. The anxiety you feel isn't so terrible—and concentrating on it only makes it worse. So just wait for it to go away. Consider it as a cold—a temporary nuisance which doesn't really require much attention. (7.3)

No. 151. Become extremely assertive and goal-directed. (3.7)

No. 152. You are being super-dramatic again. Get real. (5.2)

No. 153. You have had over 300 anxiety attacks. Every single time you were afraid you were going crazy, but nothing ever has happened. So big deal! This is just another one. (8.1)

No. 154. You are anxious because you learned to be and you can unlearn it. (4.6)

No. 157. You can stand to be scared for a little while. You don't have to get rid of it, or get in a stew every time you feel a little bit upset. (4.1)

No. 158. You're getting anxious in this situation because you *think* you should get anxious. If you thought you should get anxious because you picked your nose, then picking your nose would make you anxious. (3.6)

No. 159. You have no alternative. If you are going to go crazy, then it's going to happen. You can't prevent it no matter what you do, so you might as well be as happy as you can in the meantime. Go ahead and enjoy life while you still can. (8.9)

No. 160. Grow up! Stop being a little baby! A little fear isn't going to kill you. (1.0)

No. 161. Give yourself a break! There's no point in blaming yourself for your fear. You didn't try to get it, so stop attacking yourself. (4.4)

When the client was interviewed after he got over his anxiety, he said that two counters ultimately removed his fear. The first was the idea that fear had nothing to do with being crazy; it was just a learned phobia. The second was that the purpose of human life is not simply to protect oneself from every conceivable threat. Ours is the dominant species on this planet because we historically have taken risks. There are no guarantees for any of us. One can see the origin of both of these counters in the client's diary.

Comment

This client found the counter diary highly beneficial. However, it deserves mention that he had a strong background in psychology and read extensively in the area of cognitive/behavioral therapy throughout the year he was under treatment. Most clients need more help from their therapists.

Further Information

Ira Progoff (1977) has developed a comprehensive set of methods, called intensive journal therapy, for the use of diaries and journals in psychotherapy. The approach has similarities to this procedure.

GUIDED COUNTERING

Principles

Because countering involves cognitive and emotional subtleties that clients often miss, it is best to guide them step by step through this process, correcting any mistakes as they occur. After several therapeutic sessions, clients usually master the technique well enough to reduce the frequency and intensity of negative emotions.

Method

1. Attach a biofeedback measure (GSR, EMG, or pulse rate). Observe the measure for five minutes to obtain a baseline reading.
2. Induce relaxation. Standard relaxation, hypnotism, deep breathing, pink or white noise, nature images, or biofeedback response reduction are all appropriate. Allow the client to stabilize on the selected biofeedback measure before proceeding. (See "Use of Altered States" in Chapter 6.)
3. Prepare a hierarchy of upsetting scenes and have the client imagine the first item on the hierarchy.
4. Ask the client to tell you the belief causing the pain. Allow all the time needed on this step, until the client is able to articulate the belief in a concise sentence or two.
5. Help the client find the underlying philosophy behind the surface thought. Probing questions like, "So what if . . . ? What's so terrible if . . . ?" can be used to root out core beliefs.
6. Analyze each core belief and help the client decide whether it is objectively true or false.

7. If a core belief is false, help the client challenge and dispute the thought as deeply as possible, using all the evidence available to expose it as untrue. Continue this attack until the biofeedback measure shows a reduction in the painful emotion.

8. Repeat the exercise, speeding up the procedure until the client's biofeedback reading remains the same while the scene is being imagined.

10. Encourage the client to speak out loud during the entire procedure. This will enable you to assess the client's ability to counter and dispute.

Example

The following transcript is an excerpt from a guided CRT session with Martin, a 35-year-old professional man with multiple problems. This client fluctuated between periods of anxiety and depression, had a history of drug and alcohol abuse, and avoided all major risk-taking behaviors.

After several sessions, we found Martin's core philosophy: Everyone, he believed, should respect him all the time, in every situation imaginable. He panicked at the mere thought of rejection and felt deeply depressed when he experienced it. Apparently, he had learned his other-directed philosophy from an overly perfectionistic father, who had pushed for impossible achievements. As is true for many clients with this background, he felt he would never accomplish enough to gain his father's respect.

Hence, he constantly searched for respect. He became tense whenever he anticipated rejection and coped by increasing his perfectionistic demands on himself, creating intense internal pressure. His anxiety would then accelerate into panic—which only produced more failure. Trapped in a vicious cycle, he would then redouble his demands on himself, until the only way out was to turn to drugs and alcohol to soothe the pain.

Biofeedback techniques were used to teach Martin relaxation. A measure was used to read his skin conductivity. The unit has a skin resistance range of 5000 to 3,000,000 ohms, and a meter/tone resolution $<0.2\%$ of base resistance of $0.8F(.05C)$. Inputs consisted of external finger electrodes. Output was provided on dual sensitivity meter graduated into 40 units, which could be switched to a sub/superior displacement of 40 additional units, creating an 80-unit range.

During the first 15 minutes of the session, Martin practiced relaxation while being monitored for skin conductivity, producing a decrease of 35 units. He maintained this rate during a five-minute base reading period, after which the meter was reset at the central zero displacement level.

The following is a transcript of the instructions given to the Martin. The figures in parentheses are the amount of time elapsed, in minutes and seconds, and increases ($+$) and decreases ($-$) in Galvanic Skin Response (GSR).

I would like you to close your eyes and imagine the next scene in your hierarchy that causes anxiety. Imagine it as vividly as you can and use all your senses until it is clearly in mind. When you see it, indicate (this) by slightly raising your finger. (43 seconds; +12)

Very good. Now keep imagining the situation, but concentrate on what you are saying to yourself. Take your time, but focus on the first thought that pops into your head that's connected to your anxiety. Try to capture it and see if you can put it into a sentence. Indicate when you are ready. (23 seconds; +16)

Now, as we have discussed before, I want you to look underneath the surface. Imagine your thoughts are constructed like an upside-down pyramid. At the top, the shallow beliefs sit, but the one on the bottom holds up all the rest. I want you to start moving down the pyramid to find the core. Look at the first belief and ask yourself the question, "So what if . . . ?" (Martin was imagining he had to supervise 20 employees who were all previously his peers. Because of a new promotion, he had to supervise people he had worked with for several years as a recent college graduate. His first thought was that everybody would be very angry at him for being promoted over them, to which he countered, "So what if they are angry?")

Take all the time you need, but wait until you have an answer. (12 seconds) ("Then they wouldn't like or respect me.")

Now keep on asking yourself the question, "So what if?" or "Why?" Take your time until you have an answer, and move on to the next statement. Continue until you can find no further beliefs. (1 minute; +8) (The most basic thought Martin discovered was, "It would be absolutely horrible if somebody didn't respect me.")

Keep imagining the same situation and keep repeating the thoughts to yourself until you are sure you can remember them. Indicate when you are done (55 seconds; +8)

Take some more time just to relax. Make your muscles loose, limp and slack. (30 seconds; −8)

Keep relaxing but get some distance from yourself and start looking at each thought, one at a time. Make a coldly objective, non-emotional decision as to whether each thought is true or false, using all the techniques I have previously taught you. Take your time but be sure to make the most objective decision you can. (1½ minutes; +6) (He decided the first thought was true, but the next two were false.)

Imagine the situation again and picture thinking the first thought that you judged false. Keep doing this until it's clearly in mind. (54 seconds; +10) Now attack, challenge, contradict that thought in every way you can. Convince yourself that it is false, using all the evidence you can find against it. Continue until you feel a definite lessening in the belief. Indicate when you are done. (4 minutes; + 2) Take the next false belief and do the same thing. Dispute it as hard as you can and keep doing it until you feel it reduce. (2½ minutes; – 3) OK, now relax again. (45 seconds; – 20)

Now just as a check, imagine the first scene again just as you had first imagined it. (98 seconds; – 12)

We repeated the exercise twice more, increasing the speed during each repetition. When the test scene was presented the last time, Martin's GSR reading was – 27, from the baseline relaxed state, where it remained throughout the session. In later sessions, we used the same technique to reduce his anxiety about the other hierarchy items.

Comment

The guided approach is an extremely useful therapeutic technique. Almost all clients have used it during therapy. Much of the research described in the Appendix used this approach as one of the core procedures. Without the guided technique the therapist can never be sure the client knows how to counter maladaptive beliefs. With it, the therapist can pinpoint and correct a range of key problem areas.

Further Information

A form of guided countering called VCI has been discussed in four previous works (Casey and Mc Mullin, 1976; Mc Mullin and Casey, 1975; Mc Mullin et al., 1978, and Mc Mullin & Giles, 1981).

2

Perceptual Shifting

The most innovative techniques used in cognitive restructuring therapy derive from perceptual shifting theory. This chapter discusses 17 perceptual shift techniques which we have found to be very useful in meeting the needs of thousands of clients over the past 15 years.

The focus of these techniques is the client's perceptions and the impact of those perceptions upon the therapeutic process. Other chapters in this book examine the client's use of countering, which emphasizes "self language," and the influence of conditioning, which treats beliefs as individual stimuli. We are not concerned here with changing a client's isolated thoughts, but, more broadly, with modifying the general pattern of his or her thinking. This broader focus deals with perceptual patterns, or gestalten, schemata, or themes.

Many of the techniques described in this chapter make a creative use of analogies to help clients who are preoccupied with damaging beliefs to understand the nature of the perceptual transition that they must undergo. Hence, clients might be shown an ambiguous picture, representing raw data which they must organize into a meaningful representation. In the transposing technique some clients will see an old woman in that picture, although others will see instead a young woman. In like manner, it can be explained to clients, different individuals will respond differently to the same raw data, for a whole complex of reasons that therapists are only beginning to understand. Thus, a harsh word from a spouse will be interpreted by one client as proof of his innate inferiority and by another client as proof of his spouse's innate inferiority.

Our thesis here is that, more often than not, client unhappiness derives from mistaken perceptions that might have their roots in the earlier stages of human experience and development. Once implanted, these false, irrational beliefs color clients' interpretations of all subsequent inputs, which then weave into a coherent pattern of thought. The coherence of this faulty memory pattern is even more important than the contents of the pattern. Life is only livable against a backdrop of order and consistency which constitutes each individual's "reality." Even if that reality is founded upon damaging beliefs, many clients prefer it to no reality at all. Many techniques discussed here have proven successful in helping clients to switch from a false reality to one more positive and functional.

History is also recognized as a important factor here. Mistaken patterns arise from earlier, unfortunate learning. Errors often occur before the brain has developed the ability to reason formally (i.e., before the age of 11), and clients often fail to correct these mistaken perceptions during the normal process of maturation. It is also possible that many of the misperceptions are recorded in the nondominant hemisphere of the brain, and are therefore not coded into language. Because they are unlabeled, they are not subject to linguistic manipulation. When the dominant hemisphere develops, it does not synthesize the uncoded data, and the erroneous patterns resident in the more primitive right brain can cause negative emotions and irrational behaviors.

The underlying theory here is speculative, but there is much evidence in support of it scattered throughout psychological literature, and encompassed under such phrases as:

• Sleep and dream research
• Attitude change theory
• Ambiguous pictures
• Gestalt psychology
• Insight "Aha" experience
• Rapid cognitive changes
• Conditioned seeing
• Operant seeing
• Contexual organization in cognitive psychology
• Contingency vs. contiguity in classical conditioning
• Personal "meanings" and conceptual "clicks"
• Religious conversion, "brain washing," dramatic life changes

- Logotherapy
- Flooding
- Perceptual focusing
- Split brain hemisphere research
- Frontal lobe vs. brain stem functioning
- Visual perceptual psychology
- Cognitive developmental theory
- Cognitive neuroscience
- Neural networks
- Linguistical prototypes
- Connectionist vs. serial digital information processes

Although they differ greatly in their methodologies, all these techniques reflect certain common assumptions, including the following:

1. The brain selectively screens sensory and proprioceptive data.
2. The brain forms data into patterns.
3. The pattern the brain forms is influenced by the incoming data, but is separate from it.
4. In most cases, these gestalten are learned in the same way the brain learns other information. But some patterns are instinctual and trigger automatic emotional and behavioral responses.
5. Considering the infinite number of patterns possible, the brain uses only a few, personal schemata.
6. Themes once formed have a tendency to persist, unless unlearned.
7. Most patterns are taught by significant others.
8. The more a pattern is repeated, the stronger it gets and the more difficult it will be to remove or replace.
9. Cognitive schemata are formed more easily, and have more staying power, in the younger brain.
10. Emotional and behavioral responses are triggered by the brain's gestalten, not by the individual stimuli that are often mistaken to be the sole sources of a client's unhappiness.
11. Classical and operant conditioning can associate emotions and behaviors to the patterns.
12. Environmental stimuli can get conditioned to the themes so that later these triggers alone develop the ability to produce the pattern.
13. Language and images are ways of describing the patterns but these perceptions occur before language or visual representations.
14. Changing the representational description of the patterns may loop back and change the gestalten, but it is not a one-to-one relationship.

15. Themes are not generally formed on a logical basis, but more usually through emotional-experiential learning.
16. Some schemata, once formed, may be immutable.
17. The quickest, most complete method of modifying negative emotions and non-adaptive behaviors is by changing the patterns that elicit them.

The techniques listed in the chapter are grouped as follows.

1. Various Types of Shifts

    a. Basic Perceptual Shifts
    b. Conceptual Shifts
    c. Philosophical Shifts

2. Transposing Techniques

    a. Transposing 1
    b. Transposing 2
    c. Difficult Transpositions
    d. Progressive Image Modification (PIM)

3. Disentangling Techniques

    a. Depersonalizing Self
    b. Public Meanings

4. Techniques that Compel Change

    a. Forcing Perceptual Shifts
    b. Creating Dissonance

5. Bridging Techniques

    a. Bridge Perceptions
    b. Hierarchy of Values Bridges
    c. Stories and Fables

6. Perceptual Shifting Techniques from Other Therapies

    a. Cognitive Focusing
    b. Rational Emotive Imagery
    c. Resynthesizing Beliefs

In the pages that follow, we briefly introduce the underlying principles and assumptions for each of the 17 techniques, summarize the steps that should be taken by the therapist in executing each technique, provide examples of the successful use of each technique, and then end each discussion with helpful comments and a list of references that might be consulted for further information.

Two key points deserve emphasis here. First, for the purposes of this presentation, the techniques are covered in detail, but one at a time. The singularity of our focus in presenting each technique, unfortunately, might serve to obscure the extent to which a skilled therapist could combine any number of these techniques into a coordinated strategy for positive change.

Second, the author presumes that each therapist has all of the skills necessary to help him or her determine which of these techniques, singly or in combination, might be most suitable for each client. In a few instances, helpful pointers are provided to assist the professional in gaining confidence in the use of some of the more innovative techniques, but in the main we rely upon the professional judgment of our readers in making the best use of the array of client support tools that are presented here.

BASIC PERCEPTUAL SHIFT

Principles

While analyzing subjects' dreams, Hobson and McCarley (1977), two Harvard researchers, discovered some interesting facts about the human brain. Their research not only makes sense out of how the brain functions during sleep, but also gives clues about how it works when awake.

According to Hobson and McCarley, the brain does more than receive, store, and retrieve neurochemical information. It transforms information, organizing raw bits of data into schemata, patterns, and themes. The senses feed the brain most of these raw data when the organism is awake. When asleep, the brain uses more internal data from long- and short-term memory, emotions, and the organism's present physical stimulation. In both states, the forebrain organizes the data provided by the rest of the brain into coherent patterns, synthesizing the data into larger wholes. In sleep the brain's syntheses are called dreams. Awake they are called beliefs, attitudes, and thoughts.

Many negative emotions occur because clients synthesize raw data into maladaptive themes, continually organizing information into fearful, depressing, or angry patterns. A long history of thinking distortedly — along with the strong emotional arousal this creates — makes these themes prepotent, so that the brain consistently selects the same interpretation from its repertoire, no matter how inappropriate it is to the present circumstances.

As an example, consider the following dots in Figure 1 as raw, unorganized data. Since the brain rejects randomness, what pattern could the brain form out of the dots?

If the brain organizes the first two groups in terms of a triangle, it is more likely to organize the third into a triangle. Though a square would be more parsimonious, many people perceive a triangle in the third because they saw it in the first two. Likewise, neurotic clients may organize their experiences into "I am inferior" or other destructive themes simply because the brain has habitually concentrated on this theme.

It follows that bad experiences alone do not create clients' problems; most people have endured many negative things in their lives. It is the conceptualization of these experiences — not the experiences themselves — which produces

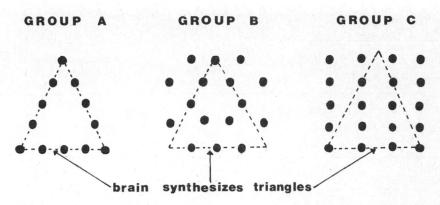

Figure 1. Analogy of the forebrain's ability to synthesize incomplete data.

the damage. Because of early traumatic learning or bad modeling, some clients consistently organize their experiences into damaging themes. Maybe these themes once reflected events accurately, but they became irrelevant as the environment changed. Or maybe they were always false and distorted. In either case, they cause the client much distress, and therefore need to be removed. The neurotic is not cured until the habituated theme is changed and a more realistic, less damaging pattern replaces it. In other words, the client requires a "basic perceptual shift" in how he or she perceives a given experience. Only then will the negative emotion be removed.

Method

1. Have your client draw four columns on a large piece of paper (see Table 1).
2. In the first column, have the client list every thought or belief that causes negative emotions in a particular situation (e.g., "I am afraid to fly in planes because I could get scared and all the passengers would see it," or "Planes are dangerous because you can't escape."). Obviously, the list can't go on indefinitely. However, even if some of the thoughts seem repetitious, it is better to include them than to leave a major theme unrecorded.
3. In the narrow second column, help your clients decide whether each belief is true or false. Look for the evidence both for and against it. Which is stronger? It is essential that the client make a decision based on objective data — not subjective feelings. (Chapter 5 provides several methods.)

Table 1
Perceptual Shift Worksheet

Thought/Belief	T/F	Best Argument Against Thought	Evidence from Own Experiences Proving Best Argument

4. In the third column, have the client record the best argument against the theme. Ideally, this argument will be emotionally persuasive as well as rationally sound.
5. The last column, in which the client lists evidence in support of this argument, is the key to the perceptual shift technique. With the assistance of the therapist, the client should prove the argument is correct by searching

out evidence from his or her own life experiences. For instance, remembering that 20 panic attacks never caused a psychotic break effectively argues against the thought that panic attacks cause insanity, and it does so using not just abstract logic, but the client's own experiences.

6. To bring about the actual perceptual shift, the client should meditate at least 30 minutes a day on those critical past incidences which disprove the irrational theme.

Example 1

In the 20 years I have counseled agoraphobics, I have found that one basic false belief produces most of their anxiety: "I could lose control over myself." Using the cognitive techniques incorporated in this book, most clients are able to purge these and other beliefs, significantly reducing or eliminating their panic attacks. They don't shift their perception quickly, for many work for more than a year. However, based on self-reports, objective tests, behavioral measures and collateral reports, we have determined that the average client is able to reduce anxiety significantly. (See Appendix.)

But even after shifting the core belief, almost all clients still feel some residual, low-level tension. Even after they are panic-free for a year, they often describe still feeling slightly on guard.

Ten years ago, one of my patients described this feeling. She asked, "If the panic I used to have is called agoraphobia, what is this tension I am having now called?" I didn't have an immediate answer. I said, "Let's call it 'Harold'." Since that time, I have told many clients of "Harold" and often use the name to describe the post-agoraphobic feeling of vigilance and tension.

What is Harold? Why this low-level tension? It is my hypothesis that clients create "Harold" to protect against the panic of agoraphobia. Harold guards against losing control. As one client described it:

> I have to be on guard and feel a little twinge of anxiety because then I will be prepared for my panics. If I get too relaxed then the panic may sneak up on me.

Harold is like a sentry always watching out for agoraphobic panic, and this tension lasts long after the need for it is gone. Thus, the agoraphobic fear may have disappeared for several years and the client is certain he or she will never again fear losing control, but Harold continues unabated. Often it seems more difficult to remove the guardian of danger than it was to remove the danger itself.

Harold is not a mysterious entity. Like any other fear, it is made up of a series of thoughts and beliefs. And like any other fear, it can be shifted, using the basic perceptual shift, as the following case history demonstrates.

Denise initially came to see me for agoraphobic anxiety. Afraid to travel far from her house, she had restricted herself to a five-mile "safe" radius (the agoraphobic's typical "territory"). Using other cognitive techniques, in six months' time she had eliminated her fears, and had flown alone on several occasions to visit her relatives—some two thousand miles away—without feeling any panic. By the time she returned for additional therapy, she no longer feared losing control or becoming psychotic, as she once had. However, she still felt low-level tension (Harold) and wanted to do something directly to reduce it.

Her worksheet looked like this:

Column 1. Harold Themes

1. If I don't constantly watch out for agoraphobia it could sneak up on me.
2. I must be prepared to escape in case agoraphobia comes back. I must make sure all my escape paths are clear.
3. A watched pot never boils. Watched agoraphobia never boils. (If I keep looking for it, it is less likely to happen.)
4. I need to think about my past agoraphobia all the time, because then I will have all my tools ready when I need them. If I forget how to use my tools, then agoraphobia could get me again.
5. I must never let myself be calm, relaxed, or too happy, because then my guard would be down.
6. It will come back unless I always think about its coming back.
7. Any time I feel calm I'm just fooling myself, because agoraphobia may always be lurking in the background.

Column 2. True or False

This client rated all the beliefs false, but only after thinking of an analogy. She imagined a man who, believing plants could infect him with a terrible disease, was afraid of touching them. She also pictured that he had erased his irrational fear and now was able to touch any plant he wanted. Despite this, however, he still felt some tension whenever he was around plants, though it served no purpose. In other words, his continuing fear around plants was as unnecessary as her continuing fear of losing control. Specific reasons behind this belief became evident in the third column of her worksheet.

Column 3. Best Argument Against Belief

1. Since I can't lose control and go psychotic, then I don't have to guard against it.

2. My watching out for the danger will increase my fear without reducing the danger.
3. Since there is no real danger, there is no real reason to guard.
4. It is better to get anxious once a month for an hour or two than to spend the whole month worrying about getting anxious.
5. Watching for anxiety doesn't reduce the chance of getting it.
6. Letting myself forget that I was an agoraphobic will just make me feel better, and it won't make it more likely that the agoraphobia will return.

Column 4. Best Evidence in Support of the Counter Belief

1. The client remembered all the incidents where she got panicky despite watching for it, and all the times it didn't occur when she wasn't watching. She concentrated on the plant analogy and reminded herself that guarding against a terrible plant disease doesn't reduce catching one, if plants don't give terrible diseases.
2. She remembered the scores of times when she feared the agoraphobia would return, but it didn't. Her fears had given her pain without any real protection.
3. She thought about childhood fears, such as monsters under the bed, or tigers in the woods, and how silly it is for a child to run away from them. She related these childhood fears to the fear of going crazy or having a nervous breakdown.
4. She speculated about all the things she could have done instead of guarding against agoraphobia, such as reading books, taking courses, renewing friendships, playing with her children, smelling roses.
5. She reflected on all the pots in life that boil whether we watch them or not. Children grow up. Love dies or deepens. Our world changes.

In keeping with the last step of the process, the client rehearsed the perceptual shift technique on a decelerating schedule. In the beginning, she practiced every day, then every other day, then once a week, then only as needed. She was instructed to try to shift Harold only during the practice periods. At other times she was told to concentrate on other aspects of her life.

Comment

The perceptual shift technique has a great advantage over many other techniques, in that it can be effectively used in a crisis and it attacks all the relevant themes causing the crisis.

Since it is an advanced technique, the therapist should employ it only after more preliminary cognitive approaches have been presented.

Further Information

This treatment is a variation of a technique described by Mc Mullin et al. (1978) and Mc Mullin and Giles (1981).

Further evidence supporting the contention that the brain organizes data into coherent themes comes from cognitive psychology's discussion of contextual organization (see Biederman, Glass, and Stacy, 1973; Palmer, 1978; Pomerantz et al., 1977). For research on insight and the "aha" experience, see Gardner (1978), Greeno (1978), Hayes (1982), Johnson (1972), Newell and Simon (1972), Simon (1978), and Vinacke (1974). And for more on perceptual organization, see Gibson (1950, 1966), Kosslyn and Pomerantz (1977).

CONCEPTUAL SHIFT

Principles

The human brain is systematic and selective in the way in which it organizes the information it receives into gestalten. It scans all inputs, looking for impressions that seem compatible with those already held, excluding those that are not compatible, and weaving all the accepted inputs into a consistent pattern of thought. The goal is to create a consistent, coherent background, which we often refer to in this book as a given client's "reality." Each thought must fit neatly within that pattern, and even if the pattern is illogical that does not negate the emotional response.

Problems arise when those original inputs, which define the character of the overall pattern, are unrealistic. The entire pattern can become contaminated. Hence, a client who has somehow formed the rudimentary impression that he is inferior to the rest of mankind will interpret any subsequent inputs that have bearing on his self-image in that light.

Precisely how the brain creates these often damaging patterns is not fully understood, but German Gestalt psychologists articulated some important theories about that process during the early part of this century. Although their work was mostly done on a person's perceptual organization, their results can be readily applied to the concepts presented here. The major principles that the brain uses to create the most consistent pattern are:

a. *Proximity.* Elements close together in time or space are associated. Clients associate thoughts that they had during the same time period.
b. *Prägnanz.* Gaps and omissions are ignored so the fit is stable and closed. Clients ignore contradictory elements in their irrational beliefs.
c. *Similarity.* Similar elements are grouped together. Clients associate thoughts of the same logical types.
d. *Organizational set.* Once the brain forms a fit, it continues organizing in the same way even though the stimulus pattern changes. Clients continue to perceive the same irrational thought in a variety of situations.
e. *Direction.* Present best fits are evolved from earlier ones. Clients are likely to perceive, as adults, the same irrational thoughts that they had as children, even though their life circumstances may have drastically changed.
f. *Absorption.* Stronger forms absorb weaker ones. Clients will give up an irrational belief if the counter belief is a better fit (simplicity, better articulation) of their experiences.
g. *Resistance and stability.* Strong organizational forms resist disintegration. Clients will hold onto their irrational thoughts even though these thoughts cause them significant emotional pain.

Once clients have established a damaging pattern of thinking about themselves and the world around them, that pattern must be dismantled before a new and more wholesome pattern can take its place. That dismantling process usually will not occur easily or quickly, though the ease and pace of it will vary from client to client. The conceptual shift technique is one method for accomplishing that goal.

Method

1. Have your client list all the thoughts connected to a target negative emotion.
2. Collapse the thoughts into one major, negative, core belief or theme. These themes are the previous best fit that the client has formed.
3. List a great number of situations (past and present) which are connected to the core theme. The situations should be listed separately.
4. Develop a list of alternative, more positive beliefs for each negative thought.
5. Summarize and collapse the positive beliefs into one core theme, a new best fit or a new way that these beliefs can be organized.
6. Help your clients reinterpret the past and present situations in terms of the new fit. Go through each individual thought and situations and show them

how the new fit parsimoniously explains what happened and how they misinterpreted the situations.

7. Your client should practice by reviewing more and more situations and by reinterpreting them in terms of the new theme.

Example

Daniel was a 39-year-old orthopedic surgeon who entered counseling because of strong feelings of depression, which had been recurring in his life ever since his adolescence. Two intake sessions indicated a cause. Whenever he felt less dominant than others—which was often—he would get depressed. His most recent depression resulted from his thought that his business partners were taking advantage of him.

An analysis of his belief system indicated that Daniel's most common thoughts were that he should always act dominant, assertive, forceful, cool, calm and collected. He would get depressed whenever his actions differed from these thoughts, and they often did. He would often spend more time than other surgeons with his patients to answer their questions and soothe their fears about an impending surgical procedure. Many of his patients were poor, and he extended them credit for many years without even charging them interest, with the result that he earned much less money than most of his colleagues. He would allow interns and nurses to question and disagree with him; he listened respectfully to their ideas without demanding absolute obedience to his will. He viewed this latter behavior as a clear sign of weakness, and at times would try to act like, in his words, "a real doctor." But no matter how hard he tried, he would always shift back to what he called "wimpy behavior."

After some preliminary instruction, we decided to use conceptual shifting.

Step 1: He listed all his negative thoughts connected to his depression:

• I back down when I am confronted.
• I am afraid to press my opinion.
• I lack the ability to demand respect.
• People always take advantage of me because I am weak.
• Women see my lack of masculine behavior and are disgusted by it.
• There is something about my basic nature which is lacking the personality force that most men seem to have.

Step 2: We collapsed these thoughts into one core attitude:

• I am a puny, weak man.

Step 3: A great number of situations elicited the core belief. They were subdivided into different areas of his life.

- *Career*: Letting clients pay late, having only a moderate income, doing home visits, keeping his fees low.
- *Lover*: Not being able to pick up women in a bar.
- *Athlete*: he would sometimes let his racketball partner win when his partner was having a bad day.
- *Teacher*: he would listen to students' opinions even though they disagreed with his.
- *Divorced parent*: he wouldn't punish his son if he felt he had a reasonable explanation for being late.
- *Friend*: he would take time out of his schedule to console his friends, or stay with them if they were sick.

He judged all such behavior as puny and weak.

Step 4: We changed each negative belief to a more positive perception.

Negative	Positive
I back down when confronted.	I listen to others' opinions.
I am afraid to express my opinion.	I don't demand others accept it.
People don't respect me.	People respect me a great deal for my competency, intelligence, flexibility, and kindness. They don't respect me in the way that people respect a rigid tyrant.
People take advantage of me.	The vast majority of people don't, but most appreciate my openness. Those few that do would try to take advantage of me no matter how I acted.
Women are disgusted by my lack of masculinity.	Women appreciate my openness. If masculinity means being inflexible, arrogant, and noncaring, who needs it?
I lack the personality force to be aggressive.	Unlike many others, I care for and appreciate the basic worthwhileness of all people. I do not look at all relationships as competitive.

Step 5: We collapsed his new beliefs into one core thought:

- I am a compassionate, humanistic man.

Step 6: The counseling continued by reinterpreting over one hundred situations from the past and present so he could discover that a better explanation (a better fit) was that he was humanistic rather than wimpy. He practiced until the new fit became automatic.

Comment

The therapist must cope with strong client resistance to changing their gestalten. Repetition, confrontation, and encouragement are necessary to help clients make the shift.

Further Information

The principles and research of Gestalt psychology can be found by reading some of the works by the founders. Although much of their work is in German, the reader may find some good translations and summaries. See Hartmann, 1935; Koffka, 1935; Köhler, 1947; Wertheimer, 1945.

PHILOSOPHICAL SHIFTS

Principles

The concept of the "intervening cognitive variable" has been described in a variety of ways by therapists, depending upon whether they subscribe to semantic, rational emotive, or cognitive behavioral schools of thought. Hence it is known variously as "self-talk," "internal sentences," "covert stimuli," "S d's," or "covert conditional responses." Cognitive restructuring therapists believe that this concept may be considered very globally as a maladaptive personal philosphy. While acknowledging that the cognition is a major source of distress in a client's life, we recognize that a core epistemological mistake may also have more wide-ranging ramifications than generally recognized.

In addressing this concept, the therapeutic goal must be to change the client's philosophy, not merely a single viewpoint. Such a change should be calculated to positively affect every aspect of the client's life, including his career, his self-concepts, and his personal and professional relationships and goals. Such broad changes require a broad therapeutic technique. In the exercise of such a technique, the therapist develops a list of questions, explores those aspects of the client's philosophy that appear to be malfunctioning, and helps the client to realize the damaging effects of the old philosophy. The aim is not only to remove unpleasant symptoms, but also to help the client obtain a richer, more satisfying, more useful perspective.

Method

1. Find the client's core mistaken philosophy. If more than one philosophy exists, write them all down. To the extent that doing so might be helpful in clarifying the parameters of the belief, it is useful to discuss the source of each mistaken philosophical view.
2. After extensive discussion, the therapist should help the client to develop an alternative philosophy which is more valid, logical, socially fulfilling, and functional.
3. The therapist should then assist the client in his efforts to formulate a strategy for incorporating the new philosophy into all areas of his life. Each area should be listed separately, and the contrasting effects of both the old and new philosophies, as they relate to each of these areas, should be specified. For example, the therapist might ask the client, "How did your old philosophy hurt you in your career? If you believed in the new philosophy, how would your relationships change?" Following is a partial list of client areas that could be affected if a client shifted from his old philosophy to a newer, more functional one:

- Career goals
- Relations with members of the opposite sex
- Relations with members of the same sex
- Relations with family members
- Relations with children
- One's strategy for handling negative emotions
- One's religion and ethical code
- One's perspective on social issues and propensities for community participation
- One's perceptions of the relative values of fame vs. fortune
- One's ability to manage conflicts with others
- One's physical and psychological health
- One's ability to cope with old age and the inevitability of death
- The pace and direction of one's intellectual growth

- One's ability to control one's own actions, as well as the actions of others
- One's ability to cope with catastrophic events
- One's self-monitoring and self-directional skills
- One's attitudes toward protection and safety
- One's ability to handle criticism and rejection from others
- The extent to which one is passive, aggressive or inclined toward assertive behavior
- The extent to which one values freedom and independence
- The extent to which one seeks the approval of others
- The extent to which one is willing to seek from or offer help to others
- How one handles failure
- The extent to which one perceives life to be imbued with purpose and meaning
- The extent to which one is inclined to trust others

4. *Remember*: It is not sufficient just to talk about the new philosophy. The discussions can help, but they are meaningless unless reinforced by action. The new philosophy needs to be incorporated into a new plan of action. So the final step for the therapist is to escort the client through a process of taking each perceptual change and designing a step-by-step behavioral plan to actualize the covert changes.

Example

Mary initiated therapy as a result of a problem that neither she nor her therapist could immediately define. She was suffering from moderate depression, despite the fact that her life was characterized by valued friendships, economic security, and what she reported were satisfying personal and professional achievements. She was haunted by a vague feeling of meaninglessness and a lack of purpose in her life.

After considerable searching, we discovered the symptom—inertia. The cause derived from a mistaken philosophical view that Mary hadn't even realized she held. Apparently, because of a series of childhood experiences, Mary had developed the view that her role in life was to be a passive observer of events. She viewed herself as an inert sponge, just taking in the world around her, but never initiating any action in that world. She wasn't trying to avoid the painful realities of the world around her; nor was she necessarily afraid of the challenges life held in store for her. She simply didn't see herself as a creator of energy, a force in her own right who could modify—at least to some extent—the environment around her.

The result of this philosophy was passivity, depression, and the creation of a façade of cool, effortless élan. To be happy, she would need to change her philosophy.

Her new philosophy would have to serve the purpose of helping her to clear away the noxiousness of her inert attitudes. Under the new creed, a high level of personal energy and a greater propensity for personal risk-taking would have to become the *raison d'être* for growth, enrichment, and expansion. The new creed might be summarized as follows: The purpose of existence is not to actively avoid the more fearsome possibilities of life, but rather to take whatever risks seem warranted for the chance of greater personal happiness.

The next two paragraphs summarize the key components of Mary's philosophical shifting.

Old Philosophy: In many areas of her life, Mary's philosophy was damaging. She was in a boring, no-growth job, but wasn't willing to take a chance at a loss in income by looking for a new position. She had a seven-year relationship with her boyfriend, who was refusing to consider cementing the relationship by marrying her. Still she kept the relationship going because, she felt, it wasn't worth the effort of looking for a better relationship. Her family rejected her lifestyle, and she hadn't seen them for six years. She had wanted to take some courses in the community college for several years, but had never gotten around to it. Whenever she had a conflict with her friends or work colleagues, she would pretend it had not happened, and would wait for the problem to fade away. She had no long-term or short-term goals, and lived one day at a time.

New Philosophy: Step-by-step, Mary started to change her philosophy, and to take action in the various areas of her life. She applied for a transfer to another job which, although more risky, had a far better opportunity for advancement. She ended her relationship with her boyfriend, and after going through some grief, started to go out with more appropriate men. She contacted her family, visited them, and discussed openly their past difficulties in a genuine effort to resolve them. She took two courses at the college. The hardest thing for her to do was to confront problems with her colleagues, but gradually she was able to try to resolve the difficulties by taking action. Sometimes the actions worked, and sometimes they didn't, but she felt that at last she was becoming more and more of an initiator in her life, even when her decisions were wrong, and she found that being an initiator pleased her much more than it frightened her. And this switch in philosophy, eventually, removed her depression.

Comment

Mary and many others like her struggle with the need to make a philosophical switch in their lives every day. They view any philosophical change as threatening and resist implementing it. The therapist must be sensitive to the reality that this kind of change is not easily effected. Chances are that the foundation of the old philosophy has been laid over the period of a lifetime. It will not be easily or quickly uprooted. Care must be taken to nurture within clients a desire for positive change, to assure them that they are capable of making that change, and to ensure that they are the primary agent for change in their own life.

Despite our best therapeutic efforts, some clients will not make the switch. Others, like Mary, make the change only after months of work. Counselor persistence in these matters seems to be a crucial variable in ensuring the overall success of this process.

Further Information

Much of the logotherapy by Viktor Frankl involves helping clients shift their philosophies. See Frankl, 1959, 1972, 1977, 1978, and 1980.

TRANSPOSING 1

Principles

We have made frequent use of a transposition technique to illustrate to clients how their brains organize the same information into different patterns, and how they must learn to shift from those patterns that are harmful to them. The pictures themselves are not curative, but are employed as analogies, usually in an early session with a client, as part of the general process of orienting him or her to the therapeutic process.

The technique involves showing clients reversible drawings or embedded figures in which the raw material for a wide range of concrete images is hidden. The clients' minds extract one or the other image(s), depending upon the manner in which they are conditioned to processing information. Hence, one client sees an elephant in a drawing, another sees a dragon, and a third insists that he sees nothing at all.

Most clients concoct some sort of image from one of these drawings within minutes, and there the analogy fails. An actual shifting of personal perceptions usually takes *months* of diligent effort on the part of both client and therapist. That reality must be carefully explained at the outset. The primary purpose of these analogous transpositions is to help clients understand the goal of the therapeutic process and use transpositions with their own beliefs.

In the following pages, we will introduce two examples of how transposing might be used, and then comment briefly on the results of research into how clients really undertake the task of effecting these transpositions, both in the drawings and in their own attitudes and behaviors (see Figure 2).

Clients usually extract either the image of a witch or the image of a young woman from this assemblage of black ink lines on white paper, but neither image is really there. What we perceive is the result of our mind's effort to organize the raw material into a meaningful image. The raw material reflected on our retinas is the same, but different observers will *interpret* different images.

If, through conditioning, we associated pain with the image of the witch, and pleasure with the image of the young woman, then the result of these perceptions would provoke either the positive or negative emotion. Remember, the raw material of the drawing doesn't *create* the emotions; the brain does.

Using the analogy as a guideline, we hypothesize that many clients who are unhappy, anxious, or depressed have learned to see the witch. Or more precisely, since the witch is not "in" the picture, they have learned to see witches in ambiguous data. To remove their negative emotions, we should help our clients see the young woman.

Any of several strategies might be employed in helping clients to de-stigmatize the witch. Through conditioning, we could pair relaxation with the perception of the witch (see our discussion elsewhere in this book on cognitive desensitization). We could also train the client to see only the young woman, thus avoiding any discomforts that might be incited by the other image.

A key point to be emphasized here is that what is true for clients' perceptions of this drawing is also true for clients' perceptions of themselves. If clients form gestalten that screen out most positive data, they will "see" a negative self-concept. If their brains keep organizing ambiguous stimuli into danger, they will feel anxious. And if they organize their environments about being unjustly treated, they will feel chronic anger.

The transposing technique emphasizes changing clients' general patterns

Figure 2. Old women-young women visual analogy of transposition (Figure 2 was drawn by cartoonist W. E. Hill and was originally published in *Puck* November 6, 1915. It was later published by E. G. Boring, 1930.)

of thinking, their gestalten, the way their brains organize their experiences. Using the analogy of embedded or ambiguous figures, we have been able to get clients to restructure their gestalten into more realistic, less damaging conceptual wholes.

Method

1. Assemble a useful collection of reversal and embedded pictures. (See Figure 3, and 4, and "Further Information" for additional references.)
2. Show clients a series of embedded or reversible figures. At least six figures are used. Show them one at a time, and ask your clients to tell you what they see. Then ask them to try to see the alternative figure embedded in the pictures. Give hints one at time until the clients are able to perceive the new figure. The hints come from the subcomponents of the picture, i.e., "This part could be seen as either the witch's nose or the young woman's chin."

    While showing the pictures explain to the client that the whole process is analogous to what they must do to change their negative beliefs. Teach your clients that what they are doing perceptually to transpose one figure into the other is the same thing they must do to change one belief into another. Have them carefully monitor how they are switching one figure into another.
3. Draw a line on a piece of paper. (Both you and your clients should have paper in front of you.) On the left side write all the components of the clients' negative gestalt, one at a time. Make it an exhaustive list. At the bottom of the column summarize all the details of the old perceptions into one major theme.
4. On the right column, transpose each detail of the old perception into a more realistic, less damaging new perception. Discuss each transposition with the client until you both agree that the new way of perceiving each detail is acceptable. At the bottom of the column, have the clients summarize all the subparts of the new perceptions into one global gestalt or theme.

In our example, the old perception is of an old woman. The new gestalt is of a young woman. The transposition of the subparts is:

Old Woman	*Young Woman*
tip of nose	tip of chin
eye	ear
mouth	neck band

Old Woman	Young Woman
wart on nose	nose
looking at us	looking away
chin	lower neck
hair on nose	eyelash

5. Have your clients practice transposing perceptions by reading the old way of believing and trying to transpose it into the new gestalten. Continue practicing until your clients can readily transpose each detail, and the total theme, from one view to another.

6. Have your clients practice transposing every day until the new gestalt forms automatically and they have difficulty remembering the old perception.

Example

Jeannette came to see me at the suggestion of her physician, who had heard of my treatment in helping local athletes improve their skills. She was concerned about her deteriorating performance in an athletic event. She had started the sport about eight years before, and had made remarkable progress in state and regional competition. But recently she had become more and more anxious right before each competition, and her performance had started to deteriorate.

An analysis of the cognitive component of her anxiety revealed a person high in need achievement, perfectionism, and a severe dread of failure. Her background showed that she was constantly disapproved of by her father, who kept pressing her to succeed. Despite early success, economic circumstances and an early marriage prevented her from ever achieving her full potential. As an adult she strove for success in sports, since she felt other areas for achievement were closed to her.

The following is an outline of Jeannette's chart, representing her old and new gestalten.

Old Gestalt

I must be very successful; otherwise no one will ever love me, approve of me, or accept me, and then I will be totally alone.

Subparts:

1. The worst thing in life is to fail.
2. If I don't totally win, I fail.
3. Success is an illusion; failure is real.

Figure 3. Reversible figure test drawing: Maurits C. Escher, "Circle Limit IV (Heaven and Hell) (Escher, 1971).

4. One must be in control of everything (self and environment) or one will fail.
5. If I can't do something perfectly, I shouldn't do it at all.
6. I am running out of time to succeed.
7. If I worry about failing, I'll be more likely to succeed.
8. I must have everybody respect and approve of me.

Figure 4. Hidden figure test drawing: Napoleon and tomb at St. Helena. (Figure 4 was drawn by an unknown artist between 1821 and 1836. It was reproduced by Fernberger, 1950.)

New Gestalt

Success, love, respect, and acceptance are all by-products of accepting myself. They may or may not come but mean little in themselves. Unless I accept that I am a good, worthwhile person just the way I am, I will never by happy. I am not bad, wrong, or inferior.

Subparts:

1. The worst thing in life is to be motivated solely by a fear of failure.
2. If you don't win you just don't win.

3. Success and failure are both illusions.
4. Many times you just have to let life happen.
5. If something is not worth doing, it is not worth doing well.
6. Success is irrelevant. There is no time limit to happiness.
7. Worrying doesn't change anything; it just makes me feel bad.
8. If I didn't respect myself it wouldn't matter if everyone in the world respected me.

Jeannette eventually transposed to the new gestalt. By concentrating on shifting the subparts, she perceived the new way at looking at herself. Initially the new gestalt was fleeting and she could only see it occasionally for a day or so. Gradually, through practice, the new perception became more prominent and the old theme faded.

Comment

It is important that clients not feel rushed during the transposition exercise. Encourage them to relax and take their time. Since new perceptions, once acquired, are often fleeting, it is also important that clients practice this technique frequently.

Further Information

Reversal and embedded pictures can be found in Attneave, 1968; Boring, 1930; Dallenbach, 1951; Fernberger, 1950; Fisher, 1968; Mach, 1959; Martin, 1914; Newhall, 1952; Wever, 1927. One of the best sources for these drawings is the work of M. C. Escher (1971).

––––––––

TRANSPOSING 2

Principles

As was noted earlier, transpositions are analogous to the process by which clients shift their perceptions. Several years ago we became interested in discovering the methods by which clients transposed their visual perceptions during these exercises, on the assumption that those same methods might be in use during the more protracted process of transposing personal beliefs.

Our curiosity on this point led us to conduct a survey among 30 of our clients. The clients were evenly divided into two groups, a control and an experimental group, and the members of each group were given a set of 11 cards, each of which contained a unique reversible drawing. One of those drawings is illustrated here (Figure 5).

As you can see from this example, each of the 11 drawings had an "A" section and a "B" section. Our clients were asked to rate each section of each drawing, using a 10-point scale, to indicate which of the two sections appeared most dominant in each drawing. For the above example, most of the clients in both groups rated Section "A" as 7 and Section "B" as 3, meaning that they were far more likely to see form in the "A" side than in the "B" side. Several described Section "A" as a cut-out of the Sesame Street character, Kermit the Frog.

All of our clients rated the 11 cards on three separate occasions over a period of two weeks. We found that they rated them reliably. We then randomly divided the clients into two groups: one an experimental group, and the other a control group. The control group simply rated the cards at 13 different times over a period of 2½ years. (The regularity of the ratings varied, depending upon our ability to reach them.) The experimental group, however, was instructed to do different things to try to make the weaker image (rated at 4 or less) stronger (6 or more). They each devoted half an hour to a conscious effort to perceptually change the image. After the "experimental period," this group rated the cards 13 more times, just like the control group.

The members of the experimental group tried a number of different approaches in their efforts to make the weak image stronger. For example, they tried just staring at the weak side—trying not to see the strong. In the effort to forcibly bias their perceptions, they reinforced themselves by eating a candy bar whenever they saw form on the weak side, or punishing themselves by snapping a rubber band when they saw the strong side. They tried relaxing when seeing the weak side and tensing their muscles when they saw the strong. But just repetition or reinforcement did not result in any changes in their perception of the drawings.

At the close of the 2½-year research effort, we found that none of the control group rated the drawings any differently than they had originally, but the majority in the experimental group was able to switch the dominance of the images. We also discovered that the members of the experimental group had all used a similar technique, which is detailed in the following example.

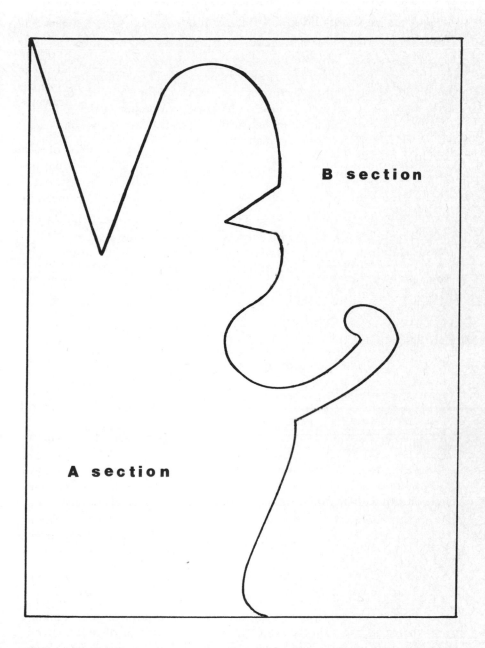

B section

A section

Figure 5. Experimental reversable drawing

Example

Frederico, a member of the experimental group, made a dramatic shift in his perception of the drawing illustrated above (Figure 5). He was seeing me for depression over a divorce, and before our sessions he would rate the pictures. His first rating of the picture in Figure 6 was 7 for "A" and 3 for "B". After the experimental period, however he rated the dominance the opposite (3 for "A" and 7 for "B"). Even though he didn't practice further, he continued to rate the "B" section more dominant throughout the 13 follow-up testings during the next two years.

He described the way in which he was able to switch the dominance of the above picture as follows:

When I first saw the picture I could only see the "A" section. It looked like Kermit the Frog. Only with effort could I see anything at all in "B." When I was told to work real hard and try to make side "B" stronger than side "A" it took me most of the half-hour but I was able to do it. Side "B" became real when I started to see a figure from one of my daughter's Atari games. She had always loved playing a game called "Adventure," where a knight had to take a golden chalice from three evil dragons. You had to first kill the dragons with a sword. This picture ("B") looked like one of the dead dragons. Once I thought of my daughter's dragon, I saw it immediately every time I looked at the drawing; in fact, it was difficult to see side "A" again. I can only remember once seeing Kermit again, and that was when I had forgotten, for a moment, the dragon.

Method

The methodological implications of our research on this matter seem clear. From our item analysis of the responses of experimental group members, we have come up with an outline of the possible ways in which clients can practice transposing one belief to another.

1. After developing a list of the core irrational or damaging client gestalten, develop the rational beliefs for each.
2. Have the client practice transposing the old beliefs to the new ones by making the new belief more vivid, using the following principles.

   a. Tie the new belief to a strong client memory. In the above example, the client had seen the dead Atari dragon hundreds of times.
   b. The new image should be a general gestalt, not a subpart. The client saw all of side "b" as the dragon, not part of it.

c. The client should make the new theme as personally and emotionally significant as possible. Seeing the dead dragon was significant to Frederico because it was associated with his young daughter playing a game in happier times—a very emotional image to the recently divorced man.
d. Simple repetition of seeing the new belief is not effective. The client must fill out the image until it becomes personally very meaningful. Once the subject saw the dragon in part "B," the transposition took place. He did not have to repeat it to improve its habit strength.
e. Although repetition doesn't increase the strength of the transposition, it does help the client remember what transposition was made. When the subject forgot that he looked at side "B" as a dragon, the dominance shifted back to the original perception.

Comment

Therapists might prefer to make up their own two-sided drawings in order to illustrate the above principles to their clients.

DIFFICULT TRANSPOSITIONS

Principles

Following is another example of the use of transpositions in the therapeutic process. This example uses more difficult drawings than our first illustration to demonstrate the rigor necessary. The difficulties clients have in this exercise often exactly replicate the type of problems they will have in transposing their own beliefs.

Method

1. Show the clients one of the pairs of pictures in Figures 6–11 or the hidden images in Figures 12 and 13.
2. Inform your clients that Form "A" (on the left) is embedded within Form "B" (on the right). Ask them to trace the outline of Form "A" with their fingers where it appears within Form "B."

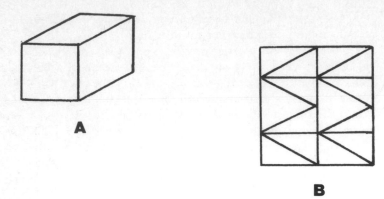

Figure 6. Difficult transposition drawing.

3. Explain to your clients that the drawings are like their beliefs. Trying to see the rational thought in their lives is like trying to see the "A" in the "B."
4. While clients are doing the task, instruct them to report any and all stream of conscious thoughts and feelings. Write down all comments and your observations as they occur.
5. Look for all client problems doing the exercise. Pay attention to self-accusation, frustrations, anger towards the pictures or towards the therapist. Look for giving up, denying that Form "A" can be found in Form "B," refusing to continue, or feelings of inferiority, etc.

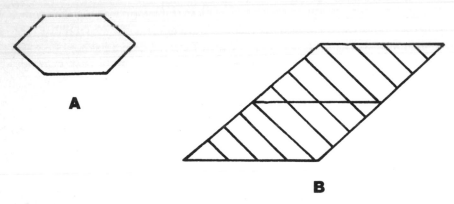

Figure 7. Difficult transposition drawing.

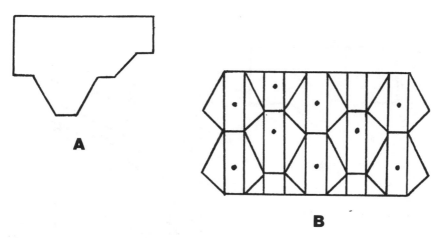

Figure 8. Difficult transposition drawing.

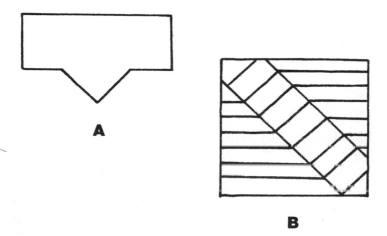

Figure 9. Difficult transposition drawing.

6. Tell clients that their frustrations, self-anger, or feelings of inferiority about this task are likely to be the same feelings and thoughts they will have about working on their beliefs. Discuss the relationships between the two in detail.

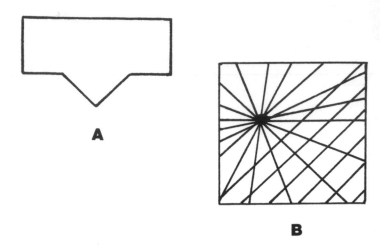

Figure 10. Difficult transposition drawing.

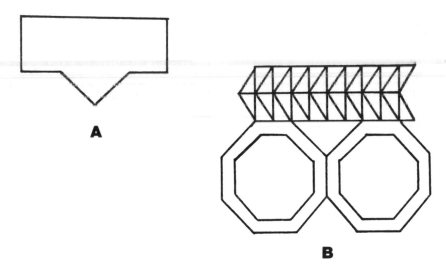

Figure 11. Difficult transposition drawing.

Figure 12. Hidden figure difficult drawing: hidden Christ. (Figure 12 was drawn by Dorthy Archbold and published by Porter, 1954.)

7. Help your clients solve these problems so that they successfully complete the task. If they are too tense, teach them relaxation while doing the exercise; if they are self-condemning, help them counter the beliefs; if they wish to give up, encourage them to continue. In any case, sustain your help until they can do the exercise successfully.
8. Show the clients that the way they solved the puzzles is the same method they can use to transpose their beliefs. List each correction and have them record them for further reference.

Example

Terry was referred to me by another cognitive therapist. She had been seeing him for about four months about a relationship problem. The therapy had been helpful for the relationship, but wasn't helpful in reducing a constant, low-level anxiety. After our intake sessions, it was clear that she was a social phobic. She was afraid about being scrutinized by others and worried about doing things others would consider shameful. She avoided public exposure whenever she could.

We followed the traditional cognitive restructuring approach, and she was making good progress. However, when we started using the transposition

Figure 13. Hidden figure difficult drawing: concealed cow. (Figure 13 was drawn by Leo Potishman and published by Dallenbach, 1951.)

technique, she had difficulties. She was doing her homework (at least a half-hour practice a day), but she reported that she wasn't able to shift her thoughts. We decided that the "difficult pictures" might give us some clues as to how she might be sabotaging her own efforts to transpose her beliefs.

The following is a transcript of part of the session where the difficult transposition approach was used.

THERAPIST: I am going to show you some drawings. The task I will ask you to do is theoretically similar to what you have been trying to do at home. But the drawings are a lot simpler and they may help to clarify some of the problems you may be having in transposing your beliefs.

But, I would like you to do something special while doing the exercise. Please tell me what you are feeling or thinking during the exercise. Most of the time we don't report these thoughts or feelings; we censor them. But for the exercise I would like you to focus and report these automatic thoughts and feelings just as you experience them. Okay?

Look at the following drawings. Notice the figure on the left labeled "A." I would like you to try to see that figure in the form on the right labeled "B." Try to see the rectangle on the left in the figure on the right. Take all the time you need.

(The client started the exercise and reported these thoughts and feelings.)

CLIENT: This looks tough. . . .
I'm not sure I can do it. . . .
I don't see it at all. Are you sure it's there?
Is it the same size or do I have to turn it?
I don't like doing this. . . .
It's no good. I can't do it. . . .
Wait, I almost had it. Nope it's gone again.
This is silly. I don't see why I have to do this. It's a dumb exercise. I really want to stop.

(Throughout the exercise the therapist encouraged her to continue.)

CLIENT: I am not smart enough to do this. Maybe your other clients are brighter. . . .
This isn't going to work for me.
I see where it is supposed to be but I can't see it. . . .

(The above remarks covered a period of about 10 minutes. During this time the client became increasingly agitated. She started to push herself harder and harder to see the form.)

CLIENT: It is no good. I can't do anything right.
You must think I'm really stupid. Do any of your other clients take this long to see it?

(After a few more minutes during which the client made similar remarks, I decided to intervene.)

THERAPIST: Okay. Stop for a moment and let's talk about it. Do you notice that what you are thinking and feeling while doing the exercise is similar to what you think and feel when you are at home trying to change your beliefs?
CLIENT: Yes! I have trouble with that too.

THERAPIST: Well, let's analyze what you are thinking and feeling. In fact, I would appreciate it if you would write it down.

First you told yourself it was tough, and that you probably couldn't do it. Next you attacked yourself for not seeing it by calling yourself stupid. Then you worried about what I would think of you for not seeing it, and finally you got angry at me for giving you the exercise. Is my summary accurate?

CLIENT: I'm not sure.

(We recorded the session, and I had the client listen to her remarks on the tape.)

CLIENT: Yeah! I sure did attack myself!

THERAPIST: Yes you did! And did you notice that you were getting more and more anxious the harder you tried, and the more you attacked?

CLIENT: Sure, I was getting pretty nervous.

THERAPIST: Okay, let's try something different this time. You noticed that the more you attacked yourself, the less you were able to concentrate on the task. Well, let's try to change things a bit. This time I want you to look at the pictures in a very relaxed way. We will practice by going back and doing some relaxation exercises we did a few sessions ago. Whenever you start feeling tense, I want you to stop what you are doing, take a deep breath, and relax your muscles in the way I have shown you. In addition, whenever you start thinking those self-attacking thoughts, I want you to quietly say, "stop, calm, relax," and then immediately concentrate on the task again. Whenever your mind wanders in any way from the task, stop the thinking and return again to seeing the picture. Instead of pressuring yourself to see the pictures, I want you do relax and just let the picture come. Do you understand?

(We practiced the relaxation for about 15 minutes. Then she returned to looking for the pictures. Whenever she appeared to be tensing up, I told her to relax. If her brow started to frown I told her to stop the thought and calmly return to the task without pressuring herself, to just wait and let the picture come of its own accord. After about two minutes she could see the rectangle in form "b" and showed me by drawing it with her finger. We then did two more drawings and she got them both in less than a minute.)

THERAPIST: All right, I think we learned something here. It's probably the reason you have had difficulty doing the transpositions at home. When you push yourself to try to get yourself to see something, it just makes you more tense, you start criticizing yourself, and you are less likely to see it. What you did here is probably what you need to do at home. So I would like you to start practicing relaxing, do the "stop, calm, relax" technique, and let the transpositions come instead of trying to make them appear.

Comment

Using the difficult pictures is not a technique in itself, but rather a method of determining problems clients are having when practicing other perceptual shifting approaches. It is a way of measuring client process variables.

The relaxation instructions given in the example above are not a standard part of the procedure. It was based on my assessment of what the client needed at the time. For other clients, it might be more appropriate to have them concentrate on seeing the drawings, even if doing so subjects them to a certain amount of pressure. The therapist uses his/her clinical judgment to see what corrections are needed to help clients make effective shifts.

Clients shouldn't see the pictures immediately. If they can, select some other drawings that are more difficult. For example, most people find it difficult to see Christ in Figure 12 and even more difficult to see the cow in Figure 13.

It is important that clients keep practicing until they can complete the exercise successfully. Stopping before completion would give them another failure experience. Give them all the help they need, but make sure they are ultimately successful.

Further Information

The geometric drawings were originally made by Julius Sprinker and copied by Kurt Gottschaldt (1939). Additional examples can be found from in W. Ellis' *A Source Book of Gestalt Psychology*, 1939.

The brain's special ability to process difficult conceptual data, is receiving support from outside the profession of psychology. Some cognitive neuroscientists, linquists, and computer scientists are recognizing that serial digital computers, no matter how elegant, could not interpret the hidden difficult figures presented in this section. They suggest a new theory of informational processing is needed, and have created concepts such as neural networks, linquistical prototypes and pattern connections. See Hopfield, 1982; Kahneman et al. 1982, and Lakoff, 1985.

PROGRESSIVE IMAGE MODIFICATION

Principles

Progressive image modification (PIM) is another example of the process by which the damaging perceptions of clients might be gradually transformed into more rational perceptions. Like the transposing technique discussed earlier, PIM is also analogous, so that an illustration like the one in Figure 14 (Fisher, 1968) can be used during early sessions with clients to help them to gain an overview of the transformational process that must take place within their personal belief patterns.

The drawings in this illustration are progressively modified from the face of a man in #1 to the body of a woman in #8. Let us assume that whenever the client saw picture #1, he or she got anxious, but the client was not anxious seeing #8. When would the anxiety be reduced? At #4, #5, or later?

For therapeutic purposes, clients don't have to shift to #8 if seeing #5 would remove their anxiety. Further shifting would be an unnecessary waste of therapeutic time. The purpose of progressive shaping is to get clients to disrupt their patterns just enough to remove the source of the negative emotion. From that point forth, through a process of gestalt shaping and repetition, clients should be encouraged to work backwards toward the original pattern (#1) by progressively imagining no anxiety response, until the first picture is disconnected from the emotional response.

The change process reflected in this analogy accurately describes what clients experience in shifting their perceptions. With the help of a therapist, they are led gradually through a process of changing various components in their general belief structures until they can isolate the source of the discomfort that first brought them into therapy. Once the source of that discomfort has been isolated, clients are taught to practice the pattern without the problem component. The effect is comparable to surgically removing a cancerous section of tissue. Practice is the mending ingredient. Clients must rehearse seeing the pattern without the problem component until doing so becomes automatic.

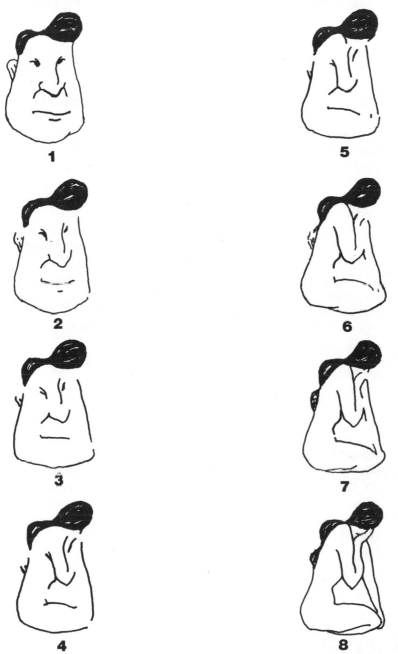

Figure 14. Visual illustration of progressive images: man-women figures devised by Gerald Fisher (1968).

Method

1. Have clients concentrate on the key general pattern connected with their problem, and ask them to describe it fully. It is ideal if clients can form the theme into a visualization.
2. After employing some relaxation to help clients concentrate, have them imagine the theme again, but to change some component of the pattern. You can change some visual component, the emotional component, or some other aspect of the pattern.
3. Continue changing aspects of the theme until clients report no emotional disturbance.
4. Once this occurs, clients concentrate on visualizing the elements in the changed pattern which have removed the anxiety. These should be described in as much detail as possible.
5. Once the key element has been isolated, have your clients picture the other themes again, but this time change the element so that no anxiety occurs. If you have correctly isolated the key element, the clients should be able to imagine the scenes without any emotional disturbance.

Example

Chad was a 27-year-old man who asked for counseling because he was deeply depressed. He was an exceptional young man, bright, creative, and empathic, but not particularly successful. He felt he was inferior to almost everybody.

Chad's overall mistaken theme was a picture of a person basically inferior in intelligence, social skills, and emotional stability. After teaching him relaxation, we concentrated on changing various aspects of this image. Initially we had him visualize that he was inferior in everything but work, then in everything but work and going to parties, then everything but work, parties, and love relationships. But Chad still felt depressed.

We changed tack and had him imagine another series of images. He progressively modified the concept of the objective trueness of his inferiority. In his first picture he imagined that his belief was 100% true, that in objective reality he was as inferior as he imagined, and he pictured himself feeling and acting inferior. In the next picture he imagined that the thought was only 75% true. We continued until the fifth image, where he imagined that his belief in his own inferiority was totally untrue, a figment of his imagination, 0% true. It was just a false superstition.

Throughout the practice, Chad would always visualize that he continued to act, feel, and think as if he were inferior even though, in decidable truth, he was not. And this led to a very important insight for him. He discovered that his behavior and feelings were totally controlled by what he thought, not by what was confirmable. So simply thinking he was inferior caused him to act that way. He acted and felt just the same at the 25% level of truth as he did on the 75% level. The truth or falseness of his thought did not affect his behavior or emotions; only his belief mattered. By separating confirmable truth and falseness from the perception of truth and falseness,* the client could go back to the original gestalt and see his mistake. He was using *acting* inferior as evidence for *being* inferior. But the progressive modification process showed him that no matter how he acted or felt, the truth based on evidence had nothing whatsoever to do with his perception.

---

*The philosophical underpinnings of cognitive restructuring are analytic philosophy, linquistical analysis, and their parent logical positivism. It is not phenomenology, relative subjectivism, or neo-idealism.

In the world of this philosophy truth and falseness can be ascertained and are not relative. Of course this truth has a small "t." We are not talking here about the big "T" TRUTH of a warmed-over Platonic idealism where truth lives in a perfect Arcadian park, and everything outside of the park is false or at least a poor reflection of the TRUTH. Such concepts are metaphysical and their truth or falseness are not knowable by us creatures on this little planet.

But this little truth is knowable. How? Because we concentrate on the truth or falseness of statements not the absolute truth or falseness independent of human observation. The little truth is very important and practical; none of us would survive well if we couldn't find it out. For example, it is very important to know the truth of falseness of statements like:

• "There is a big fire in your kitchen."
• "The airplane's engines don't work."
• "AIDS is contagious through breathing."
• "I am inferior to all other people on this planet" (Chad's view).

To determine whether these statements are true, one needs to know three things (Wilson 1967): (1) What the statement means; (2) the right way to verify it; and (3) good evidence for believing it. If we know these things then we can determine whether the statement is true. Thus for the first statement—"There is a big fire in your kitchen"—we know what "big," "fire," "in," "your" and "kitchen" mean. We also know the right way to verify it—go to the kitchen and look! And if we walk into the kitchen and see the fire, we have good evidence that the statement is true. Now, one of our house guests could argue that our "truth" is relative, that we can't absolutely prove there is a fire. Maybe we are negatively hallucinating; our senses are fooling us. He could say, "I mean, really isn't it just your poor unsubstantiated, subjective view of reality and how can you absolutely be sure the fire is objective reality independent of your senses?" Meanwhile, of course, our clothes ignite and we start charring as the discussion hurriedly terminates.

Although with more difficulty, the truth or falseness of the Chad's statement can be obtained following the same three steps mentioned above.

When I say truth, falseness, objective reality, etc., in this book I mean little "t" truth. And I insist this kind of truth is indeed knowable and without it we wouldn't have lasted long as a species on this planet. Little "t" is an essential concept to most cognitive therapies.

Comment

The therapist usually doesn't know in advance what the problem component might be in each client's gestalt. He or she must therefore be flexible in modifying the pattern to find and then isolate that component.

Further Information

We conducted some informal experimentation with pictures like the one presented in the analogy. Using 15 clients, we found that they could see the alternative image only after they had gone through at least four modifications. Our clinical experience with concepts, rather then drawings, indicates a comparable response.

Progressive image modification can be found in the work of Bugelski, 1970; Klinger, 1980; Lazarus, 1977, 1982; Sheikh, 1983a; Sheikh and Shaffer, 1979; Singer, 1974; Singer and Pope, 1978.

DEPERSONALIZING SELF

Principles

"Depersonalization" — dissociating oneself from one's own self-image — is sometimes considered to be a neurotic, and even a psychotic, symptom. It is a condition in which the self becomes unfamiliar, detached, or unreal (Cameron, 1963). So damaging is this condition viewed that most mental health professionals wouldn't consider advocating any technique that might possibly contribute to its emergence; however, our experience suggests that there are often advantages to be gained by encouraging a limited degree of depersonalization.

Depersonalization seems to exist on one extreme end of a continuum. On the other extreme of that same continuum is an equally damaging condition which we call "hyperpersonalization." Individuals who hyperpersonalize subjectify everything to an excessive extent, seeing themselves as being the cause of everything that happens around them. Too much of this kind of self-focusing can lead to serious dysthymic disorders and to obsessive introspection.

Midpoint between these two extremes falls the pattern of rational, realistic beliefs and behaviors that we characterize as "normal," though there are times when "normal" people experience mood swings toward either extreme. Our continuum can thus be illustrated as follows:

hyperpersonalization — normal — depersonalization

Hyperpersonalized clients consistently misattribute the causes of events. They judge all causes as proprioceptive. When they have problems in their lives, they try to change some hypothesized deficiencies in themselves rather than attempting to modify their environments. For example, agoraphobics try to solve anxiety by getting more control over themselves, rather than by trying to find the environmental stimuli.

Therapists who find themselves confronted by hyperpersonalizing clients can work to consciously shift their perspective from that extreme on the continuum back toward the depersonalization extreme. The goal is *not* to move them all the way, of course, but it might be necessary, depending upon the intensity of their tendencies toward self-blame, to move them even a little right of the "normal" zone, on the assumption that they will probably experience a certain degree of posttherapeutic slippage in the direction of their prior preoccupation.

The first step in depersonalization is to change the overpersonalized cause attribution. The therapist must help clients look at themselves as others look at them, from the outside, subject to environmental forces, not just as self-generating entities. The client needs to focus on observable data to find causes and avoid excessive internal attribution.

Method

1. Make a list of 20 negative events your client has recently experienced.
2. Next, record the hypothesized internal self-deficiencies that the client thinks caused the events (beliefs causing hyperpersonalization).
3. Teach the client to look for the causes of these events outside himself or herself. Use the scientific method: look for stimuli, reinforcements, operants, or environmental contingencies that served as triggers of the negative events. Rewrite all proprioceptive causes as external.
4. When there are multiple causes, use the law of parsimony — the simplest explanation should be used first — to determine the most likely one.
5. Have the client practice keeping a daily log of events, supposed internal causes, and external causes. Teach her/him to see herself/himself and others as objects, subject to environmental influences.

6. Once the client has learned not to take responsibility for these influences, teach her/him the kinds of problem-solving methods that can be used to modify the environment.

Example

Many clients hyperpersonalize the loss of love. If someone they love leaves them for another, many people feel very depressed, angry, and self-blaming. In the majority of cases, the aggrieved ones do not see or even look for the external cause for the rejection. Instead they go into a stage of intense introspection, looking for some personality flaw within themselves which caused their lover to leave. They often enter therapy so that the therapist can "fix them up," so that they can get their lover back or, at the very least, learn to avoid future rejections.

Morris entered therapy with strong depression. Jill, his lover of two years, had phoned to say she had fallen in love with Grant and had been seeing him secretly for several months. She didn't want to see Morris anymore.

Over several counseling sessions we listed the following cognitions.

Hyperpersonalization of Causes

• I am less of a man than Grant.
• I am inferior to Jill.
• Jill is mine and shouldn't have left.
• I am a wimp.
• I am not good enough to be loved by a worthwhile person.
• I'll never find anybody as good.
• I overshot myself. I should have picked someone more my equal, not some one who is so much better than I am.
• Jill left me because she finally realized what a piece of shit I really am.
• I seem to have all the problems; Jill has none.
• Her rejection makes me less of a person.
• My lack of depth and substance caused the rejection.
• I am a very neurotic person. Jill is far healthier than I. Jill left because my neurosis became obvious.

Depersonalizing Causes

In fact, Jill didn't leave Morris because of who he is or because of his basic lack of worthwhileness; she left because of one or several of the following: Morris's behavior, Grant's behavior, or Jill's beliefs, emotions, and previous history.

Here are some possible causes from Morris's behavior:

- He did not reinforce Jill sufficiently.
- He reinforced Jill too much (continuously), thus satiating her, and reducing the overall level of her reinforcement. Some deprivation would have increased the reinforcing effects of the reward.
- He punished her too much, thus causing her to escape, avoid, revolt, or resist him.
- His reinforcement and punishment were not contingent upon Jill's behavior. He reinforced and punished Jill about equally, and inconsistently, keeping her from being able to predict or anticipate what you would do next. This produced confusion and anxiety, and thus led Jill to abandon him.
- Morris's reinforcing and punishing behavior was too consistent. When he was totally predictable, Jill got bored.

Grant might have been:

- more reinforcing.
- less punishing.
- more consistent.
- more inclined to offer rewards that were contingent on Jill's behavior.
- somewhat predictable, though basically more stable.
- a new experience that might, or might not last once they got to know each.
- better able to reinforce Jill in the future than Morris was (richer, more attractive, better in bed).
- a "safer" bet for future security than Morris.
- a more congenial person than Morris.

Then, there are causes coming from Jill's belief system:

- Jill might never have wanted to get married. (Perhaps Morris was too obviously inclined in that direction.)
- Jill wants to marry now! (Perhaps Morris clearly wanted to wait a while.)
- Jill wanted to have as many lovers as she could. The more the better.
- Perhaps Jill has the Delilah or Don Juan syndrome. Delilahs and Don Juans just want to get people to fall in love with them. Once that happens they win, and then they move on to the next conquest. They collect as many relationships as they can.
- Jill may be seeking a perfect mate, and will keep on changing partners until she finds one, which she never will, of course.
- Maybe Jill wanted the relationship to solve her personal problems. Since the one with Morris did not, she tried Grant.
- Jill didn't like any negatives in relationships.
- She may have wanted someone who looks and acts more like this culture's *ideal* man.

Finally, we need to consider Jill's emotions and previous relationship history:

- Afraid of getting close.
- Will reject first, so as to avoid being rejected.
- Fundamentally hates men.
- Morris was not similar enough to her dad.
- Morris was too much like her dad.
- Morris was too much, or not enough like Jill's previous spouse or lovers.
- Jill was angry and trying to hurt Morris.
- Jill was a stimulus junkie who wanted to fall in love over and over again because it was exciting.
- Jill liked to have power in relationships, and left because she couldn't overpower Morris.

Obviously, the list can continue almost endlessly.

Comment

The above is a very unromantic view of relationships. But it is precisely this romantic view which causes the hyperpersonalization of the loss. Initially, clients are reluctant to give up the romantic view, but gradually, after they have suffered more pain, they obtain the necessary motivation to shift their perceptions.

Instead of allowing the client to wallow in self-condemnation, the therapist may help the client more, (by looking at the more objective causes of losing a love)

Further Information

Depersonalization and dissociation are discussed in the context of multiple personality by Watkins (1976, 1978) and Watkins and Watkins (1980, 1981).

Causality, overly personalized and depersonalized, is examined by Taylor and Fiske (1975) and Sober-Ain and Kidd (1984).

PUBLIC MEANINGS

Principles

In the previous section we introduced the concepts of hyperpersonalization (extreme subjectivity) and depersonalization. A parallel concept pertains to the ways in which clients view the events of their lives. Any event can be said to have both a "private" and a "public" meaning.

Private meanings are associated with subjectivity, with emotional intensity, and with exaggerated feelings of personal culpability. Public meanings are more objective and are therefore less likely to affect clients as deeply. The difference between the two is the same as the difference between one's reactions when he accidentally strikes his thumb with a hammer and those when he sees someone else succumb to that misfortune.

Helping clients learn to depersonalize their perceptions is one way to remove them from the pain of mistaken beliefs, but the success of that technique requires a great deal of practice over an extended period of time. An alternative technique involves teaching clients to shift from a private to a public perspective on any event that causes them pain.

Method

1. Teach clients to distinguish between events they perceive and their thoughts about those events.
2. Help clients observe events in terms of public and private meanings. Public meanings can be perceived by having clients practice observing the situations from another person's frame of reference. Events must be objectified. Remind clients that they already have a public view, since they have been observing others in thousands of situations all of their lives. The therapist helps clients transfer the perceptions they have of others to themselves.
3. To change private to public meanings, clients must learn to remove from their perceptions the following: emotional variables, intense self-introspection, exceptionality, and metaphysical assumptions. Obviously this cannot be done completely, but to the extent that clients can approximate their removal, they can objectively view events.

4. After the concept of public meaning has been explained, help them make a list of all the major situations they have encountered, and for each event have them list the public and private meaning.
5. Initially clients will have to interpret events publicly after they have first automatically perceived them privately. Gradually, however, through a process of shaping, clients will be able to bring the objective view closer and closer to the time of the event itself, ultimately replacing the personal with the public view during the event itself.

Example 1

Event: anxiety attack
Private meaning: I'm going to die.
Public meaning: Adrenalin and other chemicals are pumping into my blood stream.

Event: criticized by another
Private meaning: I must have done something wrong. I am inferior.
Public meaning: Someone disagrees with something I may have done. The cause of his disagreement is not known.

Event: failed in a business project
Private meaning: I'm incompetent, I'm a failure and I'm climbing down the ladder of success.
Public meaning: My planning and preparation were ineffective.

Event: I lost an argument
Private meaning: I am a weak, wishy-washy wimp.
Public meaning: He knew more about the subject than I, and may even have had more debating experience.

Event: few friends
Private meaning: Deep down inside I am basically unlovable.
Public meaning: I don't try to get friends and I don't treat people very nicely.

Event: not good at sports
Private meaning: I am a rotten male.
Public meaning: I don't have the reflexes, training or practice.

Event: 15 pounds heavier than when I was 17.
Private meaning: I have lost my self-discipline.
Public meaning: A 37-year-old woman does not have the same body metabolism as a teenager.

Example 2

The private meaning of fear is the perception that something terrible is about to happen, and that the person must escape at all cost. The public, objective meaning of fear is that there may or may not be some real danger present, and that it is necessary to look at the present environment to see if danger actually exists. Clients who need guidance in determining when it is appropriate to assume a public perspective on their fears will find the following five principles to be helpful. In general, fear is appropriate if:

1. There is a real danger to the person, and real damage could occur. It is irrational to be afraid of dragons since they do not exist and therefore cannot cause damage.
2. The level of the fear is equal to the level of damage possible. It is inappropriate to feel terrified about getting a small splinter in your foot, since the fear would be far greater than the potential damage.
3. The fear is appropriate to the probability of the danger occurring. If a person is afraid of being hit by a meteor, the fear would be irrational because of the low probability. Some clients are remarkably irrational about low-probability tragedies, while totally oblivious to such higher-probability dangers as automobile accidents.
4. The danger should be controllable. Fear of the sun turning into a supernova would not be useful, since the event is outside human control.
5. The fear is useful, as it would be in a situation in which the reality of fear keeps an individual more alert to the possibility of danger. Being alert about having a "nervous breakdown" doesn't reduce the probability of having one.

Comment

Clients who are able to switch to an public view during strong emotional arousal are able to immediately reduce the intensity of the emotion. Note that the goal here is *not* to completely remove the personal perspective, but to reduce it.

Further Information

Objectifying was first made famous in therapy by Abraham Low and Recovery, Inc. (Low, 1952). Aaron Beck uses a related concept called "distancing" (Beck, 1967, 1975, 1976; Beck et al. 1979).

FORCING PERCEPTUAL SHIFTS

Principles

It has been previously noted that effecting a perceptual shift in a client is a lengthy process. Damaging beliefs, formed and subsequently reinforced over the period of a lifetime, die hard. Depending upon the intensity of the mistaken perceptions, a client can be in therapy for many months.

And yet, a significant number of our hundreds of clients—about one-fourth of the total number—complete the shift very quickly, abandoning beliefs that they have held as long as 20 years within days or even hours!

Our research into the causes for these rapid shifts revealed that this phenomenon has been noted by many others. Early Gestalt psychologists illustrated through the use of ambiguous drawings (some of which are featured in this chapter) how rapid shifts can occur in subjects' perceptual fields. The phenomenon in cognitive psychology which is loosely described as the "aha" experience also clarifies how rapid shifts are made, as do such techniques such as insight learning, "brainwashing," and one-trial learning. Rapid shifts have also been reported throughout the attitude-change literature, and are recognized as being integral to rapid religious conversions.

There is no way to know in advance which technique will provoke a rapid shift, but by closely observing and carefully documenting examples of rapid shifts from our own caseload, we have noted that one or more of the following factors seem to operate in all such cases:

1. The old, damaging perception must be painful to clients. It must be a source of anxiety, depression or anger, thus creating a condition that clients would want to escape.

2. Clients must be aware of an acceptable alternative, a new perception, and that alternative must be clearly relevant to them so that they can make an emotional investment in it once they have escaped the old perception.

3. Clients must feel "trapped" by their old perception. Their only escape from it must be to accept the new alternative. The pain associated with the old belief should not be greatly reduced or made more tolerable through drugs or any other ameliorative strategies. Such "cures" merely make it possible for clients to hold onto their mistaken beliefs that much longer.

Clients achieve a point of readiness for a rapid shift when the pain of their old belief becomes unbearable at the same time that they become convinced that the new belief is a viable alternative for them. That critical point of readiness cannot be perfectly timed in the life of any client, but the therapist can help to bring it about by building conviction in the new belief while at the same time refusing to alleviate the pain of the old belief.

This last point is very important. Clients will not change unless they have to, and on this point many therapists may not be helping their clients as much as they intend. We all try to reduce our clients' pain as quickly as we can, using relaxation techniques, medications, or other intervention strategies. We do so with the best of intentions, to reduce their discomfort and, perhaps, to preserve their lives. But it may be that, despite our good intentions, we are actually hurting some clients in the longterm when we comply with their short-term desire for relief. If we allow them to escape from their trap, we might prevent them from coming to grips with their irrationalities.

Obviously, this technique should not be used with clients who have suicidal tendencies or who are likely to cause physical harm to themselves or others in response to their emotional pain.

Method

1. Find a core mistaken belief that is generating a major share of the client's pain. For example, the client believes his or her purpose in life is to fulfill imaginary "oughts," "musts" and "shoulds."

2. Counter the client's mistaken beliefs, introducing as many persuasive contrary views as possible. For example, oughts and musts don't exist except in the minds of human beings. The world just *is*. It has no oughts, shoulds, or musts in it.

3. Contrive a situation or exercise, covert or *in vivo*, in which the client faces only two choices: believing in the old perception or shifting to the new. For example, where two "musts" of equal strength are in opposition to each other, and both produce strong negative effects.

4. Do your best to block all escape from the conflict, except for the perceptual shift. If you don't, the client will take the escape.
5. At the peak of the conflict, keep encouraging the client to make the shift and keep identifying for the client the shift to be taken.

Example

The first major perceptual shift I encountered was with an acquaintance, not a client. Barbara, suffering from anxiety attacks, had been seeing a series of psychiatrists for several years. When she occasionally had a panic attack, she would be put into a hospital, given heavy medication, and released a few weeks later. She had gone through this cycle for ten years, and her career, relationships, and life were in total disarray.

I had lost touch with her for a while, but finally contacted her again, only to discover that her life had dramatically changed. She had a new career, was engaged to be married, and hadn't been severely anxious for two years. I asked her why. What had happened? Had she gone to a new therapist? Had she tried a new medication? She replied that none of these things had happened. Instead she had experienced a perceptual shift, which she described as follows:

> I had had another anxiety attack and I was put into a hospital again. Usually I calmed down in hospitals, but this time I was told I had to move to another wing of the psychiatric ward that had psychotics and I was very afraid to go there. So I got another panic attack. But because they had no other open beds, I had no choice. I could either go to the tough ward with my panic, or I'd have to leave the hospital with my panic. Either way I was faced with panic. I had nowhere else to run. I remember sitting in the waiting room, not knowing what to do. And then I remember feeling angry. I felt tired and frustrated. It suddenly occurred to me that I had thrown away ten years of my life fearing fear. And what did I have for all my fear and all my attempts to protect myself? Nothing but the same fear and a wasted life. It quickly came to me that it wasn't worth it. Fear wasn't worth running from any more. Panic wasn't worth avoiding. If I was going to be panicked anyway, I might as well be panicked at home instead of in a hospital. So I left. My panic left exactly at that time. I have never gotten panicked again, and I have never returned to the hospital. I don't think about panic much anymore. Instead I concentrate on making my life as happy and as fulfilling as I can.

Comment

The reader may wonder when the therapist uses this technique. Our research has found that it should only be used after all the other CRT techniques have been taught. Clients should know at least logically that their beliefs, not their environment, are causing their emotional distress; they should know the specific thoughts causing the distress, and they should have a very clear idea of what replacement perception is rational and realistic. Then and only then will the perceptual forcing technique lead to constructive changes.

While the analysis presented here is a workable one, an equally feasible alternative explanation is possible. Our analysis may be incorrect. Maybe the 25 percent who make the shift quickly do so because they are neurologically capable of doing so. The ability to make broad sweeping conceptual changes with little data is present in some of our species, but not all. The mass of humanity continues to think with gross logical fallacies, but some are less inclined to overgeneralizations, reifications, or a priori thinking. We have all experienced two clients with the same problem who receive the same treatment from us, but one makes rapid, positive changes, and the other remains exactly the same.*

Further Information

The techniques of flooding and implosive therapy may be based on the above concept. See Frankel, 1970; Marshall, Gauthier, and Gordon, 1979; and Stampfl and Levis, 1967.

––––––––

CREATING DISSONANCE

Principles

Clients unify their thoughts coherently, though not necessarily correctly. They might begin with an absurdly irrational assumption and then interpret all subsequent data in light of that mistaken beginning, with a primary goal of consistency rather than accuracy. Accompanying the resulting unified

––––––––

*Based on a personal interview with Dr. Albert Ellis, Dec. 24, 1982.

schema is a feeling of "consonance," a feeling that all is right and logical in the world, even if their unhappiness persists. That consonance, however, is like a jigsaw puzzle—disturb one element in the pattern and the pieces no longer fit together. The pattern becomes incoherent, and the earlier feeling of consonance is replaced by a feeling of dissonance.

Clients will attempt to maintain consonance even though the schema causes emotional distress, because dissonance is even *more* distressful to them and could result in an anxiety attack. The effect is tantamount to saying, "It's all right to be unhappy, if the reality is that this is your only alternative in life." Thus motivated, clients will hold to the perception that they are sick, even though it depresses them, because most of their behavior and attitudes are based on that perception. They will, therefore, defend their "sick" assessment, despite overwhelming contradictory evidence. But the key here is that "reality" is a fabrication, a product of clients' mistaken beliefs about themselves and the world around them.

One method of changing the mistaken "reality" that forms the background for clients' unhappiness is to attempt to show them the inconsistency in their thinking. The method by which this is done includes pointing out that their feeling of consonance is an illusion, that their pattern of thinking is full of contradictions, and that their thoughts couldn't possibly be true. Although clients will argue against such a confrontation, if the therapist persists he will create more and more dissonance in their mistaken cognitive system.

Once the dissonance reaches a certain point, the whole schema will be in disarray, and clients will be compelled to change it in order to gain a new feeling of consonance, based upon a new perception. It is essential that the formation of a more rational synthesis be carefully managed. Remember: clients' primary goal is consistency. They will find it just as easy to adopt a consistent pattern that is only half as erroneous as their original pattern, as they will to adopt what is for them a totally correct pattern. The burden is upon the therapist to insure that the consonance-dissonance-consonance transition concludes with the most functional reality possible for his or her clients.

Method

1. Ask your client to present his total schema about himself and his view of the world. While the client is discussing his views, the therapist takes very careful notes recording the principles, evidence, and the support the client gives.
2. Describe to your client what he has described to you, but this time ask a series of carefully prepared questions aimed at challenging the client's

prepared schemas. The probes are similar to those in "Probing for Counters" in Chapter 1, but there is a major difference. Instead of asking questions leading to counter arguments, prepare probes intended to throw the client into dissonance.

3. The client will almost always defend his schema by giving excuses and by coming up with new rationales. You must continue to ask questions to create doubt in the client's formulations. In all cases the dissonance must be maintained until the client, on his own, resynthesize the schema. It is important that you don't answer the probes for the client.

4. As the client moves to embrace a new, unified schema, monitor carefully to insure that this new perception does not encompass the seeds of future possible unhappiness.

Examples

Schema: I must constantly guard against catching germs.
Probe to created dissonance: How do you keep from breathing them?

Schema: Unless I engage in this ritual (counting my steps when I walk to my car), I will get into a car wreck.
Probe: Maybe you are using the wrong ritual. Perhaps the correct ritual is not to count. How would you know? How many accidents were you in before you began this ritual?

Schema: It is terrible when others reject me.
Probe: When you reject someone else, is it terrible for them?

Schema: Other people are causing all my problems.
Probe: How are you going to stop others from doing this?

Schema: The only way I can be happy is by taking care of everybody who needs it.
Probe: Where will you get the power to take care of everybody?

Schema: My parents' values are correct. I must follow them.
Probe: Are your parents' values better than other parents' values? Are they

the same as other parents' values? If they aren't, are all other parents *incorrect*?

Schema: If you are assertive, people will hate you.
Probe: Do they love you now since you are passive?

Schema: The only way to be happy in life is to be tough and hard, and not to let people take advantage of you.
Probe: Why would anybody want to love you?

Schema: Women keep pressuring me for a deep commitment. They won't grant me my independence. They keep getting angry with me.
Probe: If you were a woman, would you date yourself?

Comment

Clients will defend their mistaken realities against all attacks, even if these realities are a fundamental source of unhappiness for them. They even seem to take a certain pride in their unique constructions and to feel that abandoning them is a sign of weakness or, ironically, a show of irrationality. For the more adamant victims of this disorder, using a more paradoxical approach might be more appropriate.

Since dissonance is painful, the use of this technique is a classic example of having to "hurt" the client in order to help the client. Fortunately, the very nature of the disorder serves to insure that the hurt will be brief, for the moment the foundations of the mistaken reality begin to crumble, clients move quickly to replace them. The therapist need only insure that its replacement is as error-free as possible.

Further Information

Cognitive dissonance theory has been examined in a large number of publications. See Aronson, 1980; Festinger, 1957, 1964; Wicklund and Brehm, 1976.

BRIDGE PERCEPTIONS

Principles

Clients learn new information more readily if some component of that new information is already stored in their memories. That common element between the old knowledge and the new constitutes a bridge across which clients can move more easily from mistaken beliefs to more rational, functional thoughts. That transition is illustrated in the following example.

Old Belief	*New Belief*
People are not good. They are mean and spiteful.	People are people. They act the way nature planned. Sometimes we like what they do, and sometimes we don't.

The therapist might attempt to move the client from the old belief to the new belief by employing such techniques as conditioning or countering, but chances are that neither will be as efficient or produce the lasting results that could be derived from the bridging perceptions technique. This technique can best be explained using the two core beliefs described above.

Upon careful analysis of the old belief, the reader should note that there are two components, both of which serve as a bridge to the new belief: the subject "people" and the assessment that "they are mean and spiteful." The new belief is also concerned with "people," and it too acknowledges that human behavior can be disappointing, though it interprets that reality as a fact of "nature."

In this actual example from our caseload, the client hated adults for being mean and spiteful, but revealed during our sessions that she *loved* babies. Why, we asked, didn't she dislike babies, whom some people might consider "mean and spiteful" when they throw tantrums, wet their pants, or spit up their food? "That's silly," argued our client. "They're just doing those things naturally."

It was pointed out that people who yell at us because they have a cold or who withdraw when they are scared are acting out of much the same motivation as babies—naturally. If she could accept and even like babies, perhaps she could accept such adults as well.

The client practiced changing her image of adults. Every time they did something she didn't like, she concentrated on picturing them not as adults, but as big babies dressed in adult clothes, speaking in adult words, but with the underlying motivation of a baby. After picturing 43 situations with this image, she was able to adopt a new and more rational attitude toward adult misbehavior.

Method

1. Make a list of the core perceptions the client has about herself or the world that cause negative emotions.
2. Make a companion list of possible replacement perceptions, making certain that the client agrees that these would be more rational perceptions if their validity could be demonstrated.
3. During your interactions with the client, search for an attitude, already accepted by the client, that could bridge the old perception to the new. In some cases you will need a series of themes and it may take you and your client many sessions to find them.
4. Once the bridges have been found, have your client practice shifting perceptions from the old to the new. The practice should continue until the new perception replaces the old. If enough real situations do not exist, encourage your client to imagine as many such situations as possible.

Example 1

Old Belief

The client is afraid of riding a ski chairlift. "If I get anxious on the chair I won't be able to escape for 10 minutes, and I could lose control and embarrass myself."

Desired Belief

A chairlift is an opportunity to relax, look at the beautiful winter scenery, anticipate the downhill run, and talk with a friend.

Bridge Belief

The following exchange between the therapist (T) and the client (C) illustrates how a bridge might be established in this example:

THERAPIST: Skiing is a risky sport, wouldn't you agree?
CLIENT: Sure, but I enjoy it.
THERAPIST: Then you enjoy taking risks?

CLIENT: It's the only way to really enjoy life to the fullest.
THERAPIST: Aren't there more risks in skiing than in riding ski lifts?
CLIENT: Well . . . yes. I guess so.
THERAPIST: Why, then, are you unnerved by the lesser risk?
CLIENT: Gee. I don't know. I guess, now that I think about it, that that doesn't make a lot of sense, does it?

The bridge belief in this example can be stated as a more general philosophy.

> You can look at all the enjoyable, pleasurable, or beautiful things in life negatively. When relaxing on an ocean beach a tidal wave could engulf you, or a great white shark could gobble you up; you could be bitten by a black mamba when lying on soft blue moss grass next to a gentle country stream. When sailing under a silver moon on a Caribbean lagoon, you could hit a coral reef and drown. A sparrow in a English meadow could suddenly attack you à la Hitchcock. You could break your eardrums when listening to Mozart's Jupiter symphony, or your stereo system could electrocute you. When making love you could get a heart attack or catch a disease. Even if you watched one of your favorite plays by George Bernard Shaw, the theater could catch on fire. You could also worry about playing with young children because some adult could accuse you of molesting them, and you could choke to death eating a tender, juicy drumstick from your mother's Thanksgiving turkey.
>
> You could try to protect yourself by avoiding all the enjoyable and pleasurable things of life. You could retreat to your room and then worry about being trapped in an earthquake or the room catching on fire. But once you throw away the bright and beautiful, what worthwhile aspect of life do you have left to protect?

Example 2

Old Belief

From a teenage boy: "My parents prefer my older brother to myself. They give him everything and I get what is left over."

Desired Belief

"Our parents love us both, but they treat us differently because we are different people. They celebrate my individuality and wouldn't want me to be a clone of my brother. They give me what they think I need, and my brother what he needs."

Bridge Belief

The therapist discovered the following example from the client's personal history:

> Remember the two kittens your parents asked you to take care of when you were young? One was warm and fuzzy and always wanted to be petted; he loved to cuddle next to you while you slept. The other was frisky and adventuresome; he was always chasing mice, climbing trees and getting into your potted plants. If the kittens could speak, one could have accused you of giving more freedom to his brother, the other of not giving him enough love. But you loved them both and didn't prefer one over the other. You gave both what they needed. Maybe your parents are treating you the same way.

Comment

If you can find exactly the right bridge, your client's perceptions can be changed dramatically, and your client won't have to invest a great deal of time and effort in practicing the new perception. But you must search patiently with your client to find that bridge.

Further Information

Finding the key bridge perception may be the key element underlying rapid religious or other types of conversion. See Sargant, 1959.

HIERARCHY OF VALUES BRIDGES

Principles

The power of persuasion is one of the therapist's most important tools. In persuading clients that they should shift their perspective from a damaging, mistaken belief to one that is more functional, there is a danger that the therapist might rely too heavily upon rational arguments, which are the mainstays of the countering technique described in Chapter 1. Our experience shows that an appeal to personal values is a far more effective persuasive technique. Values offer the advantage of being proprioceptive and deeply rooted within clients' concepts of reality. Clients frequently will not accept a rational judgment that their attitudes or behaviors are incorrect, but they will rarely refute a proven discrepancy between their attitudes or behaviors and their actual values.

Through the careful management of the therapeutic process, the counselor can help clients to get in touch with their personal hierarchy of values. Old, mistaken beliefs are also associated with that hierarchy, but if the therapist can demonstrate that new, preferred beliefs enjoy a *higher* value on that hierarchy, he or she can facilitate clients' movement toward a more productive state of mind.

Method

1. Discover the client's personal hierarchy of values. This can be done by using a standardized value test, but a better method is to find the values through selective questioning. Make a distinction between questions which merely elicit value judgments ("How do you feel about apartheid?") and questions which force clients to *rank* their values in an hierarchical fashion ("Which would you rather have—the security that comes from having someone else take care of you or the risk of being free and thus, perhaps, somewhat lonely?") The latter type of question, repeated over a wide range of topics, eventually leads to the construction of a personal hierarchy. For example, through the following series of questions and answers, it becomes clear that the client values freedom more than wealth, and wealth more than personal relationships:

Questions	Answers
Which do you prefer . . .	
• Wealth or popularity?	Wealth
• Security or independence?	Independence
• Wealth or independence?	Independence
• Lots of friends or wealth?	Wealth
• Health or lots of friends?	Friends
• Friends or your independence?	Independence
• Being paid well or being the boss?	Being the boss

The therapist should be mindful that as useful as this questioning technique might be, it does have its limitations. Clients will be tempted to merely answer what they think the therapist wants to hear. After using the questions in developing a basic hierarchy, elicit information from your clients about their past and present attitudes and experiences, what they have actually done and thus actually believe. See if these confirm their reported value preferences. A hierarchy can also be developed by using a Q-sort technique, or fantasy analogies similar to such games as "Genie in a Bottle" or "Three Wishes."

2. Make a list of old, damaging beliefs, and have your clients associate each of these with a particular value on their personal hierarchies. (Any of the old beliefs that don't even fit on the hierarchy are immediately highlighted as being incongruous with clients' realities.)

3. Make a list of the new, preferred beliefs, and challenge your clients to associate each of these with a particular value on their personal hierarchies. Those new beliefs that can clearly be juxtaposed to higher values than the contrary, older beliefs are highlighted. The clients should then practice perceiving the higher value whenever they think of the new belief.

4. For repetition, have clients practice seeing the higher value in a variety of situations. This can be done by using images in the counseling room, or by waiting until an environmental stimulus triggers the thought.

Examples

Old belief: It would be very bad if my husband's colleagues did not approve of me.

Higher client value: Christian religious beliefs.

New belief: To truly follow Christ's teachings, we must not strive to be popular and appeal to what people think. Rather, we must use our God-given inner conscience and be true to His principles.

Old belief. Everything I try to do ends up in failure.

Higher client value: Endurance, "When the going gets tough, the tough get going!"

New belief. I am not in control of whether I succeed or not. I am only in control of my trying. I will always strive and try to learn from my failures so that I can be more successful in future attempts.

Old belief: I am bad and evil if I accept her having an abortion.

Higher client value: Humanism and love.

New belief: Her emotional health is more important than my ego needs or what others might think of me. Not having the abortion will cause her more pain than having it. Since I care most for her, I will support her decision.

Old belief: I am to blame for my father sexually abusing me.
Higher client value: Dominance, control and competition.
New belief: If I keep eating myself up with this irrational guilt, I lose and let the bastard win again.

———

Old belief: She left me for a younger, more successful man.
Higher client value: What is objectively true.
New belief: I'm good, but I am not better than all the other men in the world.

———

Old belief: I must have a man in order to be happy.
Higher client value: Self-respect.
New belief: I would rather like myself alone than hate myself living as a slave to a man I dislike.

———

Old belief: If I take this job abroad, I'll leave all my friends.
Higher client value: Stimulation and variety
New belief: I would die of boredom quicker here than I'd die of loneliness there.

Comment

In many cases it is difficult to find the client's true values. The therapist must take particular care to look for values that the client rejects in the therapist's presence because they are socially unpopular, i.e., hedonism, power, etc. Differences between stated values and actual ones can be discovered by examining clients' histories

As an aid in helping clients visualize the superiority of the new belief over the old, I have devised a three-columned worksheet on which clients are asked to record their values (Column #1) in hierarchical order, their old beliefs (Column #2), and the proposed new beliefs (Column #3), with each belief juxtaposed to the value from which it derives (see Table 2). In this way a client might see, to follow our earlier example, that an all-consuming quest for wealth, which deprives him of certain freedoms in life, is clearly contradictory to his hierarchy of values.

Therapists may ask their clients to construct their own worksheets to periodically confirm, on the basis of their own self-analysis, that they are operating according to their highest values. Such periodic reassessments can be useful, since values change, either abruptly or over a period of time. The

Table 2
Hierarchy of Values Worksheet

Column A. (Rank order of values) (highest)	Column B. (Value of old belief)	Column C. (Value of new belief)
1. _____	_____	_____
2. _____	_____	_____
3. _____	_____	_____
4. _____	_____	_____
5. _____	_____	_____
6. _____	_____	_____
7. _____	_____	_____
8. _____	_____	_____
9. _____	_____	_____
10. _____ (lowest)	_____	_____

client who suffers a near-fatal heart attack may suddenly find himself re-ranking his values in preference for those that place greater emphasis upon the quality of life.

Further Information

Research on attitude change has demonstrated the importance of the value component of people's beliefs. See Flemming, 1967; Petty and Cacioppo, 1981; Rokeach, 1964, 1968, 1973, 1979; and Smith, Bruner, and White, 1956.

Theoretically, value shifting can be viewed as another instance of Premack's principle (Premack, 1965).

STORIES AND FABLES

Principles

The tendency in the years since structured cognitive therapies have been created has been to view counseling as a tidy presentation of treatment techniques. In some circles this view is transmuted from a hypothesis into a dogma. Mechanistic counseling relies on a core conception: on the one hand, clarity of presentation, and, on the other, avoidance of sloppy subjectivism.

It was partly clients' rejection of this style and partly technique sterility and therapist satiation which led to modification of the cognitive restructuring approach. The new counseling sets out to adjust therapeutic thinking to the clients' world, where belief conviction is based more on how pleasant the belief feels than on its logical soundness.

Cognitive restructuring recognizes that there is a role for fantasy in helping clients assume a more adaptive perspective on their lives. Stories, fables, fairy tales, analogies, and metaphors are valuable means of communicating some of the complex subtleties of life to certain clients. Myths have been used by cultures to convey their most precious values to their members. Throughout recorded history, values, insights, principles, and human pitfalls to guard against have been conveyed to each new generation through the medium of fables, fairy tales, nursery rhymes, and myths. We all remember the stories we heard when young, and the morals conveyed by them, whether true or false, profound or silly, found their way into our value systems.

In using the storytelling technique, the therapist has the option of either concocting his own stories (by drawing upon either his own life experiences or the experiences of other, unidentified clients), or making use of existing media, including the published works of popular poets and magazine and book writers. The stories thus used may be long or short, funny or serious. There are only two essential requirements for the use of this technique: 1) the story must be relevant to the circumstances of each client, and 2) the story must contain within it at least the essence of a bridge between the client's old, damaging belief and a new, preferred belief.

Method

1. Synthesize the client's life experiences into a story. Each story should consist of the major situations that he has faced, his major emotional response and, most importantly, his principal themes or attitudes, noting especially those that are false or negative.
2. The therapist should then make up a story to explain how and why any evident false themes developed, and how they negatively changed the client's life.
3. Halfway through the story, the therapist should switch the themes towards a more rational, useful perception. Attach this new perception to a value higher in the client's hierarchy. Identify the positive changes that occur to the main character in the story because of the new perception.
4. The story can be a fable, fairy tale, or extended metaphor, depending upon what genre seems most useful in persuading a particular client. Prepare the story ahead of time and have the client tape it, so that the client can refer to it when needed.

Example 1

Suppose that a particular client's life experiences synthesize into the following theme or core perception: "One should avoid danger and risk whenever possible."

You could counter this theme by citing the following story, which has been told to many of the anxious clients visiting our centers. These clients tried to reduce their fears by running away, but avoidance had only intensified their pain. The story helps convince them to face their fears.

A missionary living many years in Africa observed the lion prides roaming the vicinity. She noticed that they treated their elderly members differently. While most species would let old members die because they couldn't catch their own game, the lion pride would use their elderly. They didn't have claws and most of their teeth were gone, but they could still roar. The old lions would line up on one side of a ravine, which was full of antelopes. On the other side the young lions would lie in wait. The old lions would then roar and the antelopes would run in the opposite direction, into the waiting pride. If the antelopes would have run to the roar they would have been safe (Adapted from Bakker, 1982).

Like the antelopes, most of us run away from danger and as a result never solve fear. If we face our fears and run to the roar, we could solve them.

Example 2

Helen came to see me because she felt depressed and anxious, primarily about relationships. Never having felt this strongly before, she was very concerned, particularly since she couldn't identify the cause. We discovered her core perception after some searching: "Everything should be easy." She would get upset whenever she was confronted with situations requiring effort, because she felt unable to meet any real challenges.

After working with her about the problem, I told Helen the following story.

Once upon a time, there was a little princess who was very pretty, bright and cheerful. She lived with her parents, the king and queen, in a beautiful castle. They were so happy to have such a wonderful child that they did everything for her. She didn't have to work, face problems, or save her money. Everything came easy for her. She always had the best clothes, the best grades, the cutest boyfriends. At school she got A's without working, was the homecoming queen, and was on the student council. She got use to life being like a fairy tale. The only thing she missed was being an adult, because then she could enjoy living her fairy tale as a wife, lover, mother, and grownup citizen. She didn't hope she would be gloriously happy—she expected it. After all, she had never known anything different. To her it wasn't a fairy tale; it was life.

When she became old enough, she left Mommy and Daddy's castle. She moved into a castle with the handsome prince—well, at least she thought he was the handsome prince, for he was a football star in school, was very popular, and had a great deal of "potential in business." But the expected happily-ever-after was neither happy nor ever after. She found out, to her anger and amazement, that she was expected to do the palace dishes and to clean the 50 palace rooms. She also discovered that the handsome prince was handsome to other princesses besides her, and even to women who weren't princesses at all. He also enjoyed drinking the palace wine, which he did all the time, even when there wasn't a royal ball.

Well, she had always been a very bright princess, so she thought and thought and finally came to the only logical conclusion—wrong prince! So she packed up, left the castle, and searched for another prince. Three royal weddings later she hadn't changed her conclusion—still wrong prince. It was amazing to her how many toads were disguised as princes these days.

For the first time in her life, she was unhappy. So what does a princess do when she is out of sorts? She seeks out a wizard to solve her problem for her. So she went to many royal psychologists looking for the magic solution to her problems, but alas, they lacked the magic. She was passive and didn't work at what the wizards had told her because one shouldn't have to work at magic. One should simply receive it. If you have to put out effort it's not magic, just work.

Anyway, one day, when she was particularly depressed, she started to think about her life in a totally new and different way. For the first time, it occurred to her that maybe life wasn't a fairy tale. Maybe she was not just an unlucky princess cursed by some evil witch; maybe she wasn't a princess at all and nobody else was either. Initially she felt even more depressed about her insight, for the colorful, romantic world of fairy tales was being replaced by a world of dull shades of gray. Princes and princesses are a lot more exciting then just plain humans. But gradually she realized that the world of just humans was, in a way, more interesting because, despite the pain, boredom, and failures, there were also successes, and, unlike the fairy tales, the successes were due to human effort. In the fables, if you were born a princess, you were guaranteed happiness and you didn't have to supply any effort. Any happiness you achieved was due to fate, not to effort. There is no satisfaction in gaining something that fate has decreed. But in the human world your gains and failures are mostly due to your own efforts and there are no guarantees of anything.

She also saw how the fairy tale destroyed her relationships. Spouses aren't handsome princes. They are humans, with all the weaknesses, pettiness, and imperfections of any human who is struggling in a sometimes hard and painful world. If we visualize a lover magically, and if we base this image on an ancient fairy tale, we immeasurably cheapen and malign the love we have for each other. The dignity of spouses who have spent their lives together does not show that fate preordained their relationship to work, but that they made it work, without a guarantee of success. The task is arduous enough for anyone, but it becomes impossible if the couple's roadmap is a ancient fairy tale.

Comment

Ideally, an appropriate story or fairy tale would come rolling "trippingly off the tongue" of the therapist at exactly the right moment during a session. However, therapists who lack that particular kind of creativity can still make effective use of this technique. Those who cannot devise an appropriate story will simply have to devote more time and energy to planning in advance how best to interweave stories from some other source into their overall strategy for effecting a perceptual shift in a particular client.

Further Information

Since psychotherapy began, counselors have been using stories to convey psychological concepts in a way that clients could understand, but little research has been undertaken to determine the effectiveness of such interweaving. Some exceptions have been: Lazarus (1971), and particularly the imagery and fantasy work of Singer (1974, 1976), Singer and Pope (1978), Sheikh and Shaffer (1979), and Sheikh (1983a, 1983b).

Milton Erickson is one of the best-known therapeutic storytellers. See Erickson (1982), Havens (1985), Lankton and Lankton (1983).

For other therapeutic use of fantasy see Duhl (1983), Gordon (1978), Leuner (1969), Shorr (1972, 1974), and symbolic modeling of Bandura and Barab (1973).

Our Counseling Research Institute has been examining the mythology of many cultures to abstract the core cultural themes found there. You can do your own research by examining the same material and answering three questions: (1) What core value is the cultural story honoring? (2) What belief or attitude is the story condemning? (3) How does the fable reinforce the good value while punishing the wrong one? (Usually in the story bad things happen to the hero and heroine when they follow noncultural values, such as cowardliness, antisocial actions, or overly independent thinking, and good things happen after the hero or heroine decides to conform to the prevailing social values.

The therapist will find a storehouse of useful stories in the following mythologies. For the stories and fables of the South Pacific see the *Mana* a multivolume journal of language and literature of oceania (*Mana*, 1980). Norse mythology can be found in the *Prose Edda* from Icelandic translations (Young, 1954). Australian myths are recorded in *Aboriginal Myths: Tales of the Dreamtime* by Reed (1978). Fables about the origin of the universe and the origins of man can be found in Philip Freund (1965), *Myths of Creation*. Bulfinch's classic work on more famous mythologies is a great source of cultural themes. See Bulfinch, "Age of Fable," "The Age of Chivalry," "Legends of Charlemagne," In addition, review *King Arthur and His Knights*; the Mabinogeon, *Beowulf, Religion and Folklore of Northern India* (Crooke, 1926), and that of Scotland, (Dalyell, 1835).

And don't overlook the bounty of less prestigious stories, like Mother Goose Rhymes, the Brothers Grimm, or Aesop's Fables. The astute therapist will stay alert for themes in modern, popular literature that might be tapped in helping clients gain important insights into their false perceptions.

COGNITIVE FOCUSING

Principles

Focusing helps clients crystallize their emotional reactions to certain stimuli. The technique is adapted from a well-known Rogerian therapist, Eugene Gendlin (1981). Some research indicates that it might be the active element in Rogerian therapy, producing high levels of client self-experiencing (Mc Mullin, 1972).

Within the context of perceptual shift theory, cognitive restructuring therapists have enlisted the focusing technique in order to help clients clearly identify the root causes of their personal unhappiness. Basic to the idea of cognitive focusing is the notion that feelings begin with a cognition or core belief. If that core belief is irrational, it must be shifted—i.e., neutralized or replaced with a more rational belief. After the belief is shifted, the client's identified emotion will change.

Method

1. Ask your clients to relax briefly so as to ease any tautness in their muscles. Have them recline, and they can close their eyes if they wish. (3 minutes)

2. Urge them to clear their minds and to focus inwardly while you set the scene for this exercise. If they haven't come to you with a specific problem, present them with an analogy to help uncover the major sources of their discomfort. The "storeroom analogy," one such exercise, might be presented as follows:

   Imagine that you are sitting in a storeroom cluttered with boxes. In each box is one of your problems. Each problem has a different box, and the largest boxes contain the largest problems.

   Now picture that you move the boxes, one at a time, into the corners of the room, so that you can have space to sit down. From a relatively comfortable perch in the middle of the room, survey the boxes around you carefully. Pull out the box that you most want to open, and open it.

Lift the problem out of the box and look at it. Turn it from side to side so that you can see every aspect of it. Try to step outside yourself and watch your reactions to it.

3. Once clients have selected a problem from their "storeroom," ask them to focus upon how they feel about that problem. For example, one of our clients reported feeling uncomfortable whenever she met her spouse's ex-wife. We asked her to focus on how she felt about these meetings. She tried to recreate the feeling in the present, not simply remember what she felt.

4. Instruct your clients to focus on the overall emotion that best captures how they feel about the problem. This will be more difficult for some clients than for others, and it won't be easy for anyone. Many clients are conditioned in ways that prevent them from clarifying their feelings, either to themselves or to others. Feelings are usually composites, not single entities, which could make it difficult for clients to easily sense one overall impression. Clients must subdue all of the self-squawking and jabbering that may be going on in their heads before they can recognize the overall emotion. In our example, after much effort, the client was able to label the emotion associated with meeting her husband's ex-wife as *anxiety*.

5. Once the overall emotion has been defined to the satisfaction of your clients, involve them in a careful analysis of the various nuances and components of that feeling. Since feelings are usually composites, elements of anger, guilt, resentment, jealousy, etc., could be evident in and around the central emotion of anxiety.

6. Now have your clients recall, in detail, other similar situations in which they have felt that same emotion. ("Have you always reacted fearfully when you met his ex-wife? When you met someone else, like your mother-in-law or his ex-girlfriend? Describe those other situations. Tell me exactly how you see yourself feeling about each one of them.") Have your clients resonate the situations with the feelings, so that you can confirm that there is an apparent "association" between the overall emotion (anxiety) and the meetings. The situations can be drawn from the past, as well as the present.

7. Most importantly, probe to determine what thoughts sparked the same emotion in each of these similar situations. In each instance, determine what your clients been saying to themselves. What meaning do they assign to these situations? Follow the trail suggested by each of these components to see if it leads to a mistaken core perception held by the client. Hence, in our example, the following core perception emerged: "I am not as good as her. When my husband sees us together, he will realize he made a mistake leaving her for me."

8. Now, try to help your clients switch the emotion. The first step is to ask your clients to focus on similar situations that did not incite the negative overall emotion. ("Was there ever a time when you met his ex-wife's that was *not* upsetting to you? Describe how you felt then?") Remind them to not simply recall what they experienced but to try to recreate the same feelings. (If your clients can only recall having the negative overall emotion, ask them to focus on how other people might feel in the same situations.)

9. Next, instruct your clients to focus on their thoughts, beliefs, or what they told themselves during these similar situations when the overall emotion was different. ("Describe how you thought on those occasions when you weren't anxious about meeting her.") Guide your clients through an analysis of these feelings. In our example, the resulting core perception that emerged was:

> I feel sorry for her. She is a good person just like me. Not better or worse, just another human being who has had difficult times like myself. He is with me now, not her. But he still cares for her, and I can accept his caring and learn to like her myself.

10. Finally, have your clients practice replacing the feelings that they had initially (Steps #4 and #5) with the feelings in the other situations (Step #8). The key to switching the emotions is switching the thoughts. Have your clients imagine the thoughts they had when they weren't anxious (Step #9, rather than Step #7). In our example, the client pictured believing the ex-wife was a good person, not better or worse than herself, instead of thinking her husband would regret the divorce. Depending upon the severity of the damaging preoccupation, support this practice to continue for quite some time. Teach your clients how to practice this shifting technique at home, using a variety of concrete examples from their own histories. The more they practice, the more proficient they will become at shifting from negative to positive emotions, and the more durable the positive shift will be.

Example

Lester, in his fifties, was having a great deal of difficulty with his romantic relationships. He described diverse feelings in a very confused, discordant manner. Nevertheless, he was psychologically sophisticated and a professional writer. We used the storeroom analogy to help him focus on the central problem. The main components of the dialogue, which took an hour and a half, are summarized here. (The client has already been presented with the storeroom analogy discussed above.)

CLIENT: I see several big boxes. One has my problem of being jealous when the woman I am going out with shows interest in another man. Another problem is the inner conflict I feel of wanting to be very close to her, but at the same time feeling "trapped" if I get too close. A third problem is my inability to hurt a woman whom I like as a person but don't particularly want as a mate. I can't seem to break off these relationships. Another box is the love-hate-fear-joy-anger conflict I have with a woman I have fallen in love with. The fifth box is my propensity to protect myself by always going out with several women at the same time, even though one is always special.

THERAPIST: Pull out one of the boxes from the corner—any one you wish—and put it in front of you. Open it up and lift the problem out of it. Just look at it. Get the feel of the whole problem. There are probably many aspects to it—too many to think of separately. So try to get the total feel of it. Look inside yourself where you feel things and see what comes to you as you look at the problem. What comes up when you ask yourself, "How does it feel now?" Just let the feeling come in whatever way it comes but don't go inside it. Keep looking at it from the outside. (3 minutes)

CLIENT: I pulled out the largest box, the love-hate-fear-joy-anger box. When I opened it, I saw all these swelling emotions. It felt familiar, for I have seen this box many times before. I remember noticing that at different times different emotions are dominant—sometimes the fear was strongest, other times the love, frequently the anger.

THERAPIST: What was your overall reaction to the problem?

CLIENT: Confusion.

THERAPIST: Look for a label of your overall feeling, like "sticky," "tight," "confined." Keep focusing on the overall feeling and try different words or pictures until one clicks. (4 minutes)

CLIENT: There is a feeling of great sadness and loneliness. It feels very empty. It also feels twisted—like all these emotions don't belong, like they come from somewhere else and have just attached themselves to relationships. They are very old feelings, like they started long before I dated. Mostly though, I feel regret that they are there. They seem to be muddling up what otherwise would be a clear pool of good feelings.

THERAPIST: Fine. Now I would like you to search for situations that are connected to these emotions. Find events in the present and one from the distant past. Keep focusing on your feelings until some situation occurs to you. Take each overall emotion, one at a time, and wait until an event attaches itself to the emotion. (3 minutes)

CLIENT: Every time I am with a women I feel sad and lonely. I felt this same feeling when I was in grade school. I didn't fit in and I felt I didn't have any friends and nobody liked me. The twisted impression comes a day or two after I am with a woman. I remember feeling this many years ago when I fell in love for the first time. My feelings for her didn't seem quite real; they seemed kind of neurotic or something.

THERAPIST: Okay. Keep focusing on your emotions silently but this time look for the core belief that ties the past and present situations to your emotions. Take each feeling one at a time. (5 minutes)

CLIENT: Yes, the sad and lonely comes from the thought, "I am different from others. In some way I am separate from the rest of humanity. I am not like other people."

THERAPIST: And the twisted feeling? What thought makes you feel the emotions are wrong and out of place?

CLIENT: Yes, my thought is that feeling this way is sick and I must be inferior to other men.

THERAPIST: Can you tie the two thoughts together?

CLIENT: I can begin to see what I am thinking. "I am different from the rest of humanity because I am sick." I thought this when I was in grade school, the different and inferior parts—but they turned to a feeling of being sick when I fell in love with my first girlfriend. Nowadays I don't feel this often, only when I start deeply caring for a woman.

THERAPIST: Very good work. Now let's try some shifting. I want you to focus on some different situations. Try to think of some times when you were with a woman but you felt calm, confident and healthy.

CLIENT: There have been lots of women I felt good with, but I never cared for them. If I fall in love with a woman then I get these bad feelings.

THERAPIST: All right. Then look for the times you have been with these women you love when you haven't felt these emotions. Take your time and find several situations from the past and present.

CLIENT: Well, there have been short periods of time, usually lasting only a few days, when I didn't feel them.

THERAPIST: Take some time now, silently with yourself, and focus on what you were feeling at these times. (3 minutes)

CLIENT: I can feel it. Free! Not jealous. Happy to know them, and to love them.

THERAPIST: Okay. What did you perceive during these times that you didn't perceive in the others. What did you say and believe differently? Be silent with yourself and see what comes up. (1 minute)

CLIENT: I was thinking I didn't need them. I wanted them but I didn't have to have them. See, before I felt these women I loved were my only contact with the rest of humanity. Without them I was totally alone. But at the other times I felt like I was a part of humanity, like I had my unique individuality but I was not alone. When I thought that way, my lovers were just people, not saviors there to rescue me from loneliness.

THERAPIST: Please continue.

CLIENT: There are times when I am with the woman I love when I can see things clearly. These times only come occasionally, maybe for a day or so, and then I slip back into the old murky pool. It feels like I can see her as a separate individual, with her own struggles, triumphs and tragedies. I don't think she only exists to make me feel good. It's like I lose myself during these times and see her as independent of me.

THERAPIST: Please stay with this feeling. Keep focusing on it. . . . Now, try something. While being in the feeling, look back at the old feeling. View the old felt sense of being different, twisted, and sick from the perspective of your new feeling. (2 minutes)

CLIENT: Oh my! The old feeling is not real. That's why I called it twisted. It is incredibly arrogant. What conceit and narcissism to believe that nature created me separately from others. It's like nature had two creations—everybody else in the world, and then me. That makes me as important as all the rest of humanity. I am so special I needed an independent genesis! It is a self-indulgent selfishness to demand that a woman give up herself to minister to my arrogant loneliness. Hell, we are all lonely; we are all trapped inside our own skins wishing to be part of a "we" rather than just an "I." My feeling of being different from all other people is just an exercise in cosmic vanity, an existential snobbery.

THERAPIST: Hold that perception. Tuck it away somewhere in a safe place. Call it up when your are staring at the big box of contradictory emotions. Pull it out when you are with the woman you love and are feeling angry, hurt, lonely, and hateful.

The sessions continued using cognitive focusing. The client would keep moving among situations, feelings and thoughts. When he was with his lover he practiced changing his perception that he was uniquely different, switching it to "I am part of humanity. I am not alone."

Comment

With certain clients this technique can be very powerful. But with other clients, defenses and sabotages often come up.

The danger in the use of this technique is overmystifying the process. Focusing narrows clients' attention on their emotions so that they can more easily identify the external triggers and intervening cognitions causing those emotions. The beliefs clients find are therefore more likely to be precise, and any cognitive change technique is more likely to be effective. The process is not based, in our view, on getting in touch with hidden elements inside one's subconscious or repressed emotions that need to be expunged. Rather, it focuses clients' attention on specific, manageable perceptions that can be usefully shifted.

Further Information

The theoretical, practical, and research basis for the focusing technique can be found in Gendlin's work (1962, 1964, 1967, 1969, 1981; Gendlin et al. 1968).

In addition, see Mc Mullin (1972) for research data on the importance of focusing.

RATIONAL EMOTIVE IMAGERY

Principles

Albert Ellis and other rational-emotive therapists have used a technique which aims at shifting clients' overall perceptions. Called rational emotive imagery (REI), it is included in the perceptual shift section of this book rather than in the countering section because the technique addresses clients' overall patterns of thinking, rather than their specific, individual cognitions.

In most of the other cognitive techniques described in this book, the therapist follows a basic procedure of initially identifying his clients' damaging beliefs and then applying certain predesigned exercises and approaches to facilitate his client's changing unrealistic perceptions. In this role, the therapist directs the curative process: he writes a prescription and then guides the client in the use of that prescription.

Under the REI technique, the client—not the therapist—writes the prescription. The therapist helps the client to identify clearly the source of discomfort and to focus deeply upon the core theme of that discomfort (e.g., fear, a feeling of rejection, a feeling of inferiority, an intense distrust of others). Once the dominant core theme has been identified, the therapist invites the client to focus his or her creative energies on defining strategies for reducing the intensity of the core theme. Hence, in responding to an intense distrust of others, a client might elect to use what is essentially a countering technique whereby she assures herself that some people are more trustworthy than others; or she might emphasize the need to do a better job of determining in advance who can be trusted; or she might emphasize doing a better job of not disclosing matters on which she is most vulnerable to abuse by untrustworthy people; or some combination of these approaches might be adopted. The client decides, not the therapist.

Clearly, the success of this approach depends upon three factors: (1) the extent to which the client copes effectively with a relatively unstructured therapeutic procedure; (2) the extent to which the client exercises personal creativity in defining cognitive strategies; and (3) most importantly, the extent to which the client is able to invest him or herself in the therapeutic process.

As the experienced reader will recognize, we have made some slight but important modifications in Ellis' original conceptualization of this technique. (See Step #7 in "Method.")

Method

1. It helps to have clients relax before they begin the exercise. It might improve their concentration.
2. Develop a hierarchy of ten situations in which the client has gotten upset. Be sure these situations are described in enough detail so that the client can imagine them vividly. See if you can identify any common denominators among the ten that might help you to reduce them to a few core themes. Make sure that the client agrees that the final list accurately reflects his major sources of discomfort.
3. Have the client imagine each of the situations, the feelings that are associated with those situations, and the core themes that best characterize those feelings. Ask him to keep these clearly in mind.
4. Have the client begin with any one of those core themes and focus on the associated feeling, using any strategies he can devise for modifying those feelings. Have him keep working until he starts feeling a change in his emotions.
5. Tell the client to focus on what he told himself to make the feelings shift. If it helps him to concentrate and clearly recall, have him write down the advice he gave himself. Have him become totally aware of his beliefs.
6. Have the client practice 15 minutes a day until he can consistently create the alternative emotions. Once his first choice core theme has been treated in this way, he should use the same technique with all of the remaining core themes from the list devised in Step #2.
7. To help the client gain control over his emotions, he can practice feeling

different emotions while imagining the original situations that he recounted in Step #2. He can practice feeling happy, sad, angry, confident, relaxed or any other emotion simply by alternating his self-talk.

Example

Rational emotive therapy literature gives numerous examples of this technique. We will included only one from our caseload.

Margo was a 28-year-old woman who came to me after going to at least six other therapists. With each of her previous counselors, she would try one or two sessions, wouldn't feel better, and would quit, only to move on to another therapist. This had been going on for a year.

After the first few visits, it was clear why she hadn't made any progress. She simply was not interested in really working at her own self-improvement. She was very resistant, answering my probes with a simple and abrupt "I don't know." She did none of the assigned readings, nor did she try to learn anything about the techniques or theory behind the therapy. Instead she expected, and at times demanded, that I somehow solve her depression for her. When anything was expected of her, she reacted badly to even the suggestion that she put out any effort.

Highly structured cognitive techniques weren't affective with Margo because they allowed her to be passive in the therapeutic process. She needed less counselor involvement and more client initiative. It was decided that rational emotive imagery might provide the necessary participation.

The key scene in Margo's hierarchy was her perception that all of her problems as an adult were caused by her parents. She felt, she hadn't received the nurturance necessary for her to be happy. Her depression, broken relationships with men, poor job, and financial difficulties were all her parents' fault. Apparently she had misunderstood a comment made by a novice analytic counselor five years earlier, and now she was sure her parents were to blame for everything. As a result, she hadn't seen or talked to her parents in five years.

After listening to her tirades against her parents, I concluded that her anger was extremely overblown. Her parents made mistakes, as all parents do, but it sounded like they generally supported and tried to help their daughter in the ways that they thought were best.

When we started the imagery, she imagined living with her parents and all the "terrible" things they had done. The emotion she recognized was intense rage. When she was told to shift it to a lesser emotion—anger or disappointment—she didn't. She said she *couldn't*, but it became clear from her nonverbal behavior that she *wouldn't*. She asked to do something else besides this technique. I refused and persisted in using it. Naturally she started to get angry at me for not granting her request, but I continued the same technique. The session ended in a stalemate.

Margo canceled the next three appointments. I heard later that she went to two other therapists for sessions, looking to them to solve her depression. But a month later she came back to see me, still angry but "ready to give me one last try." She expected that she had sufficiently punished me so that I would drop the rational emotive imagery, but I did not.

It should be noted, parenthetically, that this persistence is somewhat unusual in cognitive restructuring. Usually, if one technique doesn't work, I freely switch to another. But this client was a very unusual case. Nothing had worked with her. Her failure with the previous six therapists was not the fault of the therapists or their techniques. In fact, I knew two of those therapists: one was an excellent ego-dynamic counselor; the other, an outstanding behaviorist. It was necessary to do something radically different. I felt that sticking with one technique, and not allowing Margo to escape the problem, might be just what was needed. If I were to do this with ten different clients, I would probably fail seven out of ten times.

We continued the rational emotive imagery, albeit without her full cooperation. But this time she made some changes. She reduced her anger slightly, but at a cost. She said the only way she could reduce her rage was to say to herself that she was somewhat responsible. But when she said that to herself, she started to feel scared and quite guilty. I switched the imagery work to the new perception of self-blame and fear. Using rational emotive imagery she was able to reduce these feelings somewhat. We then alternated the imagery work between anger towards her parents and fear and guilt about herself. Gradually, over a period of many sessions, the client was able to reduce the guilt and the anger until her depression lifted.

Comment

The flexibility of the technique is both its greatest virtue and its vice. Some clients need more specific instruction on how to change their emotions. Others like being more responsible for their own perceptual shifting.

Further Information

The technique is described in three publications: Maultsby and Ellis (1974) and Maultsby (1971, 1976).

RESYNTHESIZING BELIEFS

Principles

The mistaken beliefs that cause clients pain are usually rooted in their personal histories. The damaging perceptions might have been implanted long before a client could process information in a rational manner, and during the years since that time an entire pattern of thinking might have evolved, based upon that mistaken beginning. A pattern cannot be altered until the original mistaken belief has been altered or entirely replaced.

This hypothesis finds support in the work of such noted theorists as Piaget (1954). He argued that thoughts, themes and beliefs accepted into the frontal lobe during the preoperational stage of brain development (ages two to seven) are likely to be based upon many kinds of logical errors. During the concrete operational stage (ages seven to 11), the individual cannot abstract reality in terms of "as if" thinking, viewing problems concretely. Any misperceptions that accrue during these two stages of intellectual development will be stored in long-term memory, and will not be easily removed as the individual matures.

Assuming the correctness of this hypothesis, it seems clear that early mistaken beliefs that were synthesized into clients' overall patterns of thought must be subsequently resynthesized if clients are to gain a healthier perspective on themselves and the world around them. The following technique explains how cognitive therapists can help their clients resynthesize early mistaken perceptions.

Method

1. Develop a list of irrational beliefs and the situations in which they have occurred. Each of these situations should be listed under "Present Situation" on a worksheet like the one presented as Table 3. The beliefs associated with each situation should also be listed there, under "Present Belief."
2. Look for critical experiences the client had prior to or during early ado-

Table 3
Resynthesis Worksheet

Present
Situation _____

Emotional Response _____

Present Belief about Present Situation _____

Early Recollection
(preformal situational events) _____

Emotional Response _____

Mistaken Core Life Theme _____

Corrected Life Theme _____

Corrected Present Belief _____

---

lescence. First, identify the preformal situational events. Have the client visualize as clearly as possible those early events.

3. Formulate into a sentence the mistaken belief that resulted from each of these events (the mistaken core life theme). Record those sentences where requested on the worksheet.

4. After careful discussion with your client, correct each core life theme. Record that information where requested on the worksheet. The early mistaken perceptions should be expunged by showing your client the correct perception of the early events. Replace all early mistaken cognitions connected to the events.

5. Once the mistaken preoperative irrationalities have been corrected, help the client change present irrational thinking.

6. Have the client regularly practice the procedure of finding mistaken beliefs, identifying their preformal origins, correcting the earlier misimpressions, and then adopting a more functional belief as a guide to his or her present life.

Example 1

Present situation: Client got anxious at party where many international students attended.

Present belief: People from other countries are dangerous.

Preformal situational event: Client was isolated from anybody not in the immediate family; was overprotected, and not exposed to usual environmental stimuli. She had never seen anyone who looked "different."

Life theme: Anything new or novel is dangerous.

Corrected life theme: The new and novel are exciting and give me an opportunity to grow and expand. The new is no more dangerous than the known and familiar.

Corrected present belief: It is interesting to meet people from other countries; I have an opportunity to learn more about other cultures.

Example 2

Present situation: Client was afraid of being alone in the evening, so much so that she surrounded herself with as many friends as possible so she would always have someone to invite over.

Present belief: I am a very sociable person.

Preformal situational event: She had been abandoned by a parent when young.

Life theme: I will never allow myself to be abandoned again.

Corrected life theme: I am not a child anymore and I don't need a person's protection like I once did. I can survive alone, and don't need to be terrified about being by myself.

Corrected present belief: I no longer need to surround myself with so friends to protect myself from running out of people. I can pick a few close friends who really mean something to me.

Example 3

Present situation: Client would never undertake any task requiring patience, concentration, and persistence.

Present belief: Routine is boring.

Preformal situational event: As a child the client engaged in extensive daydreams to make up for a socially impoverished early childhood.

Life theme: The only way to enrich one's life is through fantasy and imagination. Everyday activities are dull, drab, and gray.

Corrected life theme: Real life is at times drab and gray, and at other times a bright technicolor. Actual life is far more meaningful than fictional fantasies. True satisfaction can only come by engaging in the struggles, triumphs, and tragedies of real life, not by living in a fairy tale world of magic, where fate controls all successes. Meaning comes from human beings striving against all odds to make things better, not from escaping into sanguine fantasies.

Corrected present belief: Concentration and persistence on various activities provide the foundation for making my life ultimately meaningful and enriching.

Comment

When done correctly, this technique can provide rapid, dramatic shifts in clients' perceptions. Psychodynamic therapists often use elements of this approach in their therapeutic practice. The cognitive restructuring approach differs both theoretically and in practice, however, because of the emphasis it places upon actively correcting the faulty life theme, and because of its reliance upon the hypothesis that preoperational and concrete beliefs are readily accessible to conscious manipulation. In our view the battle doesn't rage between the conscious and unconscious, or among repressed conflicts of the ego, superego, and id; rather, the conflict is between what is verifiably real and what was once spuriously learned.

Further Readings

Piaget's works are extensive. See Piaget, 1954, 1963, 1970, 1973.

For a discussion of early preformal recollections and their importance, see Mosak, 1958, 1969. His research review demonstrates that preformal recollections reflect the basic client life themes. The most comprehensive review of preformal attitudes and their use in therapy is by Olson (1979).

3

Conditioning Techniques

Chapter 2 presented techniques for effecting perceptual shifts in clients whose unhappiness derives from a damaging overall pattern of thought. This chapter considers the consequences of irrational thoughts (paired with negative emotional responses) as individual stimuli, rather than patterns, and advocates the use of conditioning techniques in helping clients gain a more rational perspective on their lives.

Within the context of conditioning, any cognition can be viewed in several ways. It can be a conditioned stimulus, a response to environmental triggers, an operant, or a means of reinforcement and punishment.

This chapter discusses specific techniques based on experimentally established principles of learning theory. It can be divided into two major sections: classical or Pavlovian conditioning (e.g., cognitive desensitization, cognitive escape conditioning) and operant or instrumental conditioning (e.g., covert reinforcement, operant cognitive restructuring).

COGNITIVE DESENSITIZATION

Principles

Developed by Joseph Wolpe, systematic desensitization is a form of classical conditioning which pairs relaxation with anxiety-provoking stimuli to inhibit conditioned anxiety responses. There is a continuing debate about what, exactly, comprises the active mechanisms in desensitization. However, there is little dispute over the effectiveness of the procedure.

One common, though unproven, explanation is that the effective element in desensitization is counterconditioning—a procedure which pairs a positive to a negative stimulus so that the positive replaces the negative. For the procedure to work, the positive stimulus must be stronger than the negative. This is achieved by exposing the subject gradually to the feared event. Schematically, negative and positive conditioned responses look like this:

$$CS- \text{———————} CR-$$
$$CS+ \text{———————} CR+$$

After pairing a strong CS + with a weaker CS − we have:

$$CS- \text{———————} CR+$$

In the traditional desensitization approach, the CS- consists of a series of anxiety-producing images arranged in a graduated hierarchy. These images are paired with relaxation until the relaxed response substitutes for the anxious one.

Cognitive restructuring modifies this procedure by desensitizing clients' beliefs instead of their images, reducing or eliminating any negative emotions connected to those beliefs. Images are used only to provide a context or background for visualizing different beliefs.

Method 1

1. Teach the client deep muscle relaxation.
2. Develop a hierarchy of irrational beliefs that are causing anxiety. Order the hierarchy in terms of how much fear the thoughts elicit or how strongly the thoughts are believed.

3. Instruct the client to imagine the lowest thought on the hierarchy. When this thought is clearly in mind, begin deep muscle relaxation. Continue with this procedure until the client's tension level returns to zero, indicating that the thought no longer produces anxiety. For example:

> Now I would like you to think the next thought on your hierarchy. Picture this thought as clearly as you can. If you wish, you can imagine a particular situation in the past when you have often had the thought. Keep thinking the thought until it is clearly in mind. Tell me when you have it by signaling with your right hand. . . . OK, stop! Now relax yourself just as you have been taught, and keep relaxing until you feel comfortable again. Tell me when you are ready. (Biofeedback measures or a verbal report can be used instead of a hand signal.)
>
> Now I would like you to do it again. Think the thought, get it clearly in mind, and then relax yourself. You can imagine a scene where you are likely to have the thought if it helps you, but make sure it's a different situation than the one you used before.

4. Continue through the client's hierarchy of thoughts until the anxiety for all items is zero.
5. Tape the procedure so the client can practice at home.

Method 2

You can vary your technique by substituting responses other than relaxation. You can use positive physical responses, assertive responses, nature tapes (ocean sounds, country streams), positive images that a client finds personally reinforcing, or low heartbeat, GSR, or EMG readings.

Method 3

General images also can be associated with irrational thoughts as a substitute for relaxation. In most cases the therapist should help his clients interweave these images with the irrational thoughts in such a way that the emotional valence of the image transfers to the beliefs. The following images have proven useful: Superman, Wonder Woman, favorite heroes and heroines, favorite objects, sunflowers, lotus blossoms, sun, stars, moon, religious figures (Christ, Buddha, Mohammed), a wise guru, natural life forces (rivers, mountains, oceans), watching oneself in a movie, visualizing oneself as a parent, adult, or child, or imagining oneself as an animal.

Ideally, one or more positive images are interwoven with the negative CS. For instance, interweaving the thought, "I need to be better than everyone else," with the feeling a client has toward children may bring home the concept that a child is worthwhile even though an adult may be stronger and wiser and may have achieved more. Therefore, being superior is not a prerequisite for being worthwhile. Similarly, the Wonder Woman image could be interwoven with the thought, "I am inferior to other girls because I can't ride a bike."

Many eastern religions, including Zen and Yoga, have used image desensitizations for centuries.

Comment

We have found that Method #1, which pairs relaxation with anxiety-producing thoughts, is not as effective as other desensitization techniques. Some clients, particularly agoraphobics, get anxious when trying to relax ("I may lose control"). In addition, relaxation is a physiological sensory response, while thoughts are cognitive. Thus, Method #1 mixes two very different perceptual modes, which seem to dilute the effectiveness of the technique. It has been our experience that the best substitute response is in the same mode as the original negative conditioned stimulus (visual, auditory, kinesthetic, sensory, or emotional). For this reason, the third desensitization method, which counters negative thoughts with positive thoughts, is usually the most effective.

Further Information

See Wolpe (1969, 1973) for key discussions of desensitization and its variations. In addition, Wolpe's later works (1978, 1981a, 1981b) show that he recognizes and emphasizes the importance of perception in desensitization and other conditioning processes.

COVERT EXTINCTION

Principles

In a classical conditioning paradigm, a client can develop a phobia as a result of having been exposed to a terrifying event. Any stimuli present at the same time as the fear can get conditioned, so that the stimuli develop the ability to produce the anxiety. For example, a client of mine had difficulty breathing when he drove his car on a long trip. Although he did not know it at the time, carbon monoxide was leaking from the exhaust into the car. His respiratory difficulties produced a strong anxiety (UCR). He repaired the car but developed anxiety (CR) whenever he drove again. He finally stopped driving altogether. Schematically his phobia is:

$$\left.\begin{array}{l} \text{CS} = \text{driving} \\ \\ \text{USC} = \text{inhaling carbon monoxide} \end{array}\right\} \text{paired} \longrightarrow \text{CR} = \text{anxiety}$$

How can this conditioned reflex be eliminated? Even though the client stopped driving for several months, it did not remove the anxiety, for when he was forced to be a passenger in someone else's car, he got anxious all over again. His conditioned anxiety was not easily removed. Theoretically, if he had continued driving he would have been exposed to the CS without the UCS, and his anxiety would have gradually disappeared. This experience is called extinction. But because he avoided driving, the CS-UCS association never had a chance to be eliminated.

We decided to use covert extinction. The client imagined driving without breathing problems until he could picture the scene without anxiety. After practicing these images for several weeks, he was able to drive again, so that *in vivo* extinction could eliminate his phobia.

Having the client imagine the CS without the UCS is the key to covert extinction. Extinction may erase the previous association, or new learning may replace the old; whatever the correct explanation, the procedure can help clients remove phobias.

Beliefs can become conditioned to traumatic events as well as external stimuli. Thus, any thought which occurs at the time of a strong anxiety response can become a CS that alone will later elicit fear, and covert extinction can also be used with these thoughts.

Method 1. Behavioral *in vivo*

Have clients practice the feared event until extinction takes place. The therapist must be sure that the UCS will not recur.

Method 2. Covert

Have the client imagine doing the feared activity while picturing no aversive consequences.

Method 3. Belief Extinction

1. Make a list of the client's thoughts that have become associated with his sources of anxiety.
2. Have the client imagine thinking the thoughts in various situations, but without any negative emotional response.
3. The client can practice several hundred repetitions at home until the thoughts no longer produce the CR's.

Method 4. Time Extinction

Instruct your client to wait until he feels happy and confident; then have him read or think the irrational thoughts. Tell him to stop thinking or reading immediately if he begins to feel upset. Instruct the client not to do the exercise when he is unhappy.

Method 5. Neutral Images

1. Make a list of the client's irrational thoughts and the situations in which they frequently occur.
2. Develop a list of neutral images to which the client attaches little emotion, such as looking at a newspaper, eating a meal, or reading a psychological dissertation. Ask the client to confirm that these activities produce only neutral emotions.
3. Pair the irrational thoughts with the neutral scenes. You will probably need over a hundred repetitions.

Method 6. Shaped Covert Extinction

Have your client imagine a subcomponent of the CS, so that the CR is not elicited. In the earlier example of the upset driver, have the client imagine himself just sitting in the driver's seat, or just holding the steering wheel in his hands. Since the CS is not at full strength, the CR never occurs above threshold. Gradually, more and more of the CS is presented, always below threshold, until the full CS causes no response. Specifically:

1. Make a list of the client's irrational thoughts.
2. Logically dissect the thoughts into subcomponents. For example, if the client's thought is: "One is worthless if one keeps failing at things," you

can subdivide "things" into a variety of different failings, like breaking one's pencil, forgetting to put out the cat, dropping a stitch, etc.

3. Have the client image the subparts of the thoughts for many repetitions. Make sure that this focus on the subparts causes no discomfort. You can use a biofeedback measure or client self-report to determine whether the client is feeling the CR. If a CR occurs, subdivide the thought further.

4. Provided there is no emotional response, keep building the thought closer to its original form. Continue until the whole thought produces no negative emotions.

5. Another form of shaped covert extinction varies the fear-producing image rather than the thought. For example, fear of riding in an elevator can be subdivided by imagining a big elevator, a glass one, an empty elevator, one that goes up only one floor, or one that travels 40 floors. The image can also be varied by changing the client's perspective of himself in the phobic situation. The client can picture himself in the elevator on TV, looking back from the future, in an audience with friends watching a play of himself in the elevator, etc. But in all cases, the subcomponents of the image are presented so that the client's emotional response remains below threshold.

Method 7. Morita Therapy

Morita Therapy is a Japanese therapeutic technique that was developed at the beginning of this century and that seems to be based on extinction procedures. Clients suffering from dysthymic disorders are isolated for the first week in a room. During this time they have anxiety and depression but they cannot escape or avoid their discomfort. Their CR's are not intentionally exacerbated as in flooding; they simply experience their thoughts and images and let the consequences occur. Since the imagined consequences do not occur, i.e., death, insanity, total loss of control (the clients' imagined UCS's), extinction takes place. A cognitive component that helps the extinction process is the instruction: "What one thinks, imagines, or feels is less important than what one does in life. A person can carry on an active, purposeful life, despite the burden of symptoms." This philosophy helps clients realize that there are no ultimate UCS's to thinking and feeling and, therefore, there is no reason to avoid emotions.

Example

Some years ago, Kevin came to me because of severe panic attacks. The only environmental trigger we could find was that his college roommate had quit school and now he was alone in the apartment they had previously shared. After some exploring, we found the possible cause of his severe reaction to the very common experience of losing a roommate.

Kevin described an experience in which he almost drowned when he was 11. He and his parents were swimming in the Gulf of Mexico, in a place where there were underwater canyons with currents that would often pull a swimmer out to sea. He remembered the experience very distinctly. He was standing in water up to his neck, trying to see where his parents were. Suddenly a large wave hit him and dragged him into one of the underwater canyons. Fortunately, someone on shore saw what had happened and rescued him.

After the experience, he became very much afraid of the ocean, and the fear generalized to lakes, rivers, and large swimming pools. He avoided them all.

So far the client's experience was a rather typical incident creating aquaphobia. Schematically:

$$
\left.\begin{array}{l}
\text{CS} = \text{ocean and generalization to large bodies of water.} \\
\text{paired} \\
\text{UCS} = \text{almost drowning}
\end{array}\right\} \!\!\longrightarrow \text{CR} = \text{anxiety}
$$

But, unknown to Kevin, another association occurred. Not only was he in water when the panic occurred, but he was also thinking something. Through hypnosis, we discovered that at the time the wave hit he had been thinking that he was all alone. There was no one else around him, and he couldn't find his parents. He now remembered that not only had he become afraid of water, but that, ever since that incident, he was also anxious about being alone. He recalled that after his near drowning episode, he started begging his parents not to go to movies without him, and always demanded that someone stay with him. Long after his fear of water was extinguished, he remembered always being afraid of being alone. When his roommate left, he was for the first time alone for an extended period of time. Schematically:

$$
\left.\begin{array}{l}
\text{CS 1} = \text{ocean and water} \\
\quad \text{CS 2} = \text{thought of being alone} \\
\text{paired} \\
\text{USC} = \text{almost drowning}
\end{array}\right\} \!\!\longrightarrow \text{CR} = \text{anxiety}
$$

$$
\left.\begin{array}{l}
\text{CS 3} = \text{Environmental trigger (roommate leaving)} \\
\text{paired} \\
\text{CS 2} = \text{thought of being alone}
\end{array}\right\} \!\!\longrightarrow \text{CR} = \text{anxiety}
$$

We used several covert extinction methods to remove the anxiety. He listened to a series of tapes in which he imagined thinking he was alone. The scenes ranged from imagining he was alone in the bathroom to being alone on a South Pacific island with no one within a thousand miles. With each image he was told to think the thought as long as he could without any negative consequences. If he got upset or he imagined some negative consequence to being alone, he was told to stop the scene immediately, and do it again until he could think the thought in the scene without getting anxious (shaped covert extinction).

He was also instructed that outside of the above exercise he was to only think about being alone when he was feeling good and self-confident (time extinction).

After the covert treatments he was told to spend more time alone. He gave himself points for each hour he spent by himself without getting anxious, and tried to increase his points each week. He was told to stop if he got anxious (*in vivo* extinction).

Comment

One of the difficulties with covert extinction in clinical practice is that it is often very difficult to keep the UCS from entering the client's thoughts. It's hard for clients to image a negative scene with only neutral consequences. In most cases covert extinction is used in conjunction with a countering or perceptual shift technique.

Further Information

Cautela was one of the originators of covert extinction procedures. (See Ascher and Cautela, 1972; Cautela, 1971a; Gotestam and Melin, 1974; and Weiss et al., 1975.) Related concepts are Beck's (1976) neutralization technique, and habituation (Sokolov, 1963).

A subpart of shaped covert extinction is the major phobic treatment of NLP practitioners. Clients imagine seeing a motion picture of themselves in the phobic scene. The scene is varied by imagining it in black and white, as a still picture, run fast forward, backward, viewed behind a projection booth, etc. See Bandler and Grinder, 1979.

Morita Therapy has been discussed in a number of publications. See Reynolds, 1976, 1981.

OPERANT COGNITIVE RESTRUCTURING

Principles

Cognitions are strengthened by reinforcement and weakened by punishment. Thus, if a hungry man devises a strategy for getting food and it succeeds, he is more likely to resort to that strategy in the future. Likewise, the more a thought is reinforced, the more likely it will be that the person holding that thought will believe it. With years of reinforcement, some beliefs take on the certitude of dogma.

In an operant paradigm, cognitions can serve many functions. They can be discriminating stimuli or second-order conditioned reinforcements. But most importantly, they serve as operant themselves. Like behavior responses, beliefs exist because the person has been reinforced for believing them. This concept can be diagrammed as follows:

Discriminating stimuli→Cognitive operant→Positive or negative reinforcement

The reinforcement connected to cognitions can be rational or irrational. Rational reinforcement leads the organism to useful immediate rewards, without causing long-term punishment. Irrational reinforcement simply rewards a belief randomly, and has no connection with the reinforcement. Most superstitions are created in this way. Having a great day after reading a horoscope or getting a pay raise while wearing a green sweater reinforces the belief in astrology and green sweaters. Even though the associations are only arbitrary, people are more likely to believe any cognition followed by strong reinforcement.

Operant thoughts can be positively or negatively reinforced. A thought is negatively reinforcing if it removes a negative consequence, positive if it elicits a positive one. Beliefs that ultimately reduce damage to the person or return the organism to homeostasis are negatively reinforcing and thus more likely to occur and be "believed." Anxiety or pain reduction, relaxation, and physical pleasure reinforce any cognition preceding them.

Rewards can also be external or internal. The society praises its members for convergent attitudes about cultural values like sex roles, careers, and family. Divergent views are severely punished. Internal consequences are produced by the persons themselves after sufficient external reinforcement and punishment. Thus, clients who were consistently told they were bad when they were children will begin to say it to themselves whenever they engage in anticultural behavior.

To understand the cognitive aspect of operant conditioning, consider the following analogy: Imagine putting a animal in a Skinner box that has a lever, feeder, and two color lights. After you shape the animal's behavior through a series of successive approximations, the animal presses a lever and receives a food pellet whenever a green light flashes. In this typical operant experiment pressing the lever is the operant, the food is the reinforcement, the green light the discriminating stimulus.

But humans are more than animals. They have a huge frontal lobe. If we magically gave this frontal lobe to the animal, the simple operant conditioning pattern would vary. Not only would the animal's behavior change but its thoughts would be affected. Any perception, attitude, internal sense, or cognition the animal had immediately before receiving the food pellet would get reinforced along with the lever-pressing. These thoughts would more likely occur the next time the green light flashed. If the experimenter used a varied ratio schedule of reinforcement, the thoughts would recur to the point of obsession. If we asked the animal why it had this particular thought so much, it probably couldn't answer us. It would simply say it liked thinking it and believed it was true.

Method

1. Develop a list of the core beliefs that elicit the client's problem behaviors and emotions.
2. Take each belief and by a series of questions and mutual searchings try to find:

   a. What are the positive consequences of believing these thoughts (internal and external)?
   b. What negative stimuli are removed by believing them (internal and external)?
   c. What negative events occur because this thought is believed (internal and external)?
   d. What positive stimuli are removed by believing these thoughts (internal and external)?

3. Discover, through questioning, what history of reinforcement and punishment may have created these beliefs.
4. Logically analyze the rationality of the beliefs in terms of two criteria: (a) Does the belief lead to lasting reinforcement? and (b) Is the reinforcement the best that can be obtained with the least amount of punishment?
5. If you and the client agree that the belief is irrational, help the client develop alternative beliefs which are more likely to lead to reinforcement.
6. Attach new positive and negative reinforcements (external, conceptual, or imagined) to the new beliefs. Pair positive and negative punishment (environmental, conceptual, or imagined) to the old.

Example

Estelle was a client who had convinced herself that she was an agoraphobic. She maintained this belief aggressively, despite counter evidence, not wanting to give it up. After some extensive analysis, it was found that the belief negatively reinforced her. It removed from her certain pressures to which she would otherwise be subject by others. Like Berne's (1964) wooden leg example, she believed that people couldn't expect much from an agoraphobic. She could get out of taking trips when she didn't want to go, and she didn't have to be assertive (which made her feel guilty) when it came to saying "no" to others. Her alleged "sickness" was also positively reinforcing because, as a result of it, she received nurturance from her boyfriend. Unfortunately, the belief was also punishing because it provoked fear within her. She was afraid of going crazy. It also removed the possibility of positive reinforcement by denying her the opportunity for travel and enjoyable new experiences.

Estelle was thus in a bad situation. If she eliminated her belief, she would get punished in two ways: first, because she would now have to say "no" instead of saying she couldn't, and second, because she might not get all the sympathy that the illusion of ill-health had brought her. On the other hand, if she kept the belief, she would always be fearful of going crazy, and she wouldn't be able to travel.

Although unaware of it, Estelle uncovered a solution. She neither got rid of the thought nor kept it. She chose the middle zone of sometimes believing it and sometimes not. When she feared going crazy she would fight the thought and believe it less. When she wanted more sympathy, she worked herself up into thinking she was still agoraphobic. Her anxiety was correlative to her belief. It would wax and wane, according to the needs of the situation. Basically her solution to her problem was to keep herself a little bit agoraphobic and use it to get the maximum reinforcement.

Estelle and I analyzed her belief and judged it to be irrational because it wasn't useful. There were more reinforcing ways to go through life than holding onto a belief that caused so much pain. For example, she could control others more directly than by playing sick, and she could get nurturance by asking for it, rather than by manipulating those who cared about her. In addition, she could get these reinforcements without the punishing aspects of the fear of insanity and loss of traveling.

Example 2

Another client, Jessica, worked for months trying to change the belief that she was, basically, deep down inside, a "bag lady" (a woman of the streets, poor, homeless and rejected by all). Jessica believed this, despite the fact that she was a very artistic, successful, popular, and attractive young woman. Months of exposure to therapeutic countering techniques did not dislodge her negative self-perception. The following outline of the operant analysis of the belief helps to explain why Jessica's belief was so resistant to change.

Reinforcement for Believing "I Am a Bag Lady."

	External	*Internal*
Positive Reinforcement	entertained people very popular a "character" center of attention people took care of her	felt unique felt special salt of the earth in touch with all humanity

Negative Reinforcement	others didn't expect much
	didn't have to be classy
	didn't have to act in
	  a prescribed fashion
		reduced guilt
		reduced pressure to
		  succeed
		reduced boredom

Punishment	not totally accepted no deep intimacies some ridicule	anxiety attacks fear of discovery withdrawn from people

Comment

The difficulty with the operant view is not the analysis itself, for in many cases evidence supports this theory. The difficulty is removing the reinforcement of the belief. By definition insight alone does not change reinforcement history. Clients may learn that they hold onto thoughts because they have been internally and externally rewarded for believing them, but this knowledge does not change the reinforcement value of the thoughts. Unfortunately, the therapist usually doesn't have control of the contingency necessary to change the reinforcement values and must convince clients to change their own environmental contingencies.

Further Information

B. F. Skinner (1953) discusses a useful distinction between operant seeing and conditioned seeing. His "operant seeing" is equivalent to our concept of operant control of beliefs.

Operant control of covert events has been described extensively. See Epstein and Hersen, 1974; Mahoney et al., 1972. It has been tried with specific problems, including: smoking—Gardner (1971), Ingram and Goldstein (1978); weight reduction—Horan and Johnson (1971), Horan et al., (1975), Keutzer (1968), Litchtenstein and Keutzer (1969); study behavior—Coleman (1982), Genovese (1979), Nelson et al. (1977); self-concept and emotional problems—Cooke (1975), Mahoney (1971), Todd (1972), Vasta (1975).

Homme (1965) has provided one of the most comprehensive discussions of the theory behind operant control of covert events.

COVERT REINFORCEMENT

Principles

Cognitions can serve many functions in an operant conditioning paradigm. They can serve as reinforcers (e.g., "I did a good job"), as a response (e.g., "I got a pay raise because I am a good worker") or as a discriminating stimulus (e.g., "When I am self-confident, I do better work and my boss compliments me"). If a rational belief is reinforced in the presence of an environmental stimulus (such as the granting of a pay raise), but an irrational belief is not, then the rational belief will be more likely to recur in the future, and the irrational belief less likely to do so. Covert reinforcement rewards clients for rational beliefs. Schematically, this concept may be illustrated as follows:

$$Sd \longrightarrow \text{Realistic Belief} \longrightarrow \text{Reinforcement}$$
$$S \longrightarrow \text{Irrational Thought} \longrightarrow \text{No Reinforcement}$$

A number of therapeutic techniques are available for helping clients to positively reinforce their own rational beliefs. These are briefly discussed below.

Method 1. Best Possible Belief

1. Create a hierarchy of problem situations and their accompanying thoughts —about 10 or 15 items.
2. Develop a list of rational beliefs for each situation.
3. Have clients imagine the ideal way of handling each situation. Have them picture themselves thinking the most rational, realistic beliefs possible while in the situation, and have them envision the resulting emotions and behavior as outgrowths of the new thinking. The therapist might say:

   Imagine the scene but this time picture yourself thinking the realistic thought. Picture it as clearly as you can. . . . Now imagine that you are feeling realistic emotions and are acting appropriately. Keep imagining until you complete the whole scene thinking the correct thought and feeling and acting in the way that you would like. . . . Keep doing it until you can picture the whole scene easily.

4. After the above image is clearly in mind, have clients imagine the best possible consequences of thinking this new thought, not only in the situation but in all situations like it.

   Okay. Now create a picture of the best possible consequences of thinking this way. Imagine that you thought realistically in all situations like this. What really good things would happen to you? How would your life be better? Don't just think of what would happen, but try to picture it happening. . . . Keep doing it until it is clearly in mind.

5. Repeat the exercise a minimum of three times at each sitting. Continue until clients report no negative emotional reaction when imagining the original scene. Self-report or biofeedback can be used to assess clients' response level.
6. Continue the exercise, moving upward through the hierarchy that was established in Step #1.
7. This exercise is usually taped, and clients are told to practice at least three times a week.

Method 2. Standard Reinforcing Images

This technique utilizes the same steps as the above procedure except for Step #4. Instead of having clients develop their own images of the best possible consequences of rational thinking, the therapist does that task. This modification of Method #1 is helpful for clients who might have difficulty constructing positive images with sufficient intensity to be self-reinforcing.

> Imagine as you think more and more realistically that you start gaining confidence in yourself. . . . Difficulties that used to be problems for you now resolve with relative ease. . . . Career, finances, relationships start improving. . . . When problems occur, you rationally handle them and move on to new goals. . . . You start reaching and achieving all those goals and objectives that you have set for yourself.

Method 3. External Rewards

Clients' rational beliefs can be reinforced using external rewards. Using the Premack (1965) principle, any behavior that has a high probability of being chosen (eating a candy bar) will serve as a positive reinforcer for low probability behavior (thinking rational thoughts). Hence, a client might choose to reward himself whenever he replaces an irrational thought with a rational one.

Clients can consciously pair positive reinforcers with desired thoughts and behaviors whenever they wish, and should be encouraged to practice doing so. In their practice, they should be encouraged to allow small rewards to accumulate to bigger rewards, depending upon the magnitude of the perceptual and behavioral hurdles that they are attempting to leap. Hence, a candy bar might be sufficient for a small hurdle, but the client might need to set the goal of acquiring a new sports car as a reward for overcoming a truly major hurdle.

Comment

In many cases, clients find it difficult to reinforce themselves. They may be more inclined toward self-depreciation than self-reinforcement, making it necessary for therapists to help them discover the reasons behind that bent. Therapists often have to give clients permission to be nice to themselves.

Further Information

This technique is called self-reward in previous publications (Casey & Mc Mullin, 1976; Mc Mullin et al., 1978; Mc Mullin & Casey, 1975; Mc Mullin & Giles, 1981).

Many researchers have examined the effects of covert reinforcement. See Aubut and Ladouceur, 1978; Bajtelsmit and Gershman, 1976; Bistline et al., 1980; Brunn and Hedberg, 1974; Cautela, 1970, 1971b; Engum et al., 1980; Flannery, 1972; Homme, 1965; Krop et al., 1971; Ladouceur, 1974; 1977;

Mahoney et al., 1972; Scott and Leonard, 1978; Scott and Rosenstiel, 1975; Turkat and Adams, 1982.

COGNITIVE AVERSIVE CONDITIONING

Principles

In addition to reinforcing rational thoughts, the therapist can consider punishing irrational ones. If an aversive stimulus is paired with a false belief, clients will be less likely to think it, and the thought will be less likely to elicit the conditioned response. Hence, instead of eating a candy bar for thinking a rational thought, the client might be encouraged to take a dose of castor oil for thinking a negative thought.

Many stimuli can negatively sensitize irrational thoughts. Some of them are: negative beliefs, images, emotions; unpleasant physical sensations (like shock), nausea, muscle strain; or unpleasant behaviors. If there is enough pairing, and if the stimuli are aversive enough, the thoughts themselves will be experienced as unpleasant.

Method 1. Self-Punishment

1. Compile a list of the core irrational thoughts which cause the client's negative emotions.
2. Record the major types of situations in which the client is likely to have these thoughts. Each situation should be described in terms of a specific scene, in enough detail so that the client can clearly visualize it.
3. Have the client imagine one of the scenes, with its accompanying irrational thought; and when it is clearly in mind give her the following instructions.

> Okay. Now I would like you to imagine the worst possible consequences of thinking this irrational thought. What bad things have occurred because you have thought this way? What pain has this thought given you? What good things have been removed or never happened? What has it done to your self-esteem? What has it done to your relationships?

How has it hurt your life? I would like you to imagine all these negative things happening simply because of your irrational thought. Don't just *think* about the bad things, but *picture* them until they are clearly in mind, so that you can feel the negative emotions.

4. The aversive scene is repeated at least three times with each irrational thought. If you wish, you can have your client say out loud what she is imagining so that you can help her make the scenes as aversive as possible.
5. The exercise is audiotaped, and the client is instructed to listen to the tape three times a week for several weeks.

Method 2. Standard Aversive Images

1. Standard images of vomiting, a snake pit, spiders, or being despised by everyone can be used. Interweave the images with the irrational thoughts, so that the two become closely associated. For example, one client had low self esteem and was frequently depressed because she was totally dependent on others. She manipulated others so that they would handle her finances, plan her vacations, and direct her life. We used the following aversive script.

> Imagine that you are having a lot of problems in your life that need to be corrected. Your car is broken, your sink is clogged up, you haven't gotten a pay raise in three years, and you're overdrawn at your bank. For two years you have gone with a man who says he will never marry you.
> You start thinking: "Somebody needs to take care of me. I need somebody to solve these problems. I am too fragile to cope with life." As you think these thoughts, you begin to get a queasy feeling in your stomach. You feel nauseous. Small chunks of food come to your mouth and taste bitter. You swallow them back down.
> You start thinking of getting someone to help you, someone who will call the bank or find a plumber. But the thought makes you feel sicker. Your eyes water. Snot and mucous from your nose are running down into your mouth. Your stomach is turning. You think about calling your ex-husband so that he can take care of you, and about asking your mother to call your boss to complain about your not getting a raise, but these thoughts cause you to feel very sick. You start to vomit. You vomit all over yourself. It starts dripping down your legs onto the floor. You think again of how somebody must take care of you and you vomit even more. There are yellow and brown stains all over your clothes.

You start having the dry heaves. You can't stop wretching. It feels like your insides are about to come out.*

2. The best aversive images are those selected by clients, based on their own idiosyncratic fears and disgusts. Have clients describe the most disgusting, detestable experiences they have ever imagined happening to them. You can make a brief hierarchy. Then, using the above interweaving method, tie these aversive images to their irrational thoughts.

Method 3. Physical Aversion

You can have the client imagine the irrational thought and, when it is clearly in mind, associate with it an external aversive stimulus, like a mild finger electrical shock, a snap of a rubber band, tensing up the stomach muscle, holding one's breath, noxious tones, sulfur odor, or strenuous, painful physical exercise. Thought and aversive sensation must be paired repeatedly in order for the thought to become noxious.

Method 4. Red Taping

Red taping allows clients to engage in the negative thinking, but only after they have performed a variety of aversive activities. Pick a belief that clients are obsessed about, such as: "I am sick and inferior to everyone." Instruct them that they are permitted to think this thought only after they have earned their right to do so. To earn that right, they must do the following: exercise for 15 minutes, drink three glasses of water, record the time and place where they will permit themselves to engage in that obsession, and write out every obsessive thought they have for at least 20 minutes. Then they can obsess for ten minutes. If they want another ten minutes, they must do the same routine again. The response cost becomes so large that after a while most clients prefer to skip the ten minutes of obsessing.

Method 5. Removing Positive Stimuli

Another form of aversive conditioning entails the removal of something positive. The effect is similar to associating a negative stimulus to the belief. The removed positive variable can be one of many things: needed relaxation, a pleasant image, a positive emotion, or a positive belief—any or all might

---

*Adapted from Jerome Singer's (1974) quote of a unpublished manuscript by Cautela.

be removed the moment your client succumbs to the irrational belief. In the literature this technique is often called covert response cost.

Like other covert sensitization procedures, a large number of repetitions is often needed. Clients practice both with the therapist and at home, by listening to tapes of the exercise.

Method 6. Negative Labels

Words are symbols of larger concepts, and these symbols often have a negative connotation producing an aversive emotional response. By associating negative labels to the clients' irrational thoughts, therapists can help them develop a negative response to the thoughts themselves.

The following words are generally considered quite negative. Have clients say the words to themselves whenever they think or express the irrational thought: dumb, lame, muddled, asinine, bird-brained, childish, inane, absurd, foolish, nonsensical, ridiculous, laughable, ludicrous, idiotic, meaningless, preposterous, half-baked, groundless, inept, vapid, boring, monotonous, drivel, lamebrain, babble, dense, oafish, gullible.

Sometimes you may ask the clients to identify their thought by the negative label, e.g., "I had my idiotic thought yesterday, but I didn't have the silly one," or "I got upset again when I had the foolish thought that others are better than me." As in all aversive conditioning it is essential that clients label their thoughts as negative, but not themselves, e.g., "I am smart, but this thought is idiotic."

Comment

Whenever therapists use aversive techniques to change thoughts, they run the risk of clients' attaching negative feelings to more than just the targeted variable. Clients can start feeling negative about therapy, the therapist, the counseling technique, or themselves. It is essential that the therapist provide exact discrimination training to keep the aversive associations from generalizing to other stimuli.

As in the case of positive reinforcers for positive thoughts, negative pairing with negative thoughts must be commensurate with the offending thought. Clients must not feel that they should chop off an arm for a relatively minor transgression.

Most aversive techniques are used in conjunction with escape conditioning. See the next section of this chapter for an explanation.

Further Information

A great deal of research has been done on aversive conditioning. Although most of it has not been cognitively oriented, the reader can easily make the necessary adaptation. Much of the research shows mixed results as to the effectiveness of the procedures. See particularly Barlow et al., 1969, 1972, 1973; Brownell et al., 1977; Cautela, 1966, 1967, 1971a, 1971b; Hayes et al., 1978; Singer, 1974.

COGNITIVE ESCAPE CONDITIONING

Principles

Escape conditioning is most often used in conjunction with aversive techniques. Any stimulus that removes an aversive state becomes a negative reinforcer. If the therapist has conditioned clients to feel pain whenever they think a particular irrational thought, they can be taught to escape this pain by thinking a rational thought. The rational thought would be, therefore, more likely to occur, while the irrational thought would decrease in frequency.

The full aversive-escape paradigm can be diagrammed as follows. The combination is often called covert sensitization. In the example an animal is conditioned to fear a red light because it has been paired with shock. The shock can be removed if the animal presses a lever which switches the light to green. The lever pressing and the appearance of the green light are reinforced and are more likely to increase in frequency (negative reinforcement).

Noncognitive

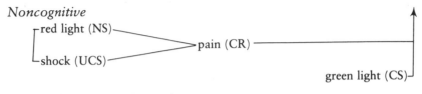

with NS = Neutral Stimulus
with UCS = Unconditioned Stimulus
with CR = Conditioned Response
with CS = Conditioned Stimulus

Cognitive

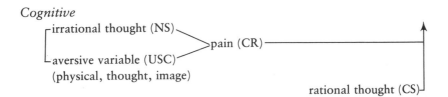

What is true for a behavior like lever-pressing is also true for thoughts. In the cognitive example the rational thought allows the client to escape from the pain elicited by the irrational thought. The neutral stimulus (irrational thought) becomes less likely to occur, while the rational thought (CS) increases in frequency. As such the rational thought is negatively reinforced.

Method 1. Relief from Aversive State

Connect an aversive stimuli to a negative belief. You can use self-punishment, aversive images, physical aversion, negative labels. (See previous section on "Cognitive Aversive Conditioning.")

After the aversive state is created, have your clients think the realistic or rational thought. When it is clearly in mind remove the aversive state immediately. If a finger shock has been used to create the aversive state, it is immediately removed upon the presentation of the rational thought. If a negative image is presented, the image is changed to a very positive picture as soon as the rational thought occurs. For example, in the aversive conditioning example mentioned earlier (p. 175), after using a vomiting scene to aversively condition the irrational thought, "Somebody needs to take care of me," the following escape scene was presented.

> You are still feeling extremely nauseous. You are about to vomit again, but then you start thinking about how you really can take care of yourself; you can solve all of your problems on your own. You can fix the car and the sink, and you can correct the overdrawn problem at your bank. You can confront your boyfriend and your boss. Immediately, you start feeling better. You take a deep breath, and your lungs and stomach start clearing. You walk out of your house and feel the fresh clean air. You feel the warm sun. There is a gentle breeze. You lie down on soft, mossy grass, underneath a willow tree, relaxing as you contemplate your strength and how you can solve all of your problems by yourself. You walk back into your house and open all of your windows. You clean everything, scrubbing floors, walls, rugs and furniture. You throw away your vomit-coated clothes, and put on new,

fresh, crisp ones. You start thinking of how you will handle all your other problems yourself, just like you handled these. You make a resolution that you won't ask anyone else to help you with problems that you can solve yourself. You feel confident and self-assured.

Method 2. Anxiety Escape

Another form of escape conditioning is called anxiety relief. This technique uses the same procedures as in Method #1, except that the client is seeking an escape from anxiety instead of from other noxious stimuli. In the escape scene the client imagines the tension rapidly subsiding as soon as the rational thought is believed.

Comment

The essential feature of all the escape techniques is that the aversive state is removed only when clients think the realistic thought. The thought then becomes a negative reinforcement. Whichever escape techniques are used, the therapist should record the procedure and urge clients to listen to the tape at least three times a week.

Clients feel a great deal better about escape conditioning than they do about aversive conditioning. The association bonds are stronger, and clients are more motivated to practice the techniques.

Further Information

Cautela has probably done the greatest amount of work on image escape conditioning. See Ascher and Cautela, 1974; Brownell et al., 1977; Cautela, 1966, 1967, 1971b; Hayes et al., 1978; Kazin and Smith, 1979. See also the references listed in the previous section.

COVERT AVOIDANCE

Principles

Avoidance conditioning is similar to escape conditioning, except that the emphasis is placed upon preventing the aversive stimulus from occurring in the first place, rather than upon escaping from it. Under this technique, any behavior which avoids an aversive emotion is reinforced, and that behavior is likely to increase in frequency. This is just as true for thoughts as it is for behaviors. Clients are likely to strongly believe any thought that keeps anxiety away. Classic examples of avoidance thoughts are:

- I shouldn't think about my problems.
- I shouldn't change; I don't have any problems whatsoever.
- It's my parents' (spouse's, boss', therapist's) fault.
- The devil made me do it!

Covert avoidance uses this same principle by having clients switch their thoughts so that they can cope more successfully. (As with all of the techniques discussed in this book, extremes are to be avoided. The goal here is not to teach clients how to "cop out" of their responsibilities at every opportunity.) The rational belief substitutes for the irrational one, and, if it avoids pain, the rational belief will become stronger.

If the client thinks a rational thought while imagining the beginnings of a negative scene, then the aversive stimulus (whether it be an image of vomiting, shock, or worst possible consequences) is avoided. If the client doesn't think the rational thought, then the aversive stimulus is presented in full, and continues until the client finally thinks of the rational belief. Clients quickly learn that rational thinking postpones or eliminates punishment.

Method

1. Make a hierarchy of problem situations and their accompanying irrational thoughts.
2. Pick the lowest item on the hierarchy and have the client imagine that

situation and the thoughts associated with it. Pair the thoughts with a negative emotion, image, or external aversive stimulus. Repeat several times until the client pairs the negative feeling with the irrational thought. The negative emotion should be strong and quite aversive.

3. Have the client imagine the same situations, but this time have him substitute a rational thought instead of an irrational thought immediately before the negative emotion occurs. If the rational thought is strongly believed, then the aversive stimulus is not presented; if not, the negative emotion is presented.

4. Keep alternating the second and third steps, moving up the hierarchy as you do, so that the client learns that rational thinking will avoid negative consequences.

Example

A number of rational thoughts can help clients avoid negative emotions. Here are some:

1. One can be happy even though everything isn't going perfectly.
2. You can enjoy your life even though you had a bad childhood.
3. I can always forgive myself for past mistakes.
4. Real dangers are almost always external. No thought or emotion can really hurt me.
5. I am not to blame for anything I cannot control.
6. I accept that there are times in my life when I will get anxious or depressed, and I don't have to push these emotions out of my life forever to be generally happy.
7. Embarrassing myself may be amusing for me as well as others. I can afford to laugh at myself.
8. My life is not so important to humanity that I have to live in dread of all possible misfortunes that may befall me.
9. I am not in the center of everyone else's universe. People are not spending their lives concentrating on how many mistakes I make.
10. The world was created by nature, not by me. It doesn't have to follow my rules of fairness, justice, or equality.
11. It is impossible for everybody to be better in everything than everybody else.
12. Nobody will care about my petty mistakes and failures after I am gone.
13. Looking back at my life even now shows that most of the things I was so worried about in the past were unimportant and insignificant.

14. The more you achieve, the more people resent you. The kinder you are the more you are liked.
15. The progression of the human species will not be permanently impeded because I don't reach my personal search for glory. In fact, most people won't even notice. They are too busy with their own searches.
16. Nature hasn't given me the power to control everything around me. Besides, it's not a whole lot of fun being responsible for the world.
17. I am not the only one losing out on the good life. Nobody has it. The guy who appears to have it—doesn't! It's just an illusion because we don't know him well enough. The millionaire sits on top of a pile of broken relationships; the movie star loses the freedom to walk down a public street without being hassled. The single person is lonely; the married person is bored. We all have our times, though. They are fleeting, but we all live for these shining moments. The only real profanity is when we pulverize these shining moments with thoughts like: "It's not shiny enough. Is this all there is? It's not as much as I was promised. It needs to last longer. I wonder if I am handling the moment correctly. Others have had shinier moments."

Comment

With most of our clients avoidance conditioning occurred naturally after the clients had practiced aversive-escape conditioning. Most clients would start to think the realistic thought earlier in the conditioning sequence in order to avoid the negative stimulus.

Further Information

The fundamental principles of avoidance conditioning have been established for many years. See Seligman and Johnson (1973) for an emphasis of the cognitive components. For noncognitive see Azrin et al., 1967; de Villiers, 1974; Foree and Lo Lordo, 1975; Garcia and Koelling, 1966; Herrnstein, 1969; Hineline and Rachlin, 1969; Kamin, 1956; Kamin et al., 1963; Mac Phail, 1968; Mowrer and Lamoreaux, 1946; Richie, 1951; Sidman, 1953, 1966; Solomon, 1964; Solomon & Wynne, 1954, 1956; Turner and Solomon, 1962.

COGNITIVE FLOODING

Principles

Flooding puts clients in the presence of a very aversive stimulus (CS) and doesn't allow them to escape. If they stay in the setting long enough, the emotion (CR) is often lessened or removed. There have been many explanations for this effect. One view is that fatigue gets paired with the CS, thus counter-conditioning it. Another is that extinction eliminates the CS because the UCS never occurs. A third view is that reactive inhibition sets in.

A cognitive explanation of flooding suggests a different account, that flooding can be understood in terms of removing a conditioned avoidance response. Avoidance is the key. It is a major component of any fear or anxiety. It is the overwhelming desire to escape. Once we feel the emotion, we will desperately look for a way to run from potentially problematical situations, even if it is not clear what we are running from.

Although our escaping makes us feel safer, and we think we have demonstrated some measure of control over the event, in fact our running away has increased our fear, since we didn't stay around long enough to prove or disprove the validity of our fears. If we are placed in a situation from which we cannot escape, two possible consequences are likely: either the damage occurs or it doesn't. Only by staying in the situation will we find out. The ultimate solution to catastrophic fears, thus, is to put ourselves into the danger and see if the catastrophe happens. It is the ultimate experiment.

However, for the ultimate experiment to work, the research design must allow no other interpretation. If clients are permitted to escape before the experiment is completed, they will conclude that it was their escape that saved them. If they are allowed drugs, a drink, a counselor's soothing words, or any other support or cop-out, they will conclude it was one of these variables that kept the catastrophe from happening. The won't see that their beliefs were irrational in the first place. A variety of flooding approaches are summarized below.

Method 1. Image Flooding

1. Have your clients imagine, in vivid detail, the feared scene and all the accompanying irrational thoughts.
2. Continue until the CR naturally subsides.
3. Whenever clients have irrational fears, instruct them to make themselves feel the emotion until they get tired of doing so.
4. Clients should make themselves afraid at various times during the day by imagining the same scene with the same thoughts again and again.
5. The therapist may find it helpful to use hypnosis in a flood-relax-flood-relax sequence.

Method 2. Verbal Flooding

Have your clients discuss, in great detail, all of their past traumatic experiences. Go through every incident many times until the clients are tired of talking about them.

Method 3. Focused Flooding

This is the same as the other methods, except clients focus on the CR's exclusively. Clients try to recreate all the physical sensation connected with the anxiety, the rapid heart beat, the queasy stomach, the disorientation, the difficulties in breathing. They keep this up until the symptoms naturally decline. Fear is experienced as deliberately as possible.

At least three half-hour sessions are necessary in using this technique.

Method 4. Negative Practice

Have your clients say all their irrational thoughts over and over again until they feel tired, bored and annoyed. Stop the practice only when they absolutely refuse to think about them anymore.

Method 5. Hierarchy

1. Help your clients make a hierarchy of their most feared situations, along with the most feared associated thoughts.
2. Imagine the least upsetting item on the list vividly with full emotional effects. Continue until the client has no CR while picturing the situation.
3. Move to the next higher item on the hierarchy and repeat the process.

Example

A modified form of flooding was used successfully with a client afraid of becoming psychotic. Justin was a psychological hypochondriac. He was very knowledgeable about certain aspects of psychopathology, and had read *DSM II*. Each time he got upset he would look in the book and pick out which psychological problem he was having today. In the course of ten years, he had thought he was a maniac, psychotic depressed, sociopath, a closet anorexic, or a closet bulimic (whenever he lost or gained a few pounds), an obsessive compulsive, an explosive personality (when he was angry), etc.

He pinpointed his anxiety to the time he was in college. He had taken some marijuana for the first time after being goaded into it by an acquaintance. It had apparently been laced with an hallucinogenic. He started to hallucinate, and panicked. He stayed awake for 24 hours, moving back and forth, in and out of panics. The next day, the acquaintance told him that the marijuana was laced and that was why he was hallucinating. His panic immediately subsided. He thought the drug caused the fear and didn't worry about it after that.

Everything was fine until about a year later. Justin was sitting in a psychology class being taught by a graduate student who was lecturing on the psychological effects of drugs. The instructor said that those who have panic reactions while taking marijuana are probably prepsychotic or at least borderline personalities. That night he started to get scared. By morning he had a full-blown panic attack. His panics stayed with him for ten years. He would occasionally have periods when he wouldn't feel anxiety, but they would stop whenever he read or saw something which reminded him of insanity. He couldn't watch TV shows about people having nervous breakdowns; he was terrified when he watched the movie "One Flew Over the Cuckoo's Nest." He couldn't stand reading science fiction about strange people on strange planets.

His core belief was easy to identify. He knew it himself: "I am close to being insane. At any moment stress could make me flip over and become permanently psychotic." We can consider his belief as a conditioned stimulus as follows:

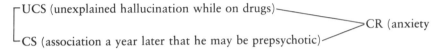

(Note: In classical conditioning, *contiguity* (the close association of CS and UCS in time) is considered important. In cognitive conditioning the *contingency* (the mental connection of one event with another, no matter what the time frame) is all that is necessary. In the above example contingency was present but contiguity was not. See Schwartz (1978) and Rescorla (1967) about the distinction.)

Justin had gone to many counselors and had tried many techniques, all to no avail. As a last resort we decided to use flooding. The client was instructed to take off three mornings over three successive weeks. He was to allow at least five hours for the technique.

Each time he was told to lie in his bed with only a dim light shining in from the next room. He had to lie there for five hours. All distractions had to be removed. He would accept no phone calls. The radio and TV had to be off. He couldn't get up and walk around, read a book, or distract himself in any way. Everything he was going to do was to be mental.

Justin was told not to fight the fear of going crazy or to avoid it in any way during his flooding time. Instead he was to think the thought of going insane, feel the anxiety intensely, and maintain the fear for as long as he was able during the five-hour period. Whenever he caught himself getting tired he was to redouble his efforts and continue to think he would go crazy. He was to keep the thought at a maximum level. After each session we set up an appointment where he could discuss his experience.

His first session was difficult. For the first three hours he panicked—not continually, but in waves. He said that he must have had at least eight panic attacks. When he felt the fear, he desperately wanted to run out of the bedroom. The only thing that kept him in the bed was essentially this thought:

> I have been scared for ten years; my life is going nowhere. I have lost my most important relationships and have not grown in my career, all because of this fear of going insane. If this fear is true, I will go insane. But what of it? It would happen sooner or later anyway, why not today? Today is as good a day as any other to become psychotic. If it is not going to happen, well let me find that out now.

So for three hours he feared insanity, but for the last two he had trouble keeping his mind on the fear. His brain started to wonder, he began to think of what he was going to have for dinner, where he was going to go on his vacation, a new car he needed to buy. Near the end of the five hours he was glad to stop. The whole exercise was boring him.

Justin's next two sessions were easier. He had trouble thinking the belief, and only had two or three waves of panic. He got bored quicker and he felt little anxiety about insanity. In the final session, the thought didn't bother him at all. He spent most of the session thinking of other things. He couldn't force himself to think about it. It seemed silly.

Flooding didn't cure Justin as quickly or easily as this account suggests. It took him several months of practice at overcoming occasional panic attacks before the problem was solved. As Justin described it later:

> The fear wasn't the same anymore. The edge seemed to be taken off it. Since the flooding, I knew the fear was just bullshit. I knew the thought was just a silly superstition. It took me a while to be sure, I had to keep on testing myself, but somewhere inside I knew.

My last report from Justin, three years later, was very positive. He would occasionally get some mild fear about insanity, about every six months or so, because he let his thinking get lazy. But he reported that he could easily get rid of it with a little cognitive work.

Comment

The key to all flooding techniques is for clients to remain in the feared scene until their bodies naturally reduce the CRs. If they escape without completing the flooding, the fear increases.

Flooding is one of the last techniques used in the cognitive restructuring repertoire because the technique is quite painful.

Of course, for flooding to be appropriate, therapists must be certain that no real UCS can occur in the flooding procedure, e.g., you do not flood schizophrenics who are afraid of losing control or depressives who are afraid of committing suicide.

Further Information

Related techniques are negative practice, massed practice, implosion, or reactive inhibition.

Image flooding and its variation is discussed by Wolpe (1958, 1969). The most comprehensive review is in Marshall et al. (1979). Negative practice was first discussed by Dunlap (1932).

External, reactive, and conditioned inhibitions have been offered as non-cognitive explanations for flooding. See Rescorla (1969) and Zimmer-Hart and Rescorla (1974). Also see Clark Hull's (1943) theoretical discussion of sEr and Ir, and Rescorla, (1967) and Schwartz (1978) for more theoretical examination.

HIGHER ORDER COVERT CONDITIONING

Principles

Language is the best example of higher order conditioning. All words are originally neutral stimuli and take on the power to create emotions only because they are paired with strong feelings.

As in language, higher order conditioning pairs a neutral stimuli with another element already conditioned. For example, a flashing red light (CS-1) can be paired with shock (US), producing fear responses (CR). If the experimenter then associates a bell with the red light, the bell (CS-2) alone can elicit the CR.

Schematically it can be represented as:

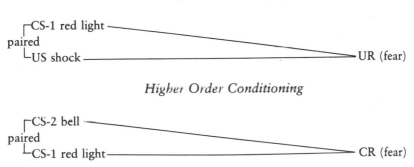

Original Conditioning

CS-1 red light ⎱
paired
US shock ⎰ ————→ UR (fear)

Higher Order Conditioning

CS-2 bell ⎱
paired
CS-1 red light ⎰ ————→ CR (fear)

With sufficient pairing, any variable perceivable to clients can be a CS-2. Cognitive restructuring generally uses two types of variables—perceptions and conceptions. Perceptions are made up of the visual, auditory, olfactory, and kinesthetic representations clients have of the traumatic event. Conceptions are their beliefs, thoughts, and attitudes about the problem situations.

Covert higher order conditioning involves taking the perceptual and conceptual CS-2's associated with a positive visualization (usually a mastery scene where the client feels very confident and self-assertive), and pairing these CS's with the target upsetting scene. After a series of repetitions, the target scene begins to be experienced with the same positive nuances as in the master scene.

Method

1. Have the client focus on the major emotion causing a problem. Label the emotion and record the SUD's level (Wolpe, 1973).
2. Have the client focus on the negative scene and create a model or typical image where this negative emotion occurs strongly. The scene should be imagined in vivid detail, using all the senses.
3. Record in writing all the perceptual and conceptual variables (CS-2) connected with the image.

Perceptual

a. *Visualization*: What the client pictures in the scene is dissected in great detail. For example, is the scene in color; is it a still or motion picture, clear or fuzzy, two- or three-dimensional? Is the client seeing him or herself in the scene? What is the focal point (the major element in the scene that draws the client's attention)? Is the scene bright or dim? What is the angle of view? What is the size of the client in relationship to objects that form the background of this scene? Are the people moving?
b. *Other Senses*: Auditory—Can the client clearly hear the sounds? What is their duration? How loud are they? Olfactory—What does the client smell? Kinesthetic—What is the temperature? etc.

Conceptual

a. Every major thought the client has before, during, and after the imagined event is recorded. The therapist helps the client state these thoughts explicitly. The types of thoughts to look for are:

   i. Expectancy—what the client anticipates will happen in the situation.
   ii. Evaluation—the assessment the client makes of himself during the scene.
   iii. Self-efficacy—the client's judgment of his ability to complete the task effectively.
   iv. Payoffs—the anticipated reward or payoff the client thinks he will get in the situation. Punishments—the aversive things the client anticipates.

     v. Self-concept—the client's attitudes about his worthwhileness as a human being.

     vi. Attributions—the attitudes and motivations the client attributes to others in the scene.

     vii. Purpose—why the client is in the scene in the first place.

  b. The therapist also searches, along with his client, for logical fallacies that might surface in the client's interpretations of these scenes. Each fallacy is written down. The most common fallacies are: dichotomous thinking, overgeneralization, non-parsimonious reasoning, perfectionism, reification, subjective error, arguing ad homineum, ipse dixit, a priori thinking, finding the good reason, egocentric error, homocentric error, self-fulfilling prophesy, mistaking probability for possibility, etc. (See "Logical Fallacies" in Chapter 5.)

4. After recording all of the perceptual and conceptual information connected to the negative event, the therapist asks the client to picture a scene he feels he has emotionally mastered. It should be a model scene, one that he handled almost ideally. The closer the content of the mastery scene to that of the negative scene, the better. Like the first image, this scene should be imagined in great detail, until it is vividly in mind.

5. As in Step #3, record all the perceptions the client has of the positive, masterly scene—visual, auditory, kinesthetic. Point out to the client the contrast between the two ways of viewing the image as the list is developed.

6. The conceptions of the positive scene are likewise recorded. The therapist should pay careful attention to finding the attributions, expectations, self-concept, and evaluations the client makes in the mastery scene. The therapist writes down the correct reasoning the client has in the visualization.

7. There is a pause in the imagery work. Therapist and client discuss the differences between the perceptual and conceptual representations of the two scenes.

8. Now the therapist is ready to do the actual higher order conditioning. The client imagines the original negative scene for two minutes. Then, gradually, the therapist introduces the perceptual and conceptual representations of the mastery scene, one at a time, with the client imagining the changes until they are vivid. The process continues until all the elements from the mastery scene are included. When this is successfully done, the client is able to imagine the negative scene, but with all the perceptual and conceptual components previously associated with the mastery scene.

9. Often the whole procedure is recorded on tape so that the client can practice the conditioning two to three times a week. With enough pairings the emotional valences of the scenes switch.

Example

Alex, an attractive young man in his late twenties, had difficulty meeting women. Although he had had several long-term successful relationships, they had all been initiated by the women involved. He couldn't introduce himself to eligible, attractive women, despite having memorized books on how to meet women and taken classes on the art of conversation.

His negative visualization revealed his problem. He described himself in a singles bar, standing close to a very attractive woman. He visualized himself as appearing very small while all the other men towered over him. (He was 6'1".) The woman was the focus of the scene; she was very colorful while he was dull and muted. He pictured a spotlight illuminating her while he stood in the shadows. She was moving in his scene while he was as rigid as in a snapshot. Kinesthetically she seemed cool and icy while he felt hot and itchy.

His cognitions revealed even more:

> purpose = To impress her.
> expectancy = "I will fail miserably."
> self-concept = "I am an inferior male."
> efficacy = "I will fail when I try to talk to her."
> attribution = "She will despise me and think me a creep."

Logical fallacies were numerous:

> catastrophizing = "It would be terrible if she rejected me."
> overgeneralizing = "If she rejects me, all women will."
> perfectionism = "I must look like the perfect male."
> pathology = "I must be really sick to have this problem."
> traitism = "I have the 'wrong stuff.'"
> musturbation = "I must get her to like me."
> egocentric error = "If I talk to her, she will focus all of her attention on me and will inspect me for any flaws."

He easily developed a mastery visualization. He pictured himself in the same bar, but he was talking to a group of men. It had recently happened. He was the center of attention and enjoyed telling jokes and stories. There were no women around.

In his visualization he was the same size as the others; all were in focus and colorful. He as well as the others were in motion. Kinesthetically, he felt warm and pleasant.

He also thought quite differently in his mastery scene:

> purpose = To have fun talking to the men.
> expectancy = none, "I'll enjoy this as much as I can."
> attribution = "Who cares what they think of me. It doesn't really matter."
> self-concept = "My worthwhileness as a human being is not involved in this in any way."
> evaluation = "I'm more interested in talking to them and finding out what they think than in how I come across."
> efficacy = "I can talk to men without any problem. If the conversation doesn't work it's more likely to be their difficulty than mine."

Instead of thinking in terms of logical fallacies, he was very realistic:

> commonplace expectations vs. catastrophizing = "No big deal, I don't need them to like me."
> discriminating vs. overgeneralizing = "If they don't like me, many other men will and do."
> realism vs. perfectionism = "There is no reason for me to try to do anything perfectly in this situation. I'll just act normally and they can take it or leave it."
> health vs. pathology and traitism = "What I am deep down inside is totally irrelevant while talking to these men. I'm just trying to have a pleasant conversation."
> nonchalance vs. musturbation = I either will like the conversation or I won't. There are no musts, oughts, or shoulds.

We now had two lists of CS-2's: those connected to the negative scene in which Alex was unable to approach the attractive women, and those connected to the positive scene in which he was talking with men. To higher order condition, we wanted the client to represent the negative scene with the perceptions and conceptions previously associated with the positive scene. The following was the beginning instruction to the client.

> Okay, Alex. Now I would like you to relax again. Narrow your attention and just focus on your muscles. Make them loose, limp, and slack. (2 minutes)

That's fine. Now please recreate that first scene where you felt so tense. Imagine right now that you are in the bar and the same attractive woman is standing close by. Picture it as vividly and clearly as you can in the same way you did before. Don't change anything. See it in the same way. When it's clearly in mind, indicate by raising your finger. (2 minutes)

Keep imagining the image, but I would like you to gradually, at my direction, make changes in what you see and think. First picture that you are of the same size (not smaller) as the other men in the bar. Imagine that until it is clearly in mind, and indicate when you are ready. (1 minute) Now keep visualizing your larger size but add motion and color to yourself. Picture that you are moving just like the attractive woman, and that you are equally colorful. (We continued switching all the other perceptions from the mastery scene to the negative scene.)

That's good. Keep visualizing and feeling the scene in the new way that you have just practiced, but now I would like you to imagine saying different things to yourself in the scene.

First picture yourself looking at her, but instead of thinking your purpose is to try and impress her, imagine that you are thinking of her in the same way you thought about talking to the men. Imagine thinking that your purpose is to have fun talking to her, rather than impressing her. Visualize this until it's clearly in mind. Indicate when you are finished. (1 minute) Now picture thinking that there are many other women you can talk to if this conversation doesn't work out. (We continued switching all the other conceptual CS-2's from the mastery scene to the negative scene.)

The session was taped and the client listened to the tape three times a week for about six weeks. He reported that with each succeeding week he found it easier and easier to approach attractive women.

Comment

There are problems with higher order conditioning. Pavlov's work indicates that the farther away the CS is from the US, the smaller the amplitude, the longer the latency, and the less permanent the CR response. The CR's have a tendency to extinguish quickly. However, the cognitive element may be a crucial addition to the conditioning. Conceptual change may help clients maintain what would otherwise be rather weak, higher order associations.

Further Information

Skinner (1953, 1974) and Pavlov (1928, 1960) did the germinal work on higher order conditioning.

NLP practitioners use higher order conditioning in many of their techniques, particularly in a technique they call "reframing," but they deemphasize conceptual changes and stress the sensory elements. See Bandler and Grinder, 1979; Dilts et al., 1979; Grinder and Bandler, 1975, 1982.

Some basic research on higher order conditioning may be found in Kelleher, 1966; Rizley and Rescorla, 1972; and Stubbs and Cohen, 1972.

OPERANT EXPLANATION OF IRRATIONAL BELIEFS

Principles

Not only do thoughts cause emotions, but emotions also cause thoughts. Thus, clients' thought systems can be viewed as shorthand representations of their emotional histories. While most clients believe that their thoughts represent purely logical, rational conclusions drawn from their past lives and present environments, thoughts might also be viewed as cognitive symbols derived from the conditioning process. For example, when a child is punished for "bad" behavior, not only is the behavior discouraged, but the concept of "bad" is also taught. Thoughts, then, may simply represent the associations of rewards, punishments, operants and discriminating stimuli in the client's history.

Example

Following is a list of some thoughts and the operant histories that might have produced them.

Thought	*Possible Conditioning History*
Everybody must like me.	Repeated punishment of independent social interaction.

Life is boring.

Little reinforcement or reinforcement to the point of saturation.

I need alcohol and drugs to be happy.

Reinforced by escape from previously aversive stimuli.

Everything is horrible, terrible, a catastrophe.

Reinforced by avoiding aversive stimuli through anticipatory catastrophizing (i.e., avoidance conditioning.)

Everything is my fault.

Learned to use self-blaming to short-circuit negative reinforcement associated with previously punished behavior.

I have the power to do anything I wish.

Superstitious learning based on random reinforcement occurring after a perception of self-power.

I ought, must and should.

a. Social aversive conditioning associated with previous behavior.
b. Superstitious learning to avoid previous social punishment.

It is dangerous.

Avoidance conditioning through a negatively reinforcing thought.

I have physical — not psychological — problems.

Avoidance of the conditioned emotional responses of guilt and self-blame.

Some things are terribly dangerous.

a. CS + UCS. Conditioned aversive stimulus.
b. An Sd preceding a strong negative reinforcer.
c. Stimuli associated with a punished behavior elicit anxiety.
d. Anxiety followed by negative reinforcement — escape or avoidance.

Sometimes I get so angry, I could kill him.

a. Escape from another's aversive controlling behavior.
b. Previous reduction in anxiety for injuring threatening person.
c. Self-mastery reinforcement.
d. Conditioned emotional response.

Life is so frustrating.

Client is on an extinction schedule.

I am confident.

Favorable reinforcement schedule.

I feel hopeless and helpless.

a. Shortage of positive reinforcement.
b. Passive resistance against aversive stimuli.

c. Person does not emit behaviors reinforced by others.
d. Reinforced for being depressed.
e. Learned to suppress behavioral responses to avoid punishment.
f. Trapped in an approach-avoidance conflict.

I want to be happier.	Heightened state of deprivation.
I don't have any problems.	Not attending to proprioceptive stimuli to avoid conditioned aversive emotions.
If I keep running the problem over and over in my brain, it will help me (obsession).	Previously reinforced for thinking, but this time thinking is not productive because it is concentrated on aversive stimuli.
I am just basically a weak, passive, shy person.	Repeatedly punished in past social interactions.
I feel so lonely.	Extinguishing of social reinforcements.
I believe that a world of magic exists.	Neutral stimuli accidentally paired with positive reinforcements.
I must have what I want now!	History of immediate gratification. Limited delayed reinforcements.

Comment

The operant histories behind the beliefs are speculative. There are other valid conditioning interpretations of these thoughts.

Further Information

Among the best sources of information on an operant definitions of beliefs are three classic works of B. F. Skinner (1953, 1972, 1974). The influence of conditioning on various types on perception has been extensively described by Taylor (1962) and Wolpe (1981b).

4

Paradoxical
Methods

Clients often seek help in overcoming the anguish caused by mistaken beliefs and false perceptions, and then resist the efforts of therapists to help them achieve that relief. In our experience, as many as one out of every five clients becomes combative toward the counselor one or more times during the therapeutic process. It is not always clear whether this behavior reflects a tendency toward self-sabotage, or a personality conflict between therapist and client, or the devotion clients show toward their mistaken perceptions. It may even be a deeply-rooted component of the problem that brought the client into therapy in the first place.

What is clear is that therapists must be ever alert to the possibility of such resistance, and ready to respond to it in a manner which preserves the integrity of the therapist-client relationship and at the same time contributes to the client's progress.

Combative clients do not respond well to the countering and perceptual shift techniques discussed elsewhere in this book. Indeed, they often exhibit an uncanny agility in sidestepping the logic of a therapist's counters. And that should not be surprising. Those who have suffered long and hard under the burden of harmful misperceptions acquire the skills and instincts of a fencing expert, and their thrust and parry can, at times, be overwhelming to the unprepared therapist.

Paradoxical methods represent a real advantage to the therapist in such instances. Using these methods, therapists don't argue against the mistaken beliefs of their clients. Instead, they assume a concurring posture, agreeing fully, even overwhelmingly, with any damning conclusions that the clients may have drawn. The consequences of such a strategy, surprisingly enough, are usually quite positive, as the following discussion and examples will illustrate.

SELF FLIM-FLAM

Principles

In 1964 James Randi, an internationally known magician and escape artist, offered to pay the sum of $10,000 to any person who could demonstrate the existence of paranormal powers under scientifically observable conditions. Since then, 650 persons have applied for the prize and 54 have made it through the initial screening. However, none has stood up to scientific scrutiny. Randi still carries the check around with him, and he is prepared to give it on the spot to anyone who can convince him of paranormal capabilities (Randi, 1982).

Randi describes those who have made claim to his prize as all falling into one of two groups. First are the outright fakes—the snake oil salesmen, the flim-flam artists. They know they are fakes and have tried to win the prize with sleight-of-hand tricks. Second are the true believers—a group far more interesting to the field of psychology. These people actually believe they have paranormal powers, and are amazed when the experiment fails to prove it. Members of this second group suffer from what might be called, "self flim-flam." They have fooled themselves so completely that they believe they have powers that they don't have. Many clients belong to this second group.

Paradoxically, these clients are often very intelligent and quite well educated, in spite of their absurd beliefs. If one is even moderately objective, it is silly to believe, for example, that a human being can be perfect, or that people should be in control of everything that happens to them. Yet some very bright people believe that they possess such "paranormal" abilities.

Another paradox can be seen in how little many clients work at changing themselves. They may spend a lot of time and money on therapy and seem genuinely motivated to reduce their anxiety and depression, but in many ways they actively work at not changing. They don't do their homework, or miss appointments, or use other self-defeating behaviors.

Often these surface paradoxes point to self flim-flam. It can be hypothesized that some clients' problems (a ballpark guess is 10%) are based on an elaborate self-deception. Their irrational thoughts are like cognitive tricks that they play upon themselves. Beliefs such as, "I could lose control and go crazy," or "I must be better than all other people to be worthwhile," may not be solely mistaken perceptions arising out of poorly synthesized experiences; they may also reveal a kind of cognitive game clients play in order to reap seeming rewards. Just as a con artist plays tricks on the public for external payoffs, so clients may trick themselves for internal payoffs—to generate feelings of security or high self-esteem, to reduce anxiety, to empower someone else, or simply to spice up an otherwise boring existence.

Self flim-flam is a dramatic play, a theatrical show, a performance in which the client is both performer and audience. Initially, clients may create the drama for external applause, but after years of practice they begin to play the role only for themselves. External payoffs may have long since vanished.

Many cognitive approaches are not effective for clients who play self flim-flam, as they often view therapy as another arena for their performance. While these clients may pretend to work very hard at therapy, they make little, if any, real progress. Sometimes they reveal their game-playing with an inappropriate smile or a verbal slip. Sometimes they withdraw altogether from the play when it endangers irrational beliefs.

To free the client from a self-delusionary belief, it is necessary to expose it as an act and then to redirect the client's thinking so it is more in line with reality. The following methods have been found to be highly effective in this regard.

Method 1. Screening to Identify Self Flim-Flam

1. Develop a list of your clients' irrational beliefs.
2. Describe the concept of self flim-flam to your clients. Be sure to distinguish between fooling the public and fooling themselves. Also make it clear that a belief can be flim-flam even if clients know it to be false, as long as they *act* as if it were true.
3. Look for the internal and external payoffs for the theatrical performance.
4. Explain the negative effects of using self flim flam to achieve these payoffs, and help your clients find more productive, effective ways to achieve them.

Method 2. The Value-Based Flim-Flam

1. What value does the client idealize and glorify? Does this value underlie the client's performance? (The client admired the concept of the noble sufferer. He read books on martyrs and those who gave up their lives for others. He felt there was nothing greater than sacrificing yourself for your

friends—always with the image of undying gratitude from the public.)

2. What value does the client reject? Is the client carefully avoiding any hint of this value in the presentation? (He hated the idea that humans are machines, bound to mechanistic responses to various stimuli. In therapy he would argue vehemently against finding the conditioned triggers to his anxiety.)

Method 3. Looking for Telltale Inconsistencies

1. Look for what the client wants the therapist to believe. (For instance, one of our agoraphobic clients wanted the therapist to believe that he was waging a noble battle to keep from losing control and going crazy.)
2. Expose the client's belief as irrational. Confront the inconsistencies among setting, appearance, manner, behavior, emotions, and other beliefs connected with the drama. ("If you're really afraid of going crazy," we asked our agoraphobic client, "how come you don't take your Librium as directed? Why do you take risks like flying to New York?")
3. State that you don't accept what the client is saying. ("I don't think you really believe you'll go crazy.")
4. Describe the setting for the performance of the irrational thought. Point out the stage, props, and costumes the client uses. (Our agoraphobic client would get anxious only when he was with others whose attention he wanted. If they didn't pay attention to him, he would start feeling as if he were going to go crazy. He always carried his tranquilizers when he anticipated these scenes, and would wear loose shirts so "my breathing would be free.")
5. Identify the gestures and mannerisms in the client's performance which give it away as a drama. (The client would always smile proudly and speak dramatically of how he, the great warrior, once again had fended off psychosis.)
6. How does the client want the therapist and others to react to various thoughts, emotions, and behaviors? (He wished unabashed admiration.)
7. How have previous audiences participated in and supported the performance? (His wife and some of his friends had reinforced the drama by telling him what a fine person he was to do so well, despite having the agoraphobia.)
8. What errors has the client made in the performance which caused the audience not to be convinced? (The client's wife was getting suspicious of the validity of his agoraphobia, since he was able to venture into public

places with no anxiety whatsoever when he thought no one was watching.)

9. What "dirty work" is hidden in preparation for the performance, and what errors or inappropriate behaviors are concealed? (Whatever the client was thrust unexpectedly into an agoraphobic situation it would take him time to get anxious. On several occasions, the situation was over before he had time to work himself up. On another occasion, he showed an inappropriate behavior in the middle of a counseling session. He had been describing a particularly bad week in which he had four panic attacks. I had to leave the room for a minute, and on my return noticed he was humming to a song on the radio. I confronted him and he said with a slight smile he was just trying to keep his courage up.)

10. In summary, the therapist can zero in on clients' game-playing by answering the following questions.

   a. What role might the client be playing?
   b. What payoffs does the client get for playing this role?
   c. Who is the client trying to convince? Is the client aware that a game is being played?
   d. Has the client actually convinced the audience?
   e. When does the client perform the role, and when not?
   f. Does the audience play a counter game?
   g. Is it successful?
   h. Does anyone point out the game?
   i. Does the client play the same role in many different situations?
   j. How long has the role been played?
   k. What are the negative consequences of playing the role?
   l. What actions could the client take instead of playing the flim-flam?
   m. What specific response is the client trying to elicit from the audience?
   n. How does the client try to get this response?
   o. Why is the desired response reinforcing to the client?
   p. Why does the client have to play a game instead of asking for the response directly?

Most clients—like the agoraphobic client described previously—are not aware that they are "faking" their anxiety. Nor are they intentionally engaged in self flim-flam. The key element that sustains the flim-flam is the internal reinforcement it offers. Typically, clients are unaware of any self-deception until it is revealed to them by the therapist, or until they catch themselves verbalizing a gaping contradiction which cannot be rationalized away.

Example 1

The following is a transcript of the opening session with Maurice, a very successful, attractive, divorced man in his thirties who had lots of women interested in him. Unfortunately, he also had a history of ruined relationships, all of which ended the same way — with the woman leaving him for another man.

> I am in the same situation that I have been in many times before. It's always very painful and I need your help. . . . I am doing something wrong in my relationships. I get involved in a love relationship, and it goes real well for a while, and then something starts happening: I get jealous, I get suspicious, I get manipulative, I get angry, I get childlike, and I start sabotaging the relationship. . . . It always ends up the same — the woman gets disgusted and I get real hurt and feel real inferior.
>
> I have been going with a woman for about a year and a half now. She is a very attractive woman, bright, vivacious, spirited. She might be better than me, socially more popular, more gregarious. Men have always been interested in her. I think I feel inferior to her, and I am scared. She told me recently that she may be beginning to feel love towards another man. . . . He is a macho type, rich, powerful and has high status friends. I am not. I am bright, creative, emotional — but I am not powerful.
>
> I could feel the pain and hurt in my gut when she said it. So as I often do in situations like this, I did a strange thing. I said, "Thank you for telling me; I really admire your honesty. Clearly there is only one thing to do in a situation like this. You must pursue the other relationship as hard as you can, you should sleep with him; spend a lot of time with him and see what happens to your feelings towards him. See if you fall in love with him. And then, if you are, that will be it for us. If you're not, then we can go along as we were. I don't want to see you until you find out how you feel towards him." She protested, but I insisted that she should not see me until she makes up her mind. She said she loved me and wasn't sure about him and wanted to see me. I said, "Well, maybe we could, but we couldn't have any sex."
>
> . . . that's kind of a typical example of the problem I have. I do the opposite of what I want. I said and did things and I don't know why I did them. I keep doing things that go contrary to what would be to my advantage.

Even in the first session the client was beginning to see that he was engaging in some kind of self flim-flam. Later sessions revealed what this flim-flam was about.

I play this martyr role with women. They hurt me or I get jealous, but instead of yelling at them, I trick them. I pretend I am kind, wise, forgiving, interested only in their welfare. I show them I will sacrifice myself for their happiness in true martyr fashion.

The game is really sickening. I say things like, "You go ahead and marry him. Be happy. I hope it works out. You are a wonderful person. I want to release you from me. I don't want to hold you down anymore."

It's totally bullshit. I don't believe a word of it. The payoff I get is twofold. First I get back at the woman for hurting me. I make her feel guilty, and she can't attack me back for being kind, caring and nice. Secondly, I fulfill my little heroic martyr image of myself by thinking what a terribly compassionate, kind, courageous man I am.

It took the client many more sessions to continue to explore the martyr flim-flam. At times he would forget he was playing a role and start acting like a martyr again. But gradually he saw the performance and its damaging effects. He practiced being straight about his anger, and he started to show who he really was—a normal human being with fears, angers, and jealousies, not some sacrificial lamb for man—or woman—kind.

Example 2

Phillis had heard of my work and insisted upon seeing me, but I was initially unwilling to accept her as a client. She had already been in therapy with some of the top cognitive therapists in the field for over ten years, with no evident progress toward alleviating her periodic depressions, which were punctuated by severe temper tantrums. I was very candid in telling her that, although I use some techniques slightly different from those of my colleagues, I was not optimistic about my ability to help her in light of their inability to do so. But she insisted upon entering therapy with me anyhow.

We worked well together for several months, but then, inexplicably, our relationship began to deteriorate. She stopped doing her homework, stopped faithfully exercising the techniques on her visits to the clinic, and began complaining about an increased frequency of depressive episodes. Despite my best efforts, progress stopped. We terminated the relationship, and I refered her to another therapist. But a year and a half later she was back again, insisting that I accept her as a client.

I had been working on the flim-flam theory during this time, and recognized she was probably a major game-player. I told her what I thought; to my surprise, instead of rejecting the concept outright, she said it could be true for her. We started therapy again, but this time we worked only on under-cutting the flim-flam.

After several sessions we both agreed that she was playing a type of flim-flam we called "poor me." Automatically, whenever she started to feel a little bit tense or slightly depressed, usually for fairly realistic reasons, her brain would immediately click on "poor me." She mostly played the drama for herself as the audience, but sometimes played it for other significant persons in her life, like her husband, other relatives, and therapists. The role had many components. The major feature was to exaggerate to herself how unhappy she was—"everything is my fault; I am inferior to everybody in everything." But there were other sub-roles, like "spoiled brat"—I should get everything I want when I want it"; martyr—"I must be unhappy and miserable to make others' lives a little bit better"; hysterical—"every minor frustration will cause me to go insane"; "wooden leg"—"you can't expect one so sick to do anything in life except to lie in bed all day"; temper tantrums—"anyone who doesn't accept my 'poor me' role is attacking a cripple and I have the right to hurt them back."

This time around in therapy, she recognized quite early that she was playing this game, that she really didn't feel as upset as she was pretending. She played the game because she wanted comfort and sympathy from others. She wanted someone to take care of her and treat her as a sick, helpless child. She also knew where she learned this role; her mother had played a major league game of "poor me" all her life.

With her cooperation we developed an attack against "poor me." I instructed her to do the following:

a. Recognize and identify all the components and subcomponents of the game as soon as you can after you have played it. (She would do this by expressing her "poor me" feelings on a tape recorder and then listening to how she sounded.)
b. Identify the audience the role was being played for: herself, husband, relatives, therapists.
c. What is the payoff for playing the role? (Almost always she wanted sympathy. Even when she was her own audience, she would mentally comfort herself for having to endure such a hard life and retire to her bed for two days.)
d. Prove to yourself that the role is phony. (Although it sounds difficult, she was often able to see through the role. She recognized that her supposed despair didn't quite ring true. She would often say that she didn't really feel as bad as she sounded.)
e. Actively remind yourself of all the damaging effects of playing "poor me."

(She had been basically playing the role her whole life, and had accomplished very little except feeling chronically depressed and anxious.)

f. As soon as you can, stop the role and be as honest and straightforward as you can. (She would practice on a tape recorder over and over again until both she and I felt she was communicating honestly without flim-flam).

Throughout the therapy sessions with her, I would immediately confront her on any "poor me" portrayal and insist that she correct the misrepresentation until it was clear of the "poor me" component.

The counseling wasn't easy for her; it was probably the hardest thing she ever had to do. She constantly wrestled with herself—a part of her wanted to play the flim-flam while another part wanted to stop it. Gradually she was able to stop and correct the flim-flam sooner and sooner after the portrayal. After a while she would interrupt herself in mid sentence and say, "That's a lie. I'm not really feeling that. It's just "poor me" again. Then she would correct what she said and say it honestly.

At times she stops her anxiety and depression immediately now, whenever she choses, by attacking her self flim-flam.

Comment

This approach is most successful with hysterics, but must be used with care, as damaging results can occur. Clients will defend their beliefs angrily if they feel attacked, so it is best to build good client-therapist rapport before exposing self flim-flam. Moreover, if the therapist mistakes a conditioned response for a flim-flam, more guilt and confusion will be added to the client's already negative emotions.

Further Information

The name of the technique is taken from the title of Randi's (1982) book. Further readings in the area will give therapist more tools to deal with excessive self-deception. See Gardner (1957) and particularly *The Skeptical Inquirer*, the Journal of the Committee for the Scientific Investigation of Claims of the Paranormal, Buffalo, NY.

Social psychologists and sociologists have examined social performances, roles and presentations. See the work of Erving Goffman (1961, 1971, 1980).

FORCED CATASTROPHES

Principles

While countering is a highly effective technique in most counseling situations, it does have its limitations. Even before submitting to their first therapy session, most unhappy clients will have tried to reason themselves out of a harmful mindset. These early attempts at self-help can complicate the therapeutic process. Clients often feel that they have already traveled the path of logic being taken by the therapist, to no avail. Some may, out of sympathy, tolerate what they perceive to by the therapist's pointless probes. Others will explode with impatience, exhibiting some of the very aggressions that warrant paradoxical techniques.

One technique for moving clients beyond their harmful preoccupations is called "forced catastrophes." (The reader will see certain similarities between this and the cognitive flooding technique, discussed in Chapter 3.) Under this technique, clients are challenged to follow their fears to their worst possible conclusions. When the worst is never actually realized, they are forced to acknowledge the fallacies in their prior thinking.

Method 1

1. Make a list of clients' core irrational beliefs.
2. Instruct clients to try to make happen exactly what they fear. There are several ways of doing this.

    a. Behavioral. Have clients look for situations they can throw themselves into which they have previously avoided. They should try to make the situations as aversive as possible. For example, they are to seek out phobic situations like snakes, long flights in planes, social embarrassment.

    b. Cognitions. Tell your clients to try to think and believe the irrational thoughts whenever they are in trigger situations. For instance, whenever they are criticized, they should try to intensify their thoughts of inferiority.

c. Affective. Tell them to try to feel as emotionally upset as they can while imagining the situation with its accompanying irrational thought.

Method 2

1. If the fear behind the irrational thought is proprioceptive, like fear of going crazy, losing control over oneself, or hallucinating, set up a time when the client will try to create the catastrophe intentionally.
2. The time allotted should be at least four hours, where the client tries to make himself "go crazy, lose control, hallucinate," etc. Nothing should be done to alleviate the effects of his worst expectations, should those be realized (e.g., the client should not lock himself in a cell or chain himself to a bed post). He must try to create the catastrophe simply by thinking it. Since the client fears that his own brain can make these things happen without outside influence, then the client ought to be able to create these phenomena independent of outside resources.

Example

Ogden was a 33-year-old man who came to me after going through therapy with several cognitive behaviorists. He reported only minor changes, despite the fact that I knew these therapists were excellent. He complained of feeling inferior, having marital problems, being depressed, and acting passive. He said he had gone to the other therapists with the same complaints. My view of the problem differed from his perception.

He described feeling weak, inferior, and non-assertive, but his behavior in the early sessions belied his description. He aggressively argued against my suggestions, made up scores of excuses for not doing any homework, and seemed to actively resist therapeutic intervention of any sort. In my judgment his goal in coming to counseling was to confound the therapist—not to reduce his negative emotions. It seemed clear to me that his previous therapy consisted of his trying to "show up" the therapists by demonstrating that there was nothing they could do to help him.

I decided that a paradoxical approach might break Ogden's pattern. It seemed to me that his key irrationality was his belief in his own passivity. He demonstrated aggressiveness, while thinking he was passive. I felt that the paradoxical technique could most effectively intervene on his passivity.

I instructed Ogden to practice the following techniques for at least a month.

a. Find situations wherein you are likely to be passive, seek them out, and put yourself in them.

b. When in the situation try to think the irrational thoughts as hard as you can; try to get yourself to believe them. (His particular thoughts were, "I am weak, inferior a nerd." "Other people have power over me." "People don't respect or like me. I allow others to manipulate me." "I never stand up for myself.")

He was told to keep a daily log of his passivity points and to earn as many points as he could. The more points the better. Each week he was to aim at getting more points than the week before.

As the reader might suspect, the client had a great deal of difficulty getting any points at all for the first two weeks. Despite his claim that he was naturally inclined to be passive and overly compliant, he found it extremely difficult to act passive even in very minor situations. He did a little better the next two weeks, but he barely averaged .05 + in passivity for most of his attempts.

This technique showed him very clearly that his problem was not as he had envisioned. He was not passive at all. Because of the exercise he realized that he was overly aggressive and hostile. Previous therapeutic attempts to make him feel stronger and more assertive were misdirected; what he really needed was to resolve his hostility and anger towards others. The therapy was redirected towards examining the underlying thoughts that were causing his aggression.

Comment

Paradoxical intentions rarely are curative, but, as in the above example, they often clarify an important issue for the client. The technique is particularly useful for those clients who imagine that they should have control over all of their feelings. After trying the technique, they realize that they have as much difficulty making themselves feel angry, anxious, or depressed as they have had trying to remove those feelings.

The procedure is similar to flooding, except that in flooding the client simply tries to stay in an aversive situation, while paradoxical techniques press the client to make himself feel as bad as he can while in the situation. In addition, flooding is more systematized, and generally more carefully monitored by the therapist.

Like other techniques in this chapter, this approach is contraindicated for clients with directly conditioned emotional responses.

Further Information

Paradoxical intention, developed by Frankl (1960, 1978), is similar to forced catastophizing.

Ellis' (1985) risk-taking exercises have a paradoxical component. Also see Giles, 1979; Goldfried, 1977; Haley, 1973; Jacobson and Margolin, 1979; Weeks and L'Abate, 1982.

SWITCHED ROLEPLAYING

Principles

Elsewhere in this book we have noted the passion with which clients often cling to their mistaken beliefs, even when they cause them pain. They might even do so with a certain amount of pride and feel guilty if they allow themselves to be too easily dislodged from false perceptions they have harbored for a lifetime. This devotion might result from clients' belief that they derive certain payoffs from enduring the handicap. Sometimes the motivation is far more basic: clients simply do not want to appear to be "giving in" to the persuasive logic of their therapists. Switched roleplaying is a technique that preserves clients' self-image, lowers their resistance to therapy (because the therapist assumes a passive, accepting attitude toward their irrational beliefs), and hones their countering skills so that they are better able to monitor their own attitudes and behaviors in the future.

Method

1. Identify your clients' irrational beliefs.
2. Teach your clients the preliminaries of cognitive restructuring therapy, i.e. finding beliefs, analyzing them, and disputing and shifting them.
3. Tell your clients that, for purposes of this exercise, you are going to adopt their irrational beliefs (though you won't want to label them as such), and charge your clients with persuading you otherwise, using the techniques you discussed in Step #2.
4. Reverse roles. Have the clients try to counsel you out of your beliefs. You defend the irrational thoughts, while your clients try to use logic and persuasion to convince you that you are wrong.
5. Continue the roleplaying long enough (at least half an hour) so that your clients submit to *their* roles without thinking about it.
6. If during the roleplaying your clients present rather convincing evidence

that the irrational thoughts expressed by you are faulty, you should acquiesce. Continue until your clients have developed a good repertoire of counterarguments.

Example

The following transcript summarizes a significant portion of my exchange with Barton, a client who sought counseling because his close friends had been telling him for years that he didn't trust people enough. They had told him that he must be paranoid. This transcript is near the end of the switched roleplaying session.

THERAPIST: This thought that people can't be trusted is absolutely true. There are probably a thousand examples of your being taken advantage of by someone whom you had thought you could trust. It's best not to trust anybody, but to treat all people like they are trying to manipulate you, and to guard against their doing so.

CLIENT: But some people have treated me fairly.

THERAPIST: For now! But just wait till the future.

CLIENT: What do I get for covering my ass all the time? No friends and lots of enemies.

THERAPIST: At least you won't be taken like you have been for the last 15 years.

CLIENT: But that's a bad exchange. No friends, lots of enemies. And what do I get for all this protection? I can put a banner on my wall when I am dying alone and friendless. It will read, "HE NEVER LET ANYBODY TAKE ADVANTAGE OF HIM!" Big deal! It wouldn't be worth it.

THERAPIST: But if you let yourself get taken it will show everybody what a schmuck, what a weakling you are.

CLIENT: It would only show that I win some and lose some, like everybody else. A real schmuck would be a guy who throws away all closeness just so somebody doesn't take advantage of him. Now, that would really be dumb!

THERAPIST: How could you have any self-esteem if you don't protect yourself from others?

CLIENT: Do I have any self-esteem now, with my present attitude?

THERAPIST: That's because you have not done a very good job of guarding.

CLIENT: I don't know of anybody who guards more than I. And I have paid the price for it. I have no friends, no lover, and despite all the guarding, some people are still able to take advantage of me. It's not worth it anymore. Better I stopped protecting all the time an open up to people, and if I get hurt, then so what. It would still be better than what I have now.

THERAPIST: You have a good point there. I can't argue against it.

Comment

Besides being a good treatment technique, switched roleplaying can be used to assess how solidly clients have incorporated their counters. Clients who have just memorized counters are unable to argue with the therapist. They give up the argument quickly and agree with the therapist. In the above example, the client demonstrated that he had fully mastered the disputing technique—not just the words but the counter philosophy behind it.

Further Information

Role-switching is used in many forms of psychotherapy. See Corsini, 1957; Greenberg, 1974; Moreno and Zeleny, 1958.

———

OBTAINING GOALS—TIME PROJECTION

Principles

Clients who feel unhappy about their lives are usually convinced that if they could only acquire what they do not now have, they would be considerably happier. Time-honored rationalizations, such as "The grass always looks greener on the other side of the fence," begin to hint at the flaw in that perception, but such expressions are only words. They are not felt realities, and therefore hold little meaning for a truly troubled client.

A paradoxical approach begins with an acceptance of clients' complaints about the voids in their lives, but then encourages them to imagine that those voids are suddenly filled. They must imagine fully, completely, all of the details associated with having everything in life that would make living worthwhile for them. If they undertake this envisioning process in earnest, they will be able to see the negatives of their "dream world" just as clearly as the positives, and should emerge from the exercise with a great sense of perspective on their current lives.

Method 1

1. Have clients develop a list of desires (those things or circumstances that would make them happy).
2. Relax the clients and then ask them to fantasy that their beliefs and desires have magically come true. In the fantasy, assure them that their fulfillment can never be changed, taken away or lessened, and that keeping the state permanent will never require the least bit of effort on their part.
3. Then have the clients fantasize a completely accurate description in detail of what life would be like after all their wishes come true. Be sure to help them visualize the negative components of their lifestyle, since most clients will glorify the fantasy.
4. Repeat the fantasy for each belief on the list.

Method 2

There are many variations of the above technique. One includes the popular fantasy of finding a genie in a bottle or a wizard who grants three wishes. Fictional literature is replete with examples of the negative effects of such windfalls: Midas, who starved to death because all that he touched turned to gold; the jilted lover who got his beloved back with a magic love potion, only to go insane because he can't escape from her; Faust, who sold his soul to gain material wealth, only to discover that the wealth was illusionary, but the loss of a soul was eternal.

Example

Irrational belief: I am inferior to everybody.
Corrective belief: I am better than everybody.
Negative effects of correction: You would never be content. Many would be jealous of you for being better and would hate you for it. You would always worry about not maintaining your position. You can't cuddle up with "betterness." A lot of people would refuse to accept you as better. You would die of boredom since you would not have anything to strive for.

———

Irrational belief: I am unhappy because I can't control all my negative emotions.
Corrective belief: I must instantaneously control all feelings.
Negative effects of correction: You would lose all spontaneity. All pleasant emotions would be controlled, and your life would deteriorate into a series

of meaningless mechanical routines. Motivation, drive, desire would be gone. You would have no empathy or understanding of others, and would lose the ability to get close to anyone.

———

Irrational belief: My spouse isn't the way he/she should be.
Corrective belief: My spouse becomes perfect.
Negative effects of correction: You would immediately feel very inferior. You would become constantly guilty, since all problems in the relationship would have to be your responsibility. The relationship would lose all interest since it would be too predictable. There would be no challenge, no hope of it getting better, no problems to work on, no justified anger, nothing to gossip about, no tensions to be resolved, no making up after fights. In short, there would be no reason for a relationship at all.

Comment

When my clients have used this exercise, most of them have discovered that perfection, or reaching all their goals, may be the worst condition a human being can attain. Happiness, they discover, is more in striving for a goal than in reaching it.

———

TEACH THYSELF

Principles

Teaching has always been a very effective technique for learning, as graduate assistants who have lived through the shock of preparing their first lecture series can attest. Suddenly, the necessity to advocate and defend, rather than simply parrot, the basic tenets of law, literature, or sociology has a way of focusing the mind more thoroughly than any of the more material incentives offered by academe. You must know your subject or face the humiliation of being defrocked by your *students*!

In the teach thyself method, clients are asked first to clearly identify their harmful core beliefs and any related emotions, and then to devise a curriculum by which they can teach others how to acquire the same misperceptions they now hold. The technique capitalizes upon several important therapeutic advantages. First, there is the element of surpise. The resistant client is caught off guard. Instead of having to defend his or her misperceptions, the client can now pontificate upon them, which—at least at first—also implies a certain level of acceptance of them by the therapist.

Second, when they are forced to assume the role of teacher, clients are forced to distance themselves somewhat from their preoccupation and the intensity of their interactions with the therapist. That distancing allows an opportunity for greater objectivity to creep into their deliberations.

Third, the pressure to do well (not to be embarrassed in front of your students, or the therapist) can motivate clients to give a lot more attention to the possible sources of their own misperceptions than would be likely otherwise.

This technique uses a paradoxical approach toward helping clients gain a clear understanding of the sources of their unhappiness. Beyond that, any of a wide variety of cognitive techniques might be employed to help them gain a more rational view of themselves and their world.

Method

1. Develop a list of clients' core beliefs associated with their negative emotions.
2. Divide the beliefs into their key logical components. For example, the thought, "I am inferior to my brother," can be broken down into the concepts "I am," a state of being, "inferior," which can be broken down further into what traits, to what degree, during what times, etc., and "to my brother," which implies family history, relationships, etc.
3. Instruct clients to imagine in exact detail how they would teach each subpart of the beliefs to someone else. For example:

   Picture that a young, bright, psychologically healthy person is given over to your care for ten years. You have the power to control his/her environment for this time. Now let us suppose that you had to teach him/her to be as upset as you have been. What would you do? Specifically, how would you get him/her to believe he/she was inferior, sick, stupid, or any of the other beliefs that you have about yourself? And what are the key subcomponents of each of these beliefs that you would have to first teach? How would you teach these subparts?

4. After they have exhausted their description, ask clients to explore whether

some significant people in their own environment may have taught them (albeit unintentionally) in the same way. Go through their history in detail to determine how the beliefs and their subparts may have been learned.

Example

Belief: "I am bad if I ever hurt someone, even unintentionally."

Resulting emotion: Guilt, fear of punishment.

Environmental triggers: The client would feel guilty if any person he had contact with even casually was upset or unhappy. He always thought that he should be able to do something to help this person and felt guilty if he couldn't.

Belief subparts: To believe the complete irrational thought a person must first be taught:

a. People can be classified into two categories—good or bad.
b. Individual traits can be evaluated into good or bad.
c. Global judgments and blanket statements can accurately describe individuals or their traits.
d. People have traits which are part of their "being."
e. There are metaphysical states of being, badness, and intentionality.
f. Individuals have the power to psychologically hurt others.
g. One negative example ("ever hurting someone") indicates the existence of the whole trait ("being bad").

How a client might "teach" subparts:

- Model overgeneralizations, e.g., blacks are lazy, Irish drink too much, and women don't have the head for math.
- Teach an idealized metaphysics, e.g., have person memorize Plato. (Truth, beauty, virtue, justice, goodness, and badness exist as independent realities.)
- Instruct about Schopenhauer's concept of universal intentionality. People's actions are full of will, volitions, and purpose. Therefore, any behavior that goes awry can be traced back to the creator of the action.
- Teach cosmic responsibility. Since the world is the creation of multiple wills, any injustice, pain or suffering can be attributed to the evilness or badness of one or more of these wills.
- Teach individual responsibility. Each individual is responsible for any "badness" in his or her environment. If people don't immediately correct evilness, they are culpable for creating it.
- Teach perfectionism. The world and all the people in it, including oneself,

should be perfect. Thus, any pain or unhappiness is not part of the natural order of things and needs to be immediately corrected.

Further Information

Several books employ the contradictory approach. They can be useful to the clinician in helping analyze the exaggerated subcomponents of a client's thinking. See Buchwald, 1977; Feirstein, 1983; Greenburg, 1964.

REDUCTIO AD ABSURDUM

Principles

Reductio ad absurdum (reduction to absurdity) is a method of disengaging clients from their irrational beliefs by caricaturing those beliefs until they appear utterly ridiculous. In order to continue to embrace them, most clients keep their irrationalities just within the bounds of acceptable logic. Therapists can use a variety of techniques to exaggerate these harmful beliefs beyond a point at which clients can defend them, until they prefer not to be identified with them.

Method 1. Blowup

1. Make a list of the client's irrational thoughts.
2. Record the typical scenes which accompany them.
3. Have the client imagine the worst outcomes possible in these scenes. Describe these outcomes in detail. For example, the worst outcome for a client who was afraid of getting anxious in a plane was:

   I am in the plane 30,000 feet up and I'm getting anxious. The plane is packed with people. I start sweating and my head starts shaking. I begin to moan out loud. People around me start staring at me. I start screaming and everyone in the plane turns around and glares at me. The stewardess comes up and tells me to be quiet. But I scream even louder, telling everyone I'm out of control. I can't sit still any longer and start running up and down the aisle yelling and waving my hands. Everybody looks at me like I'm a crazy man.

(When imagining a phobic event, most clients stop the scene at this point, usually while experiencing strong anxiety. But the key to the blowup technique is to continue the image to the ultimate conclusion.)

When the plane lands, I am met at the airport with at least 100 people crowding around. Everybody I know is there—my mother, father, second-grade teacher, spouse, children, boss, and all the other important people in my life. As I walk off the plane they are all pointing accusing fingers at me, calling me "wimp, sissy, coward." They are all booing loudly. My wife throws her wedding ring at me, and walks away, arm in arm with the pilot. My mother and father disown me. My kids laugh and make jokes about me. My boss fires me on the spot and says I'll never get another job again if he can help it. They don't bother to take me to a hospital. (Why waste taxpayers' money on such a weakling?) I look at the daily paper, which has a half-page picture of me on the front page with the caption: "SISSY, WEAK, MILKSOP, FREAKS OUT ON PLANE." On a local TV news program, I see my therapist saying to the press, "Some people just don't have the 'right stuff.'" Everybody laughs at the funny things I told him in therapy. I wander around the city, and everybody points at me and laughs derisively. I can't even get a place at the Salvation Army because none of the winos wants to be seen with me. I spend the rest of my life wandering from place to place, eating out of garbage cans.

4. After the scene has been prepared during the counseling session, have the client write a script describing the blowup in detail. The client should read the script daily.

Method 2. Absurd Situation

1. Make a list of the core irrational beliefs.
2. For each belief, think of extreme situations which would show the absurdity of the thought.
3. Analyze the extreme situations to determine exactly why the thoughts are irrational. List each reason.
4. Check to see if the same absurdity exists in the present situation.

Example

Irrational thought: People's problems are always their fault.

Extreme situations: Being born handicapped, being short, having an alcoholic father, growing up in a slum.

Reasons irrational: Assumes control of things people have no power over, like their heredity, early childhood environment, and who their parents are.

Irrational thought: I must never make mistakes.

Extreme situations: Breaking a pencil; betting on the wrong team.

Reasons irrational: As human beings we make hundreds of petty mistakes each week. We do not have sufficient knowledge not to make them.

Irrational thought: Outside events make people upset.

Extreme situations: If things I am afraid of are truly dangerous, then nobody should take elevators, handle snakes, or speak in public.

Reasons irrational: If situations cause fear, then everybody in the situation will have the fear.

Method 3. Absurd Inconsistencies

Take each of your clients' thoughts and demonstrate to them that although they are saying what they believe is true, they are not acting as if it were true. Their behavior contradicts their beliefs. For example: a client who believes that he could never be helped has been to therapists for the last 10 years; a wife who has been saying that her spouse is a terrible mate throughout their 20-year marriage; clients who say they want to get better but never do their homework; employees who can't stand their five-year-old job; depressed patients who call up all their friends and relatives saying that they have decided to kill themselves.

Further Information

See cognitive flooding (Chapter 3) for related concepts. Blowup is described by Lazarus (1971). Confronting the inconsistencies between client thoughts and actions is practiced by many therapies, but see particularly Berne, 1961, 1964, and Fagan and Shepherd, 1970.

———

UTILIZATION

Principles

Instead of fighting clients and their misperceptions, therapists often find it helpful to put clients' penchant for self-harm to more constructive ends. This utilization strategy begins with the therapist's affirming the right of the client to express himself openly and clearly. The therapist appears acquiescent in his or her willingness to accept the client's self-deprecations, but he or she then imposes one critical criterion: the client must amass as much evidence as possible in support of his or her damaging belief.

The beauty of this technique is that it is not, in itself, a deception designed to cure a deception. Logical, critical thinking is to be applauded wherever it is found. Such thinking is inherently medicinal, insofar as harmful misperceptions are concerned. When clients adopt such thinking in support of their misperceptions, they are destined to fail. Their ultimate victory is all the sweeter, and more durable, because it is *theirs* not the therapist's.

Method

1. Develop a list of your client's basic irrational thoughts.
2. If your clients are constantly arguing that these thoughts are rational, ask them to continue their argument, but to make their disagreement more persuasive by shoring it up with logic, evidence, and emotional conviction.
3. Tell them that the reason they should argue against the therapist even harder is that they need to develop more of a critical sense; they should accept no authority—particularly that of the therapist—on faith alone. The more they disagree with the therapist, the more they will be able to resist the suggestions of others which have previously damaged them.

Example

Are you willlng to cooperate with me? I think your arguing against me is good. It increases your ability to be critical and, as I have said, that ability to think critically is essential to changing your own irrational beliefs. So please continue to argue but argue stronger and try to make your arguments more logical, because I think that will help you.

The therapist continues in this manner, encouraging clients to keep up what they are doing but to do it in a slightly different way (i.e., more logical, more evidence, argue in a more objective manner). The approach continues until the client starts questioning the irrational beliefs themselves, at which point the therapist reverts back to a more standard cognitive restructuring approach.

Comment

As with most paradoxical approaches, the therapist may unintentionally reinforce the client for being resistant.

Further Information

Milton Erickson and his followers have done extensive work on utilization. See Erickson (1982), Erickson and Rossi (1981), Havens (1985), Lankton and Lankton (1983), Rossi (1980), Rossi and Ryan (1985), and Weeks and L'Abate (1982) for extended discussions of the concept of responsibility underlying the technique.

RESIGNATION AND ACCEPTANCE

Principles

When I first described the resignation and acceptance technique to a friend, his laconic response was, "That sounds like a technique from the 'Do-Nothing School of Psychology'!" Harsh, but pretty much to the point. Under this technique, therapists basically listen agreeably and assent. They do not dispute their clients' self-depreciations. They are primarily "listening posts," hoping thus to force clients to recognize flaws in their own thinking.

Clients who come into therapy hoping for a "quick fix" are frustrated by this approach, and it is not recommended for clients who are more likely to respond positively to a more directive approach. It can be very frustrating, and therefore very beneficial, to clients who are prone to the self flim-flam phenomenon discussed elsewhere in this chapter.

Method

1. Develop a list of ten situations, harmful core beliefs, and their associated emotions.
2. Discuss each situation and confirm that each belief and emotional response are understandable and appropriate to the situation.
3. When clients ask what they should do about it, respond by saying that all they can do is to try to avoid the situations that produced these thoughts and feelings.
4. When clients insist that they can't avoid some of these situations, or that it would cause more problems to avoid them than to face them, agree with the clients and suggest that they might as well accept feeling upset, since there is nothing they can do about it.
5. If clients come up with alternatives to avoiding or accepting, agree with these suggestions. Keep on doing this until the clients have discovered the irrationality of their own thinking, without your pointing it out.
6. Be prepared to handle clients' anger at the therapist's lack of responsiveness. "You aren't helping me!" Be prepared to answer that if the client is perceiving correctly, there is little that you can do.

Example

The client in this dialogue had anxiety attacks about going to office parties.

CLIENT: So, you see, it's terrible if I make a mistake when other people are watching.

THERAPIST: Yes, now that you have explained it to me, I see. If your reasoning is right, you would lose your job and your wife would leave you.

CLIENT: Well, what can I do about it?

THERAPIST: Well, it certainly seems that you are in a hell of a bind. I guess all you can do is to avoid those parties.

CLIENT: I have tried that for five years! I can't avoid them all!

THERAPIST: Well, I guess you have to try not to make mistakes.

CLIENT: But I keep on making them. The more I try not to make faux pas the more I make them.

THERAPIST: Well, if you can't avoid the parties and you can't keep from making mistakes, then you can't do anything. I guess you will have to resign yourself to getting upset.

CLIENT: But then my wife would leave me and I'd be fired.

THERAPIST: Boy, that would be really tough! I hope that doesn't happen.

CLIENT: But that would be terrible!

THERAPIST: Sure would. But you would have to accept that. Lots of people aren't married, and there are a lot of people unemployed. So you would survive, but it would be really nasty. Looks like the only thing is to accept the pain and hurt and stop trying to push it away.

CLIENT: But I must do something! I just can't let these things happen. Isn't there is something you can do?

THERAPIST: What? Me? From what you've presented here, it would seem that you're trapped. There's nothing I or anyone in the world could do. You are stuck. Completely. There is no way out.

CLIENT: Well, maybe I'm wrong. Maybe I am exaggerating. Maybe it wouldn't be so terrible.

THERAPIST: Please explain further.

For the rest of the session the therapist shifted to a more standard cognitive approach while the client looked for possible mistakes in his thinking. Whenever the client started to talk like he was trapped again, the therapist returned to the resignation approach. The therapist kept forcing the client to come up with his own examination of his own thoughts. He refused to rescue him.

Comment

This technique is most effective with a resistant, overly pampered client who has a history of "playing victim." For his part, the counselor plays the passive-aggressive game better than the client. But, to a larger degree than in any other paradoxical approach, this technique requires that the truly caring professional sublimate his or her instinct to relieve a hurting client. Whenever this approach is contemplated, the therapist should consider the possible damage to both client and therapist that could result from paradoxical communication.

There are many situations in life in which acceptance is the only logical alternative, permanent handicap and loss of a loved one being two examples. In such circumstances, resignation and acceptance are not paradoxical, but rational.

Further Information

A noncognitive therapy that uses paradoxical acceptance a great deal is provocative therapy. See Farrelley and Brandsma (1974) for numerous examples.

5

Logical Analysis

Logical analysis is a structured method for helping clients overcome the damaging consequences of their mistaken beliefs. Fundamentally, it is a method of fighting irrational imagination with logic. Since the client's discomfort began with a thought, the therapist uses the cognitive process to assess the validity of that thought and to rectify any emotional problems sparked by that thought.

The process of logical analysis includes five steps, with a variety of techniques associated with each. We begin with a unifying overview of the process in order to provide the reader with a context for each of the specific techniques discussed later in this chapter.

The five steps might best be understood if they are presented in the form of an analogy. Imagine that your client's thoughts have been put on trial in a courtroom. The client is both judge and jury and has as his or her goal the task of determining the guilt or innocence, truth or falseness (rationality or irrationality), of each belief. As in any other courtroom, this one has established procedures for clarifying claims and counterclaims, evaluating evidence that is both pro and con, and arriving at a carefully considered final verdict regarding the validity of each thought. The process is as follows.

Step 1: State Your Case. The first thought to appear before the bench is clearly stated, *but in an analyzable form!* Clients usually have difficulty at the outset in meeting this requirement. They will begin by reporting their feelings: "I'm afraid of snow!" After using such techniques as those described in "Turning Beliefs into Statements," they learn to identify and articulate the beliefs that gave rise to those feelings. In this case, the belief can be expressed in an analyzable form as "Snow is to be feared."

Step 2: Define Your Terms. That damaging belief ("Snow is to be feared!") is then subjected to a careful analysis to make certain that everyone in the courtroom understands the specific meaning of all of the key terms and phrases. In this case, the key terms are *snow* and *feared*. After consulting a dictionary, or a series of expert witnesses, the court might consider the following range of meanings for these two key words:
Snow could be either:

- a half-inch deep, slippery coating that covers sidewalks and imperils walkers, or
- a 40-inch snowfall that results from a blizzard and causes destruction on a wide scale.

Feared can mean any of the following:

- a slight nervousness about the prospect of a snowfall;
- feeling saddened and disappointed about the possibility of snow;
- feeling utterly panicked about a forecast of snow.

If the reaction (panic) is clearly out of proportion to the subject (a half-inch snowfall), it may be possible simply by clearly defining these two key concepts to help clients at least begin to alter their damaging beliefs. Later in this chapter we consider two techniques that have proven useful to clients during this phase of logical analysis: "Defining Beliefs" and "Finding the Meaning of Concepts."

Step 3: Decide Upon Your Rules of Evidence. Both the therapist and the client must agree at the outset upon the criteria for assessing the validity of the client's thought. (This would be roughly tantamount to such standard courtroom rules as the defendant's right to cross-examination, the prohibition against "hearsay" evidence and the presumption of innocence until guilt has been established.) In our example, the rule of evidence boils down to one central question: How will you know if snow is really to be feared?

The court can decide (and your client must concur) that the real test of the validity of this thought lies in the answers to such questions as the following:

• How many other people agree that snow is to be feared?
• How many people have been *killed* as a result of snowfall, in contrast to other common causes of death?
• How many people have been *injured* as a result of snowfall, in contrast to other causes of injuries?
• How much destruction of property occurs as a result of snowfall, in comparison to other natural disasters?

Two specific techniques are offered in connection with this step: "Distancing" and "Scientific Attitudes." The goal of both techniques is to help clients adopt an attitude that is favorable to the logical analysis process. It should also be acknowledged here that, under this step, the therapist has a key role in (1) helping clients formulate a set of "rules of evidence" that will conclusively demonstrate the usefulness or detrimental consequences of their beliefs, and (2) making certain that clients adhere to those rules during the remaining steps of this process.

Step 4: Examine Your Evidence. The evidence (the answers to the above questions in our example) should be presented for the consideration of the judge and jury (i.e., the client). Many clients have difficulty in evaluating evidence objectively. This difficulty results in part from the failure of our educational system to emphasize the acquisition of critical thinking skills, and in part from emotional considerations. Clients who derive certain payoffs from their unhappiness, or who are inclined to sabotage the therapeutic process, or who have an emotionally unhealthy attachment to their mistaken beliefs, will find it very difficult to abandon those beliefs, no matter how much convincing evidence has been amassed. Those special cases can best be treated using some of the techniques discussed in Chapter 4.

We assume that most of the clients who are helped by logical analysis make the best use of it once they are able to incorporate the following skills into their analysis of the evidence:

a. The ability to form hypotheses, i.e., to discern meaningful patterns in a mass of evidence and to engage in inductive reasoning. I present a technique for bolstering this skill under "Forming Hypotheses."
b. The ability to clearly recognize cause and effect relationships. For example, is the evident fear of snow related to the occurrence of a snowfall or to some other factor that is manifested coincidentally during snowfalls? Two of the techniques addressed in this chapter help the client in this aspect of his analysis: "Finding the Causes" and "Graph Analysis."
c. The ability to use a self-probing technique in assessing the truth or falseness of a particular belief. Here we offer the "Disputing Irrational Beliefs Analysis."

d. The ability to recognize logical fallacies in one's thoughts and in the manner in which one expresses oneself. Fallacious thinking can contribute to a misinterpretation of the evidence that has been presented for analysis. Hence our section on "Logical Fallacies" is designed to acquaint both therapists and their clients with classic examples of this kind of thinking, in the hope that they will thus learn to avoid them.

Step 5: State Your Verdict. On the basis of the information gathered and analyzed in Steps #3 and #4, the client (our judge and jury) decides whether snow is to be feared.

The client might logically conclude that certain degrees of snowfall are to be feared, which is fine. If weather forecasts suggest that a dangerous blizzard is on the way, it would be wise to limit one's movements, hoard essential supplies in anticipation of a long siege, and take any other appropriate precautions. But this kind of analysis would prevent a client from panicking at the mere suggestion of a pending snowfall. The client would thus have better control over his or her cognitions, which is the goal of cognitive restructuring therapy.

TURNING BELIEFS INTO STATEMENTS

Principles

Clients often have difficulty expressing their thoughts precisely. Sometimes the problem derives from their inability to clearly recognize what they are feeling, in which case such techniques as focusing might be used to help them over that hurdle.

When clients finally seek therapeutic help, they have probably been compelled to do so by emotional discomfort. They are most likely to express their discomfort in words that describe their feelings, not the thoughts that provoked those feelings. They must be helped to understand that when they say, "I hate men," what they are really asserting is, "Men deserve to be hated." If the latter were not so, they could not, in all honesty, hold onto the belief.

It is a simple but very common mistake to assume that a true and natural cause and effect relationship exists between the two key variables in a statement such as "I'm afraid of snow!" The point to be emphasized in this phase of logical analysis is that descriptive, emotion-charged statements in themselves cannot be analyzed. Only when we look behind the statement to challenge the *assumed* cause and effect relationship among the variables within it, can we recast the statement into a form whose validity can be tested.

Method

1. Have your clients present a list of problem feelings, but require them to state those feelings as completely as possible. Hence, instead of accepting the statement, "I'm afraid," require that they spell out more fully what they are afraid of: "I'm afraid of snakes (or rejection, or being poor, or getting too fat, etc.)."

2. Once you have cataloged a complete list of your clients' discomforts, assist them in recasting those statements in a manner which is disputable. ("Snakes are to be feared, etc.") If particular clients have very long lists of these emotions, complete the first few restatements with them, so that they learn the technique of teasing out these assumed relationships; then have them complete that same procedure on the other statements in your

presence, so that you can confirm that they have acquired the necessary skills.

3. Certain clients might be encouraged to continually practice hearing these assumptions in what they say, or what they hear others say, and recasting beliefs into assertions that are suitable for analysis.

Examples

Following is a list of client statements, followed by a recasting of those statements to reflect what the client is *really* asserting in a more disputable, analyzable form.

Client's statement: "I am scared."
Client is really asserting: "Something is scary."

———

Client's sentence: "I need to be competent to feel worthwhile."
Client is really asserting: "Self-worth = competence."

———

Client's statement: "Love conquers all."
Client is really asserting: "All human problems can be solved by feeling the emotion called love."

———

Client's statement: "Life should be good."
Client is really asserting: "Human existence is required to follow certain rules. Wishes = oughts."

———

Client's statement: "I can't survive without a man."
Client is really asserting: "Men are physical necessities."

———

Client's statement: "I need to be sure in order to decide."
Client is really asserting: "Certainties exist."

———

Client's statement: "It awful when I feel unhappy."
Client is really asserting: "Having an unpleasant emotion is an exceedingly bad thing that can happen to a human being."

Client's statement: "I hate mistakes."
Client is really asserting: "Lack of perfection should be despised."

Comment

Once your clients are able to recognize and respond to harmful assumptions, you will want to encourage them to practice the skill continually. One way to reinforce this positive habit is to encourage them to be alert to such statements when they are made by others and to mentally practice recasting the statements into analyzable assertions.

Further Information

Stating logical assertions in the correct form is discussed in detail in philosophical analyses. See Flew, 1952, 1953, 1956; Macdonald, 1954; Munitz, 1981; Urmson, 1950; Wilson, 1967; Wittgenstein, 1953.

DEFINING BELIEFS

Principles

Once a belief has been stated in an analyzable form, we must be as clear as possible about its true meaning. Language is, inherently, an imperfect medium for communication, and human beings tend to complicate the communication process even more by resorting to vague abstractions, emotional outbursts, or sugar-coated platitudes—whichever best suits their mood at a given moment—in order to express their feelings and the cognitions that gave rise to those feelings.

After they have learned how to recast descriptive statements into analyzable statements, clients can be very glib about that process. They might blurt out a "men deserve to be hated" assertion and immediately begin to test the validity of that statement. It is most important that the therapist slow them down, force them to concentrate fully upon the variables in that statement, and require them to define those variables in very specific terms before they continue. Just doing this could have the effect of making the falseness of certain client beliefs undeniably apparent.

Method

1. Have your clients write a list of their core beliefs, expressed in the form of analyzable assertions.
2. Take one assertion at a time and go through each word in it carefully. Ask the client to make each word as specific and concrete as possible. You may wish to use the following instructions.

> Words have different levels of abstraction. To analyze thoughts we should use the lowest level. For instance, "this table" (pointing to a table near me) is a specific thing. Only one table in the universe is "this table." But we could say more abstractly "table" in "the room"—there are several—or "furniture," or even more abstract—"object in this room." In each case I am moving from the concrete to the abstract. But notice what happens when we reach the abstraction "object in this room." It's too abstract to mean much. For instance, if I asked, "True or false? Is the object in this room brown?" you would be unable to answer me because "object" is too abstract. To know the color, you must know what "object" means.
>
> Your thoughts are like that too. If we wanted to know if you "need to be highly successful to be happy," we must know specifically what you mean by several concepts, like "need, highly, successful and happy." If we don't make these words specific we can't know if the statement is true or false.

3. Develop a series of questions that will help clients pin down their concepts. For example, the therapist can question the belief "I am inferior" by asking, "What part of you is inferior? Have you always been? How do you know that you will always remain inferior? Inferior compared to whom? When? All the time or just some time? In everything or in just a few ways? What does 'I am' mean? What level of 'inferior' do you mean? Are you at the absolute bottom or just a little bit inferior? What scale have you selected to judge your inferiority? Is the scale valid or do you make it up when you feel bad?"
4. After you and your clients have made each word in the sentence as specific as possible, rewrite the sentence incorporating the new definitions.
5. Have your clients practice defining their sentences during the week until they understand the need for concrete definitions.

Example

Emile was a young man who entered therapy because he constantly got angry at himself and others. He always felt frustrated when his plans didn't work out as he thought they should. His unreasonable expectations caused major problems in his marriage, at work, and with his friends.

He was exceptionally bright and we quickly found the core belief that created his problems. He believed that his mind could control everything. He thought that he should be able to make himself happy instantaneously, that he could control physical sickness just by exercising his willpower, and that he should be able to make everyone in his environment — including his wife, his boss, and his children — act according to his wishes simply by willing it. When something didn't happen the way he wanted it to, he would get angry with himself for failing to exercise his will correctly. He wanted therapy to make his willpower work more effectively.

Emile's history demonstrates the origins of his belief. He grew up with a father who was a genius, but who, unfortunately, was also erratic emotionally. Emile never felt accepted by his family. In his adolescence, he joined quasi-religious, fundamentalist cults which offered him acceptance if he acquiesced to their philosophies. Their philosophies centered around the idea that the mind was all-powerful. They taught Emile, incorrectly, that anyone could do anything he wanted to in this world if he had enough faith. A person's mind has no limits, they contended. If Emile wanted fame and fortune, it was his if he willed it.

Because he wanted to maintain the closeness with his fellow cult members, Emile accepted this philosophy. But it never worked. He always seemed to bump against limitations. When he asked the cult leaders what was wrong they said he didn't have enough faith. This made him feel guilty, so he tried to get more faith. But he never could. He couldn't seem to get enough faith to make his mind all-powerful.

After going through the preliminary steps of cognitive restructuring therapy, we got to the point of defining the words in one of his key assertions. We analyzed: "The human mind has the willpower to control anything."

At the start of our analysis, Emile defined the key words by simply giving synonyms for them. Hence, "human mind" was replaced with "inner being," and "power" was replaced with "potency." I told him that good definitions are much more than mere substitutions of one abstraction for another. I urged him to be more specific, and to use words that conveyed concrete images of what he actually meant. I had to proffer a couple suggestions in order to clarify what he was to do, but once Emile got the hang of it, he was able to offer the following suggestions.

mind = the physical organ in the skull, the brain.
willpower = a nonphysical energy (spirit) which directs all action.
control = to regulate, direct, change, or restrain something.
anything = physical things like rocks, weather, trees, etc.; people—
their thoughts, emotions, behaviors etc.; self—my bones, muscles,
genes, emotions etc.

I then asked him to create a new sentence which had his more concrete, specific definitions in it. He wrote:

My brain, the organ in my skull, has a spiritual, nonphysical energy which can direct, regulate, or change physical objects, other people, or any aspect of myself.

I asked him to substitute a specific example for controlllng a physical thing.

CLIENT: Well, like making it rain.
THERAPIST: Put that into the sentence.
CLIENT: The spiritual energy in my brain can make it rain, not rain, or change rain into snow.
THERAPIST: Do you believe that?
CLIENT: That's really stupid, No one can do that.

We then went through other specific examples, such as having his mind mend a broken leg in a day, change his heredity by turning himself into a 10′ tall woman, make other people love him, or make rocks turn into snowflakes.

After several weeks of considering his thinking, he announced, "The power of the mind stuff should win the silly putty of the year award. It's like a child's fairy tale."

Comment

On first glance, defining a client's words may appear to be an academic exercise, playing with semantics, and irrelevant to the client's concerns. Many clients will certainly feel this way.

It is crucial at this point that the therapist restate the basic rationale for this aspect of the therapy. Clients' thoughts created their problems. The outside world didn't do that. And if their thoughts can be shown to be nonsense, and clients can come to see that they are, then the core cause of their fears, depression, or anger is undercut.

Further Information

Philosophy instead of psychology has the most useful references for the therapist. Excellent examples of defining concepts and words can be found in the work of linguistic philosophers. See Ayer, 1952, Munitz, 1981; Ryle, 1957; Urmson, 1950; Wilson, 1967.

————

FINDING THE MEANING OF CONCEPTS

Principles

The defining beliefs technique just discussed might be misleading to the extent that it suggests that defining key words and phrases is simply a matter of relying upon what clients *believe* the definitions should be or of looking up a particular term or phrase in a dictionary. The definitional process is usually much harder than that. What people *want* definitions to be is often at odds with prevailing opinion, and even the lexicographers who write dictionaries are usually years behind popular usage in their definitions of certain terms.

An "establishment," for example, could be a synonym for a mom-and-pop grocery store on the corner or for a powerful stratum of society that presumably controls great reserves of wealth and can control the actions of others in society, as in "the Establishment." Sometimes the subtle nuances of meaning are reflected more in how a word is said than in the word itself, but differences that result from intonations or body language can be readily detected by the alert mental health professional who knows what to look for and how to probe for further clarification when necessary.

While definitions may sometimes be difficult, they are far from impossible. Definitions are, after all, matters of consensus. The meaning of a word or phrase is what most people agree that it is at any point in time. Hence, one could take the position that the final arbiter of any definition is the public. The following method helps clients find meanings for certain difficult terms and concepts by teaching them to resort to publicly acceptable definitions.

Method and Example

1. *Model Case.* You and your client select an example of a correct use of a key word or phrase taken directly from an analyzable assertion. The example should be ideal so that virtually anyone in this society would agree that it is a valid example of the concept.

> Daphne came to see me because she was suffering from a powerful guilt. She felt that she was bad, immoral and evil and should be punished because she had hurt the feelings of a loved one on a series of occasions.
>
> To determine whether her behavior could correctly be judged as "bad," I asked her to search her mind for a model case which virtually everyone would agree was an example of a bad act. She recalled a newspaper article she had read. Several years ago three men were hunting for deer. They had no luck and were sitting on a hilltop feeling bored. They noticed another man walking down a road in the valley below. They had never seen him before. Just for the sport of it, they started to shoot at him. He tried to run away but after several tries they hit and killed him. The men then left the dead man on the road and went home for dinner.

I agreed with Daphne that this was an excellent example of what most people would agree is "bad" behavior.

2. *Contrary Model.* Select an example of a contrary case. Pick an ideal situation as similar as possible to the first, but in which the concept would clearly (in the judgment of most people) not apply. Whatever "bad" means, this case is clearly NOT an example of it.

   My client and I selected the following example.

> A man was driving his car along a narrow street lined with large trees and foliage. It was late at night and he was driving carefully, below the speed limit, and he was a nondrinker. Suddenly a man dashed in front of his car from behind a large bush. He slammed on his breaks but couldn't stop. He hit the man and killed him. He tried to help the man but saw it was too late. He called the police and waited for them to arrive.

3. Compare the model to the contrary case and determine what key abstract principles were present in the model that were not present in the contrary case. What are the essential differences between the two? List them.

> When we examined the components of the model to determine why the men's behavior could be correctly called bad we concluded:

a. The man was killed. (Bad event)
b. The three men had killed him. (Cause)
c. They had no reason to kill him. (Unjustified)
d. They chose to kill him. (Intention)
e. They could have avoided killing him. (Free choice)
f. They knew what they were doing. (Awareness)

When we examined the contrary case we determined the only variables present were:
a. The pedestrian was killed. (Bad event)
b. The driver had killed him. (Cause)
c. The driver had no reason to kill him. (Unjustified)

4. To determine which principles or combination of principles are essential to the concept, take each rule one at a time and think of situations which included all the other rules except this one. If the concept no longer applies, then the rule is essential.

a. For example, could we judge the hunters' behavior as bad if nothing bad happened? No. If no one was killed or injured or hurt in some other way, we couldn't call an act bad.
b. Is the act bad if someone wasn't the cause of the other's death? No. If the man were struck by lightning, we wouldn't blame the hunters.
c. Is the act bad if the hunters had a good reason for shooting him? No. A policeman has a right to shoot an attacking felon.
d. Is the act bad if the hunters hadn't intended it? No. As in our comparison example, one reason the driver was not guilty of murdering the pedestrian was that he did not intend to do so.
e. Is the act bad if it couldn't have been avoided? No. Imagine an adult grabbing a child's hand and making him hit his sister. The child is not to blame for hitting his sister.
f. Is the act bad if the person isn't aware of what he is doing? No. If a psychotic veteran shoots a man while hallucinating that he is being attacked by his old enemy, he is not to blame.

In our example, all rules were necessary to call the act "bad." The way the public uses the concept, a behavior is bad if something bad happens, if it is caused by another person, if there was no good reason for the act, if it was intended, if the person has the freedom not to do it, and if the person was aware. If just one rule is missing, then the behavior cannot be judged reprobate.

The driver in the example cannot be responsible because three rules were not present in the contrary case that were present in the model case:

intention, freedom, and awareness (d, e, and f). Clearly people can't accurately call themselves bad simply because they have hurt another person without reason (a, b, c). If they do and they feel guilty about it, their thinking is false. And their irrationality is not just play for the academic linguist; it is a life-threatening, crucial distinction. Because of (d), (e), and (f) the hunters could be convicted of murder; without them the driver was guilty of nothing but an unfortunate accident.

5. Once your analysis uncovers the crucial rules, apply them to the client's own beliefs.

My guilty client found she could not accurately call any of her previous behavior bad, since at least one rule was always missing. In some of the incidents she described, none of the rules applied!

Daphne's insight into the illogical nature of her thinking enabled her to use other cognitive restructuring techniques far more effectively.

Comment

Because this approach requires a certain amount of abstract thinking ability, some clients may not be able to use it effectively without considerable coaching. Initially the counselor may use the approach to analyze clients' concepts for later challenging.

Further Information

This approach is a modification of Wilson's (1963) method of analysis. The reader should go directly to this work for a comprehensive explanation of the procedure.

DISTANCING

Principles

Step #3 of logical analysis requires that clients decide upon the rules of evidence that will enable them to determine whether or not a given, analyzable assertion is valid. ("How will you know if snow is really to be feared?") For many clients, two hurdles must be cleared at this critical juncture in the therapeutic process. First, clients must be willing to be objective about their past and present beliefs and behaviors and about the evidence that they will be reviewing in their efforts to validate those beliefs and behaviors. Second, clients must be willing to refrain from undermining this rule-making process.

Either distancing or scientific attitudes or both techniques can be used to help clients acquire the skills they need to objectively analyze their own thinking, so that they can later assess the truth or falseness of their damaging beliefs. This objectivity begins with the rule-making process, for it is too easy to make rules that are designed to satisfy subjective needs.

Our use of the distancing technique derives from the work of Aaron Beck (1976), but includes some adaptations that we have found helpful within the context of the logical analysis methodology. As in the depersonalization technique discussed in Chapter 2, clients need to learn to look at their own thoughts as objects outside of themselves. They must exercise that same objectivity in constructing rules that have bearing on those thoughts. If they have not acquired that skill by the time they are ready to formulate rules of evidence, chances are that they will not accept any rules that clearly challenge the integrity of their long-held, mistaken beliefs. Distancing helps clients to analyze their thoughts as though the thoughts belonged to someone else, thus clearing the way for greater objectivity in the rule-making process.

Method

1. Develop a list of clients' core irrational beliefs connected to their emotions.
2. Create some fantasy analogies to give clients an external vantage point from which to analyze their beliefs.

   a. A colleague of mine, Elisabeth Vollmer, developed a fantasy which helps clients look at relationships more objectively. She tells them:

   Imagine I am a Martian and have just landed. I don't have much time on earth so you will be the only person I can talk to. We Martians understand much of earth but there is one thing we have never understood, and they sent me to earth to find out about it.

   We have noticed you have a thing called "relationships." We are thinking of instituting them ourselves. But we need to know as much about them as we can. What is a love relationship? How does one get one? How many different kinds of love relationships are there? What is the difference between friends and lovers? Can you have a bad lover? Why do people stay in "bad love"? What's good love? How can one tell whether love is good or bad? Why do humans want them anyway? If humans are in bad love how do they get out of it or make it into good love?

b. Another technique is empathy training used by client-centered therapists. Have your clients imagine what it's like to be another person, looking at the world through another perceptual frame of reference. Then have them visualize how this other person would view their damaging beliefs. For example, "If you were a woman would you want to date, or marry, yourself?" or "Imagine you are someone else who doesn't have your belief. How would this other person see your situation differently?"

3. After clients imagine the new perception vividly, ask them to make a decision about the validity of their thinking.
4. Instruct clients to use the dissociation imagery whenever they get confused about the truth or falseness of their thoughts.

Comment

Although this technique is often useful, it is sometimes difficult to get clients to bridge the outside perception back to their own vantage point. Practice of distancing is important.

Further Information

Metaphors help improve distancing ability. See Duhl, 1983; Erickson, 1982 and Gordon, 1978.

SCIENTIFIC ATTITUDES

Principles

Clients who practice the distancing technique will find that the formulation of rules of evidence will proceed more efficiently and accurately, especially if they have the support and creative assistance of a therapist. But getting some of them to adhere to those rules is difficult. Clients sometimes resort to self flim-flams, sabotages, and other resistant behaviors highlighted elsewhere in this book. Such attitudinal barriers can undermine the effectiveness of the logical analysis approach. If such a problem is going to arise, it will first become manifest during Step #3, finding the meaning of concepts.

Scientific attitudes is a strategy for anticipating and circumventing a client's resistant behaviors. The main point of this technique is that clients should be taught to value the kind of objectivity that characterizes scientific inquiry and to regard their own rules of evidence in that light.

Method

1. Present a series of scientific attitudes, such as those presented on the following "Attitude Checklist," to your clients. Discuss why each is necessary, and how it is useful in discovering the causes and cures of problems.
2. Obtain your clients' concurrence in using this scientific point of view.
3. When your clients show a contrary attitude during the analytical process, refer to the checklist and ask if they have changed their minds about rules that they had previously approved. Continue the analysis only after you and your clients agree again to the scientific attitudes.

Example. Attitude Check List

1. As best you can, deal with facts as they occur, instead of relying upon opinion.
   Example: Fearing elevators is a fact; believing that elevators cause fear is an opinion.
2. Accept facts which have been substantiated even if they directly contradict our feelings. (We must then work on changing our feelings, instead of twisting the facts to fit them.) Reject the authority of science itself if the facts contradict science orthodoxy. Be intellectually honest. Let the facts contradict the theory no matter how personally distasteful.
   Example: Accepting that your present frustration may be based on being overindulged when young, even though you don't like thinking of yourself as "spoiled."
   Example: Accepting you have a drinking problem even though you hate the idea of being an alcoholic.
3. Refrain from dogmatic conclusions based on insufficient evidence. Don't consider uncontrolled case examples as evidence.
   Example: Don't jump to such conclusions as, "My marriage conflicts cause my agoraphobia. My friend got over her agoraphobia when she got divorced."
4. Recognize the difference between hypotheses and facts.
   Example: "Anger turned inward produces depression" is a hypothesis, not a fact.

5. Remain without an answer until one can be found. Don't just make one up because there is a gap in your understanding. Say that you don't know.

   Example: "I don't know why I lose my temper all the time, but I think it is sexual frustration."

6. Accept no theory a priori or permanently.

   Example: "The cause of people's psychological problems is failure to sufficiently integrate various intrapsychic systems." This hypothesis is subject to change.

7. Reject no theory a priori.

   Example: "It can't be my thoughts causing problems because I don't remember thinking anything." This theory too is subject to change.

8. Search as hard for counter evidence to your theory as you search for evidence for it. Actively attack and challenge your own theories as hard as you challenge contradictory views.

   Example: Find evidence to support the idea that emotions can cause attitudes, as well as the view that attitudes can cause emotions.

9. Examine testable theories. Abandon those theories that cannot conceivably be verified (purely metaphysical) or reframe them into testable propositions. Avoid explanations which are pure invention.

   Example: It may not be possible to test such hypotheses as "Ancient inherited archetypes cause my present emotional responses," or productive to test, "Stress is caused by an asymmetrical alignment of energy forces in the body."

Comment

Scientific attitudes guide clients through logical analysis. The therapist must be careful not to batter clients by inferring they are ignorant or worthless for not believing them.

Further Information

Many of these concepts come from the work of B. F. Skinner (1953).

Several good books and articles on the philosophy of science can help the therapist convey other principles. See Kuhn, 1977; Popper, 1959; Radnitzky, 1970; Suppe, 1974; Toulmin, 1967; Weimer, 1979.

FORMING HYPOTHESES

Principles

A great many clients have difficulty reasoning inductively—i.e., forming general hypotheses and conclusions from specific facts. Instead, they form hypotheses and conclusions about themselves, other people and life in general based on intuitive guesses, rather than facts. Often these guesses lead them to interpret events erroneously, and this in turn creates emotional turmoil. However, if these clients are taught some of the principles of hypothesis formation, they can learn to stop making random assumptions, thus short-circuiting the emotional pain these assumptions so often produce.

Method and Example

1. Teach clients inductive reasoning by giving them a series of premises and asking them to find the most reasonable hypothesis to explain these premises. Discuss the principles in the examples and correct any mistakes.

   Example 1. What is Alfred afraid of?
   Facts:

   - Alfred is afraid of the family cocker spaniel.
   - Alfred is not afraid of fish.
   - Alfred is afraid of rabbits.
   - Alfred is not afraid of frogs.
   - Alfred is not afraid of his parakeets.
   - Alfred is not afraid of cockroaches.
   - Alfred is afraid of his mom's mink coat.
   - Alfred is not afraid of his dad's leather vest.
   - Alfred is afraid of bats.
   - Alfred is afraid of bears.
   - Alfred is not afraid of snakes.

   Comment: Although any inductive conclusion is by its nature disputable, a parsimonious hypothesis is that Alfred is afraid of fur.

Example 2. What is a likely trigger for Mary's anxiety attacks?
Facts:

• Mary got anxious at a supermarket with long lines.
• Mary did not feel anxious watching a movie with her friends.
• Mary got anxious at a busy restaurant.
• Mary did not get anxious hostessing a large bridge party when her husband was out of town.
• Mary got anxious in an empty sidewalk restaurant.
• Mary did not get anxious in a supermarket with her husband.
• Mary did not feel anxious watching TV by herself in her house.

Comment: There are several possible triggers, but this client was afraid of being away from home by herself.

2. As appropriate, use symbols, rather than words, to teach inductive reasoning.

Example 1. Imagine that the letters A through L in the lefthand column represent stimuli which are possible triggers to anxiety, and that the symbols in the righthand column are your emotional response to these triggers (+ = anxiety; − = no anxiety). Using the information in both columns, identify the stimuli most likely to cause anxiety.

	Stimuli			*Emotional Response*
A	D	G	K	+
A	E	H	K	−
C	E	H	L	−
C	D	I	K	+
B	D	G	J	−

Comment: Using inductive logic, apparently the presence of D and K together causes anxiety. Either one alone is not enough.

Example 2

	Stimuli			*Emotional Response*
A	F	G	K	+
A	D	I	K	−
C	E	G	L	−
A	F	I	K	+
C	D	I	J	−
A	E	H	L	−
B	D	G	J	+

Comment: B or F are sufficient—though not necessary—causes.

Example 3

Stimuli				Emotional Response
A	D	G	J	+
B	F	I	K	+
B	F	ITL	–	
C	E	H	J	–
A	E	H	J	+
A	D	G	K	–
B	F	G	J	–
C	F	G	L	+
C	E	I	K	–
C	D	G	L	+

Comment: Anxious responses are caused by the presence of (A and J), (B and K) or (C and L). Several combinations are sufficient; none is necessary.

3. After the client has learned some of the abstract principles underlying inductive logic, list the various combinations of triggers for the client's emotional responses. Record them one at a time. Make a complete list.
4. Record those instances when the anxiety occurred (+), and when it didn't occur (–).
5. After you have compiled a complete list of stimuli and responses (A to L; + and –), analyze the relationships among them to identify the client's most likely anxiety triggers.

Comment

Most clients need to be taught only the most basic principles of inductive logic. This material may be presented in successive approximations. For instance:

What is the cause of + ?

A	B		+
B	C		–

What is the cause in this example?

A	B	C	+
C	D	E	–
A	D	F	–

The therapist starts with these simple examples and gradually works up to the more complex examples. But even in these simpler cases the complexity of inductive logic is apparent. In the first example, it is hypothesized that

A is the cause of +. But logically it also could be that the combination of A and B, with C absent, causes + to happen, or that B and C prevent + from happening, or that whenever B comes second in the sequence, it causes +. In everyday practice, however, we generally select the most parsimonious explanation. See Quine and Ullian, 1978.

Further Information

The use of inductive reasoning in cognitive psychology can be found in the works of Bruner, Goodnow, and Austin (1956), Haygood and Bourne (1965), Johnson (1972), Popper (1959), Trabasso and Bower (1968), Watson and Johnson-Laird (1972). The more complex examples are transposed into clinical cases from the work of Anderson (1980).

FINDING THE CAUSES

Principles

Your clients are now ready for Step #4 of the logical analysis process. Their damaging beliefs have been restated in analyzable form and defined in concrete terms. The rules for processing evidence for or against those beliefs have been established, and your clients have made a commitment to adhere to those rules. The analytic process can now begin in earnest.

The first step to be taken during this analytic phase should be to confirm that the relationship among the variables in an analyzable statement is a valid one. Hence, in the trial expression, "I'm afraid of snow!" it is necessary to confirm that the fear is properly associated with *snow*, and not with some other phenomenon that might have been manifested coincidently with the snowfall, such as *cold*, or *cloudy skies*, or even some sort of proprioceptive image, like a painful recollection from youth that occurred on a snowy day. Potentially dozens of phenomena that might occur immediately before or during, a snowfall might provoke the negative emotion.

In order to determine if snow is the true source of the negative emotion in our example, clients and their therapists will have to be able to sort through a wide variety of possible causes of the fear. In our own effort to address this problem, we have devised a strategy for helping clients and their counselors to meet this challenge. That strategy centers on the use of Table 4. We cannot *guarantee* that the use of this table will always pinpoint the true source of damaging beliefs, but we have found it to be useful far more often than not, and it does introduce a much-needed degree of efficiency into this phase of the logical analysis process.

Method

1. Using a chart similar to the one presented in Table 4, list the possible causes in the extreme lefthand column. They could be events, thoughts, perceptions or other emotions that immediately precede the client's negative emotions. List each possible cause on the chart.
2. Discover ten situations in which the anxiety occurred. List those situations separately on the bottom of the chart. In most cases, have your clients pick the ten worst anxieties that they have experienced. In other cases, it might be wiser to select the ten most recent anxieties.
3. Find ten more instances as similar as possible to the first ten, except that the anxiety did *not* occur. Record them also on the bottom.
4. Then go through all the possible causes and check whether they were present in the anxious and non-anxious situations.
5. A cause should be present in all anxious situations, but never occur in any non-anxious events. The greater the differences between the two types of situations (10–0), the more likely the variable causes it. In actual practice, however, such clear differentiation rarely occurs; a 9–1 or 8–2 contrast is more common.
6. Logically the chart assumes that if A causes B, then A should be present every time B occurs and it should never occur when B isn't present. But the therapist should consider several other possibilities when searching for causes.

   a. A is not the cause of B but a part of B. For example, a rapid heartbeat may always be present whenever the client gets anxious not because it causes anxiety but because an increased heartrate is one symptom of anxiety.
   b. A and B are related because B is the cause of A. Avoidance behavior is often related to anxiety, but it is far more likely that anxiety causes the avoidance than the other way around.
   c. A and B are highly correlated because a third factor (X) causes both. A fight with a spouse may cause both anger and anxiety. The two are associated because of X, not because one emotion causes the other.

Table 4
Finding Causes

POSSIBLE CAUSES	+ Panic										− Panic										(+)-(−)
situations	1	2	3	4	5	6	7	8	9	10	1	2	3	4	5	6	7	8	9	10	
1. I felt guilty	0	0	0	0	0	0	0	1	0	0	0	0	0	1	1	0	1	0	0	0	−2
2. I was passive	0	0	1	0	0	0	1	0	0	0	0	0	0	0	0	1	1	0	0	0	0
3. I felt angry	0	0	0	0	1	0	0	0	0	0	0	0	0	0	0	0	1	0	0	0	0
4. Worried about my heart	1	1	0	1	1	1	1	1	1	1	1	1	0	0	1	0	0	1	0	1	+4
5. Was very tired	0	0	0	0	0	0	0	0	0	0	0	0	0	0	0	0	1	0	0	0	−1
6. Felt inferior	0	0	1	1	0	0	1	1	1	1	1	0	0	0	1	1	1	1	1	1	−1
7. Negative external stimuli	0	0	1	0	0	0	0	0	0	0	0	0	0	0	0	1	0	0	0	0	0
8. Fear of criticism	1	0	1	0	0	0	1	0	1	0	1	0	0	0	1	1	0	0	0	1	0
9. Enclosed space	1	0	0	0	0	0	0	0	0	1	1	0	0	0	0	0	0	1	0	1	−1
10. Was trapped	0	1	0	0	1	1	1	0	0	1	0	0	0	0	1	0	0	0	0	0	+4
11. Fear of failure	1	0	1	1	0	1	0	1	1	0	1	0	0	1	0	1	0	0	1	0	+2
12. Missed my medication	0	0	1	0	0	0	1	0	0	0	0	0	0	0	0	1	0	0	0	0	+1
13. Had too much to eat	0	0	0	1	0	0	0	0	1	0	0	0	1	0	0	1	0	0	0	0	0
14. Felt strange and unreal	1	0	1	1	0	1	1	1	1	1	0	0	0	0	0	1	0	0	0	0	+7
15. Something unexpected	0	0	0	0	1	0	0	1	0	0	0	1	0	0	0	0	1	0	0	1	−1
16. Exercised	0	1	0	0	0	0	1	0	0	0	1	1	1	1	1	1	0	1	0	1	−6
17. Increase in stimulation	0	0	1	0	0	0	1	0	0	0	0	0	0	0	0	1	1	1	0	0	−1
18. Not enough sleep	0	1	0	0	0	1	0	0	0	1	0	0	1	1	0	0	0	0	0	0	0
19. Marital problems	0	0	1	0	0	0	1	1	1	1	0	0	0	0	1	1	1	0	1	0	+1
20. Sexually frustrated	0	1	0	0	0	0	1	0	0	0	0	0	1	0	0	0	1	0	0	0	0
21. Fear of losing control	1	1	1	1	0	1	1	1	1	1	0	0	0	1	0	0	0	0	0	0	+8
22. Financial problems	0	0	1	0	1	0	1	1	0	0	0	0	0	0	1	1	1	1	1	1	−2
23. Physically sick	0	0	0	0	1	0	1	1	1	0	0	0	1	0	0	0	0	0	0	0	−3
24. Depressed	0	0	0	0	1	1	1	1	0	0	0	0	0	0	1	1	0	1	0	1	0
25. Was assertive	0	0	0	0	1	0	0	0	0	0	1	1	1	1	0	0	0	1	1	0	−5
26. Ate a lot of sugar	0	0	0	1	0	0	0	0	1	0	0	0	1	0	0	1	0	0	0	0	0
27. Fought with spouse	0	0	0	0	1	0	0	0	0	0	0	0	0	0	0	0	1	0	0	0	0
28. Was being perfectionistic	0	1	0	1	0	1	1	1	0	1	0	1	0	1	1	0	0	0	0	1	+2
29. Felt lonely	1	1	1	0	1	1	0	0	1	1	1	1	1	0	0	1	1	0	0	1	+1
30. Thought of going insane	1	1	0	1	0	0	1	1	1	1	0	0	0	1	0	0	0	0	0	0	+6
31. Failed at a task	0	0	1	0	0	0	1	0	0	0	0	0	0	0	1	0	0	0	0	1	0
32. Away from home	1	1	1	1	0	1	1	0	0	1	1	1	1	1	0	1	1	0	0	1	0
33. Morning	1	1	1	0	0	1	1	0	0	0	0	0	1	0	0	0	0	1	0	0	+3
34. Afternoon	0	0	0	1	1	0	0	0	0	0	0	0	0	0	1	1	0	0	0	1	−1
35. Evening	0	0	0	0	0	0	0	1	1	1	1	1	0	1	0	0	1	0	1	0	−2
36. Felt confident	0	0	0	0	0	0	0	1	0	1	1	1	1	0	1	1	1	0	1	1	−6
37. Worried about future event	1	0	1	1	0	1	1	0	1	1	0	1	0	1	1	0	1	1	1	0	+1

Situations where client panicked	Situations where client did not panicked
1. In a class room	1. Taking test in class
2. Exercising at health club	2. Exercising at club
3. Visiting a bank	3. Shopping at store
4. Spent afternoon with relatives	4. Visiting my mom
5. At home after busy morning	5. Saturday afternoon
6. At church	6. At church picnic
7. Speech at school	7. School seminar
8. Party for friends at home	8. Friends visiting
9. Right before I went to sleep	9. Late at night
10. Driving in a car	10. In a car

    d. A may be present every time B happens simply because A is ubiquitous and present all the time (a 10–10 score). Clients may feel chronically inferior, but they feel this even when they aren't anxious. Inferiority is, therefore, not a cause of the anxiety.

    e. Occasionally you will find the opposite score (0–10), where A is never present when B occurs, but is always there without B. Such a factor may counteract B. For example, one client never got anxious when she was assertive. Her assertiveness may have prevented her from feeling anxious.

Example

In the Preface I mention that we formed some of the foundations of cognitive restructuring by studying agoraphobic clients. Our basic method of finding the stimuli to their panic attacks was using the "Finding Causes" worksheets. For two months we had our clients chart their anxieties, carefully recording any events that *preceded* them. Table 4 is a typical client record.

The table shows several possible causes. Causes can be found among those variables which occurred far more frequently in the panic reactions than when the emotion didn't occur. Several have high scores—fear of losing control (+ 8), felt strange and unreal (+ 7), thoughts of going insane (+ 6), worried about heart (+ 4), and feeling trapped (+ 4).

After discussion with several clients, we decided "feeling strange" and "heart concern" did not cause panic, but were part of the symptoms of anxiety (disorientation and increased heartrate). "Losing control" and "fear of going insane" always preceded the panic, so these two variables possibly caused it. Later analysis with other clients showed that most agoraphobics rated these as key variables.

Two variables seem to prevent the panic—exercise (– 6) and feeling confident (– 6). And several ubiquitous agents didn't cause anxiety because they were constantly present. Although before the survey clients felt these factors were causes, the survey convinced them that they were not. "Feeling inferior," "worried about a future event," "feeling lonely," and "marital problems" were present whether the clients panicked or not.

Comment

The survey controls too few variables to confidently find "true" causes. Clinically, however, clients can often identify those variables they superstitiously believed were causes.

Further Information

Descriptions of the theoretical conditions necessary to find causes are included in the general works of Brown and Ghiselli, 1955; Ray and Ravizza, 1981; and Simon, 1978.

The chart graphically represents some of John Stuart Mill's analysis of causes (see Nagel, 1950).

GRAPH ANALYSIS

Principles

Graph analysis is one of the basic topics covered in freshman statistics courses, but few mental health professionals actually employ it in their therapeutic practices. This technique might actually be used *before* the "finding the causes" exercise that was just discussed, depending upon a particular client's circumstances.

Suppose for a moment that you and your client are able to identify 20 or more variables that *might* be associated with a damaging belief—far too many to be analyzed within a reasonable period of time. You need some way to quickly determine which of the variables are worthy of being seriously considered as possible causes of the negative emotion.

An acquaintance of mine—an engineer who was working on the Apollo program for NASA—reminded me of the value of graph analysis several years ago. One day my engineer friend watched me for quite some time while I was running correlational analyses on many variables. He then suggested that it would be a lot easier and save a lot of costly calculating time, if I would get at least a rough idea of whether the variables were related before I tried to correlate them. He reminded me that I could do that by using graphs. All I had to do was to get some graphing paper and plot, on the vertical Y axis (ordinate), the intensity of each variable and, on the horizontal X axis (abscissa), its occurrence over time. Each variable, in turn, could be plotted on the same graph. Those lines that had similar or exact opposite curves were probably related and worth a correlational analysis, while the others were discarded. The total number of likely variables was thus greatly reduced to a far more manageable quantity.

Hence, aching bunions, a feeling of nausea, and the occurrence of certain holidays might be seen to have nothing to do with one's fear of snowfall, while low self-confidence and a reduction in one's personal mobility because of adverse travel conditions might correlate very highly with the negative emotion.

We use graph analysis often, usually with good results. It is also a valuable technique to teach clients, who can actually prepare and plot their own graphs as often as they find them useful.

Method

1. Ask your client to draw a line on a graph paper about how generally happy he was during different periods of his life.
2. On the Y axis, chart the intensity of his happiness using high, average or low, or +10, 0, −10.
3. On the X axis, record his age from birth to the present.
4. Have the client plot the variables you believe may be related to happiness on the same graft.
5. Discuss the similarity and differences between the lines.
6. Any client variables can be charted on the graph.

Example

In Figure 15 happiness and the quality of the client's love relationships seem to be highly correlated. The first attachment was with his mother, but this did not seem to make up for some negative school experience. From then on,

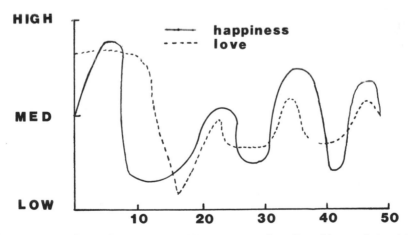

Figure 15. Correlation between overall happiness and quality of love relationships.

however, his love relationships seemed to parallel almost exactly his life contentment.

The graph in Figure 16 suggests a negative correlation between happiness and dependency. The more dependent the client was on others, the less happy she was. This client was sexually abused as a child and physically abused by her two husbands. Only when she was free of them and in control of her own life was she happy.

Public recognition doesn't seem to be related to happiness for the client whose graph is shown in Figure 17. She was an artist and originally thought she wanted fame, but the graph suggests that they are independent. Another graph for this client indicates that the key variable related to happiness is likely to be her creativity on the job. She was an extremely talented artist, happy only when she pursued her art work. It didn't seem to matter how much money she made or whether she became famous.

This client (Figure 18) suffered from agoraphobia, so we charted his panic attacks. Other therapists had suggested that the cause was his marriage, but, as can be seen by the graph, that is unlikely. The likely cause is his general self-confidence level. When he liked himself and felt he was worthwhile, his panic reduced significantly, but when he felt he wasn't good enough, he got panicky.

Comment

Any time period—an hour, day, week or year—can be graphed.

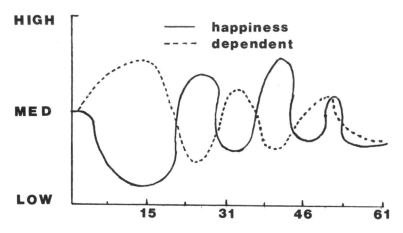

Figure 16. Correlation between happiness and dependency.

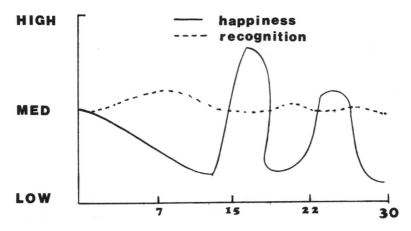

Figure 17. Public recognition correlated with happiness.

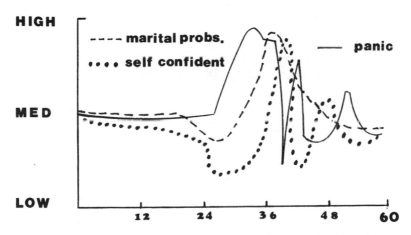

Figure 18. Relationship among panic, marital problems and self confidence.

_____

DISPUTING IRRATIONAL BELIEFS (DIB'S) ANALYSIS

Principles

The DIB'S (Disputing Irrational Beliefs) Analysis is a simple but powerful technique that is often helpful to clients who have difficulty gauging the truth or falseness of their own beliefs. With this technique, which was developed by Albert Ellis, clients are asked to articulate the thought in analyzable form and then to answer a series of open-ended questions about that belief.

Certain clients will need to bolster their objective thinking skills and to cling tightly to their rules of evidence during this exercise, if it is to be useful. Analysis requires precise thinking and a scrupulous avoidance of sidetracking, which are difficult to master. DIB'S can be useful for those clients that get entangled with higher level abstractions.

Method

1. Instruct your clients to answer the following questions when analyzing their beliefs.

    a. What belief bothers you?
    b. Can you rationally support this belief?
    c. What evidence exists for its falseness?
    d. Does any evidence exist for its truth?
    e. Realistically and objectively, what is likely to happen if you think this way?
    f. What could continue to happen if you don't think this way?

2. Have your clients practice applying this series of questions to each of their beliefs. They can do this at home, but they must come to subsequent sessions prepared to report the results of their analyses to you. Where difficulties persist, you can employ other cognitive techniques in addressing those problems.

Example

Richard came to see me because of depression and grief over the breakup of his relationship with his girlfriend. They had been lovers for about two years. The relationship had never gone well, but they both clung to each other simply because they were both lonely and the other was at least someone around. But they fought with each other all the time about their differences, each claiming that the other was wrong and should change. Finally they inflicted so much punishment on each other that the relationship became far more aversive than reinforcing. At this point the relationship ended.

Usually in this type of depression, the client believes that he wasn't good enough for her, and that's why she left. On my advice, he used DIB'S analysis to look at his belief.

1. *What belief bothers me?* I think I am not worthy of her.
2. *Can you rationally support this belief? And what evidence exists for its falseness?* No. I can't support it. My goodness or badness is a multidimensional thing. It is a totally subjective view on my part. My conclusions would be totally dependent on what aspect of her I compared with what aspect of me. In addition, there would be no way my "basic" worthwhileness could be rated or compared.
3. *Does any evidence exist for its truth?* There is no evidence that I am not worthy of her. But she does have some traits superior to mine. She is more sociable and more popular, although I think more clearly and act more responsibly. We are both equally worthy.
4. *Realistically and objectively what is likely to happen?* I will likely sooner or later forget her and meet someone more compatible.
5. *What could continue to happen if I think this way?* I'll continue to feel unworthy. I'll go out with other women feeling unworthy, and I'll continue to act without confidence so that they will reject me more frequently. When I get rejected again I'll feel more and more unworthy, etc.

Further Information

This technique is a variation of Ellis' procedure. The original can be studied by examining Ellis, 1973, 1974, 1985; Ellis and Whiteley, 1979.

———

LOGICAL FALLACIES

Principles

When our hypothetical client mentioned in the introduction to this chapter says, "Snow is to be feared because it is dangerous!" the intensity of that declaration is itself an indication of his depth of conviction. In fact, his belief that the statement is true makes it true for him, regardless of the absence of any objective evidence. Our client knows that it is true because he has heard many people say that it is, or because he knows of a couple instances (out of all the snowfalls throughout the history of mankind) in which snowfall has been associated with death and destruction, or because he feels that he would be doing society a disservice by treating the prospect of snow too casually and thus exposing innocent citizens to a potential danger. Any or all of these could be reasons why the client *knows* that snow is dangerous, but none of them is *proof* of that assertion. Indeed, they are all classic examples of fallacious thinking.

Logical fallacies are unsubstantiated assertions that are often delivered with a conviction that makes them *sound* as though they were proven facts. Some of these fallacies derive from clients' perceptual distortions (e.g., overgeneralizations), others from psychological errors (e.g., catastrophizing), while still others are logical distortions (e.g., a priori thinking). Sometimes fallacies result when people mistake correlations for causalities.

Whatever their origins, fallacies can take on a special life of their own when they are popularized in the media and thus become part of a national credo. Once they have achieved that stature, they hold a special appeal for those who seek the approval of others by resorting to these commonly held misperceptions.

Fallacies are most likely to creep into the interactions between client and therapist during Step #4 of the logical analysis process, when the client is manipulating the evidence that has been amassed for or against a damaging belief. "Better safe than sorry," our client might say, quoting a popular platitude, without recognizing that the platitude has nothing to do with the rules of evidence that he has established, and therefore cannot be advanced as proof of the claim that "snow is to be feared."

The best way to teach clients about logical fallacies during this analytical phase is by calling their attention to such utterances the moment they are expressed and immediately pointing out how they contribute *nothing* to our evaluation or whether a belief is true or false. More often than not, they are merely diversions that help clients avoid coming to grips with a lifetime's accumulation of mistaken perceptions. Put all of the logical fallacies you can assemble on one side of a scale and one piece of solid evidence on the other, and the scale will instantly tip in favor of the evidence.

Method

Once clients come to recognize how essentially vacuous logical fallacies are, the best way to teach them to avoid resorting to these linguistic diversions is by presenting them with examples and encouraging them to counter every fallacy they utter or hear until they become satiated with the pointlessness of these assertions. Following is a list of common types of logical fallacies, their definitions and some examples of each.

Example. List of Logical Fallacies

Sensationalism
Simple, innocent emotions that happen to almost everyone are built up into terrible, overwhelming, psychiatric emergencies.

• "I must be having a depression because I feel sad after my vacation."
• "It's dangerous to sometimes get nervous."

Overgeneralization
A few instances of a category are taken as representing the total category.

• "I am inferior to Mike because he always beats me in racketball."
• "Anybody who can't spell is stupid."

Personalizing
Viewing random events as a personal attack on oneself.

• "I broke my leg because God is punishing me for past sins."
• "There is a good reason for everything that happens to a person."

Anthropomorphism
Attributing human characteristics to inanimate objects.

- "The car refused to budge."
- "The thunder boomed angrily."

Permatizing
Making something temporary into something permanent.

- "I am going to be scared forever."
- "I'll never be happy."

Fault-finding
Looking for a person (others or self) to blame when something goes wrong.

- "It's my (or my spouse's) fault that the marriage didn't last."
- "All criminals are produced by bad parents."

Pathologizing
Calling a learned reaction a disease.

- "Anybody who is anxious all the time is really sick."
- "Overaggressiveness is a disease."

Perfectionism
Picking a theoretically conceivable standard for oneself or others, even though practically no one has ever been able to achieve it, and using it as the common measure for a person's worth.

- "I should never make mistakes."
- "I have to be better than everybody else, in everything."

Dichotomous Thinking
Dividing a continuum into two mutually exclusive parts (also called all or nothing, or good and bad thinking).

- "Abortion is either right or wrong."
- "If it's worth doing, it's worth doing well."
- "In this world you are either a winner or loser."
- "Some men have it and some men don't."

"Awfulizing"
Looking for the worst possible outcome of any event.

- "This pain in my leg means I have cancer."
- "My husband is late; he must be having an affair."
- "If I don't get an 'A' in this class, I'll never get into medical school."

"Musturbation"
  Making "wants" into "musts," "oughts," and "shoulds."

- "I have to get her back."
- "I need to become a great actress to ever be happy."
- "I must be sure to decide."

Entitlement
  Claiming an exceptional privilege that doesn't exist (the prince in disguise syndrome).

- "I shouldn't have to put up with all the petty things they make me do at work."
- "It's unfair that I have to show my driver's license to cash a check."
- "Why did this have to happen to me?"

Psychologizing
  Finding psychological causes for events, while ignoring other causes.

- "I bumped into the table because I was trying to hurt myself."
- "My sore shoulder must be caused by tension."
- "I forgot his name because I'm blocking it."
- "You're single because you're afraid to get married."
- "If you want to be rich, you would be rich."

Nonparsimonious Reasoning
  Choosing the more complex explanation over the simplest.

- "You don't like for me to criticize you because you had a love-hate relationship with your father, and all men represent father figures to you. So you're just transferring your infantile repressed hostility onto me."

Reification
  Assuming an abstraction (e.g., personality traits, IQ, schizophrenia) stands for a real, concrete entity.

- "He lacks courage."
- "He is basically lazy."
- "Justice, beauty and virtue are the ultimate form of reality" (Greek philosophers).
- "She has less willpower than others."
- "I'm having a nervous breakdown."

Homocentric Error
Assuming that the human race has a unique place in the order of things.

- "God made this planet for human beings."
- "The sun revolves around the earth."

Egocentric Error
Concluding that since you are the center of your world, you are the center of everyone else's.

- "Everybody should treat me nice."
- "I should get what I want in life."
- "The world ought to be fair."

Subjective Error
Believing that other people's behavior and emotions are caused by you.

- "I am sorry that I made you feel depressed."
- "I am making my husband unhappy."

Apriorisms
Deducing facts from principles instead of inducing principles from facts.

- "Women have fewer teeth than men, because they have smaller jaws." (Aristotle)
- "Melting snow could not cause the Nile to rise, because the equatorial regions are too warm for snow." (Plato)
- "When people are nice to you they are just trying to get something."

Overpowering
Attempting to solve all problems by bulldozing over them.

- "When the going gets tough, the tough get going."

• "Alcoholism can be solved by willpower alone."
• "All you need is heart."

Possibilities = Probabilities
If it is possible for an event to occur, then it is probable.

• "If something can go wrong, it will."
• "I should worry about getting diseases from plants."
• "Flying in planes is dangerous."

Anecdotal Evidence
Considering one uncontrolled case as proof of a larger principle.

• "I know someone who . . . "

Arguing Ad Hominem
Attacking the opponent instead of the opponent's argument; also called "damning the source" and "pointing to another's wrong."

• "If you aren't a recovered alcoholic, then you can't help me."
• "You can't know what you are talking about because you don't have a college degree."
• "What right do you have to give advice? You have never run a corporation."

Ipse Dixit
Asserting something is true because an authority says so; appealing to authority.

• "Freud said . . . , Skinner said . . . , Ellis said . . . , Mc Mullin says. . . . "
• "A famous study at an Ivy League college proves. . . . "
• "Four out of five doctors recommend. . . . "

Competition
Judging one's worth by always comparing to another.

• "I am not skilled because there are many people who can do better."
• "Winning is everything."

Mystification
Explaining physical events by metaphysical or esoteric interpretations.

- "Memories of past lives obtained by age regression hypnosis are evidence for a former life."
- "Many of the activities chronicled in the Old Testament about the Exodus were caused by a comet which later became the planet Venus."
- "Out-of-body experiences prove life continues after death."
- "The metal alloy Nitinol can be bent by psychic energy."
- "People can view objects from a distance even though they do not have direct physical sight of the object (remote viewing)."
- "The Nazca lines in Peru were landing fields for spaceships baring ancient astronauts."
- "The blue sky, the flickering of stars, the Northern Lights, and sun spot activity are caused by orgone energy, the basic élan of life."
- "A mother's experiences a day after conception will leave an imprint on the unconscious mind of the fetus."

Correlation = Causation

Assuming that if two variables are associated one causes the other.

- "Anger at self causes all depression."
- "Planes cause fear since I only have fear in planes."
- "Thunder causes lightning."

Internal Verification

If something feels true, it is. The stronger one feels, the more certain one can be.

- "I know he is the man for me. I can feel it in my bones."
- "Get in touch with your gut feeling. That will tell you what to do."

Ignoring Counter Evidence

Assuming that all a theory needs is good body of evidence to validate it. (That is not enough; one must also show that the evidence for a theory is stronger than the evidence against it.)

- "Since some subjects have obtained a high hit rate in psi research, extrasensory perception has been proven." (Rhine)
- "Since monoamine oxidase inhibitors, tricyclics, and alprazolam have reduced some clients' panic reactions, all panics are totally biologically based and psychological therapy of any sort is unnecessary."

Oversocialized Thinking

Overculturated persons are people who do not think independently of society's values; they uncritically accept the general cultural beliefs. A form of this fallacy called "arguing ad populum" makes statements to appeal to the common prejudices of the masses.

- "A woman's place is in the home."
- "My country right or wrong."
- "Marriage should be 'til death do us part."
- "You can't trust anyone over 30."
- "Spare the rod and spoil the child."
- "Real men don't eat quiche."

Finding the Good Reason

Defending a position by picking the most favorable sounding argument, rather than asserting the most logical or empirically correct one.

- "I haven't married her for five years because I want to make sure she has the fullest opportunity to grow and enhance her life independently of me."
- "I criticize him a lot because I love him, and I know that if he doesn't correct his mistakes other people will always reject him and he will be miserable."
- "We are aiding certain governments, not to protect our economic interests, but because we are safeguarding the citizens' freedom from totalitarian foreign oppression."

Self-Righteousness

Believing that good intentions influence the validity of one's position.

- "But I was only trying to help you."
- "Extremism in the defense of liberty is no vice."
- "Violence is virtuous if its intent is to remove injustice."
- "It's true because I meant well."

Sidetracking

Changing the subject of a discussion to a non-germane, irrelevant issue to hide the weakness of one's position. These strategies are commonly referred to as "red herrings."

a. Dishonest questions: Rapidly asking a whole series of questions, so that the opponent must stop the argument to answer them.

- "Why are you criticizing me for being late? Did you have a bad day? Why is this so important to you? Are you having that PMS problem again? Have you gone to the doctor about it? Is there something else you are REALLY angry about?"

b. Pointing to another's wrong.

- "Since you accuse me of being fat, what's that spare tire doing around your waist?"

c. Archeological blaming: Dredging up a past wrong.

- "You say I was rude at the party. What about last year's party where you embarrassed the hell out of me?"

d. Emotive language: Trying to get the other person emotionally upset by using emotionally loaded phrases.

- "You are so stupid, ugly and dumb you can't possibly know a goddamn thing!"

e. Judo approach: Overagreeing with a complaint so that the other person withdraws it.

- "You are right! I have been cruel and unkind to you. You have a perfect right to be so upset. I am really a hard person to live with. I don't see how you do it."

f. Anger attack: Trying to sidetrack people by getting angry at them. Most people will respond to the anger and drop their position.

- "How dare you criticize me! You have no damn right to do so."

g. Invincible ignorance: Totally denying there is any problem what so ever.

- "I have absolutely no idea what you are talking about. I didn't have anything to drink at the party."

Forestalling Disgreement

Phrasing one's point of view so that it would be difficult or embarrassing to disagree with it.

- "Everyone should know that. . . . "
- "As any fool can see. . . . "
- "It is obvious to anyone with any brains that. . . . "
- "Unless you don't know anything about the subject, it is clear that. . . . "

Tried and True
   Suggesting that a belief is true simply because it represents the traditional view.

- "What was good enough for my father is good enough for me."
- "Don't change horses in midstream."
- "That's our policy."
- "It's always been done this way."

Impressing with Large Numbers
   Assuming that a thought is true if many people believe it.

- "Fifty thousand Americans can't be wrong."
- "Counseling isn't helpful because I can name ten people who went for therapy and none of them got better."
- "In a recent survey, hundreds of doctors recommended that. . . . "
- "Get with it! Everybody who's anybody believes this."

Begging the Question
   Making statements which sound as if they are asserting a cause and effect relationship, but which are simply restating the same concept; a form of tautology which takes for granted the very thing in dispute.

- "I avoid flying because I am a coward" (part of the definition of 'coward' is to avoid things unnecessarily).
- "Anybody with this much anxiety must be crazy" (the client's definition of crazy is anybody with strong uncontrolled emotions).
- "I am not a real man because I didn't fight him." (Client had an adolescent definition of being a male. "Men" would beat up anybody who got in their way.)

Appeal to Ignorance
   Assuming that if I don't understand something, then no one can.

- "I can't figure out why I get depressed. It must be random bad luck."
- "This conditioning crap is just so much bullshit. All you have to do is take the bull by the horns and get some willpower and courage to overcome your fears."

Further Information

The fallacies come from a variety of sources. Some are malapropisms, two come from RET (Ellis, 1985), but most can be found in a variety of books on logic; see Fearnside and Holther (1959). Some of the examples come from Gardner (1957, 1981), Sprague de Camp (1983), and Taylor (1949).

6
Adjuncts

In each of the previous five chapters, we have focused upon a major category of cognitive restructuring techniques: countering, perceptual shifting, conditioning, paradoxical methods, and logical analysis. The reader will recognize that this attempt to batch problems and techniques is an artificial imposition of order. In reality, clients don't come to us in categories, so we cannot respond to them in that way. One client might have a range of problems, with symptoms relating to several of these categories. The therapist then assumes the role of cognitive alchemist, mixing and matching techniques and principles freely as the needs of his clients dictate.

Besides those already presented, there is a potpourri of techniques that do not fit neatly into any of the above categories, and that are designed for use in supplementing many or all of them. Hence, these are called "adjunct" techniques. They are other ingredients for the alchemist's brew, distinguished from the rest mainly because they can be applied more generally across categories in meeting client needs.

In our discussion of adjuncts, we begin with a focus on "Crisis Cognitive Therapy." Any client's problem could begin with, or evolve into, a crisis, with the client reaching a point of utter desperation. The cognitive therapy response to these situations differs slightly, but in an important way, from that of other mental health professionals.

The section on "Images Techniques" discusses the need for bolstering client skills in mental imagery, a valuable adjunct to any of the previously discussed techniques, as are the techniques covered under "Handling Client Sabotages."

Our section on the "Use of Altered States" will prove helpful in treating certain client conditions, and resorting to "Historical Perspectives" is almost unavoidable in conjunction with most of the other CRT techniques.

The last next technique presented in this chapter, "Environmental Practice," is intended to bolster clients' confidence in the effectiveness of cognitive techniques that have been prescribed for them.

CRISIS COGNITIVE THERAPY

Principles

Any mental health professional's immediate response to a client's crisis situation is to take whatever action seems appropriate to insure the client's physical well-being until his or her condition stabilizes. Then other treatments might be applied.

We take a cognitive approach to crises. The goal of this approach is to discover what the client is thinking that has provoked the critical state. If the client who is in crisis has some background in cognitive approaches, an accelerated form of cognitive therapy (CRT) might be used to stabilize the client's condition at a more comfortable level. If the client is new to cognitive therapy, counselors might try a marathon session or resort to traditional crisis intervention approaches initially and then introduce cognitive fundamentals and techniques when stability has been achieved.

Following are four possible cognitive techniques for helping clients in crisis.

Method 1. Quick Perceptual Shift

To help your client form a rapid perceptual shift, arrange all the necessary components.

a. Clearly identify the core perception causing the crisis. Make certain the client sees it clearly.
b. Point out the perception that would remove the crisis if the client believed it.
c. Do not reduce the client's tension level to zero by various ameliorative procedures. Reduction may be necessary, but some negative emotions motivate clients to make the shift.*
d. Search for the key bridge perception that can help carry the client from the old to the new perception. The bridge should be some image, value,

---

*RET has two continua of emotion: the first ranges from 1–99 and includes negative emotions like sorrow, regret, frustration annoyance, etc. and the second begins 101 to infinity, like depression, anxiety, despair, hostility and self-pity. Having two continua shows clients that even strong negative emotions like frustration, annoyance, and displeasure help motivate them while weak motivations of rage and self-downing help restrict them. (Ellis, 1986).

or belief firmly implanted in the client's experience. It should have a strongly positive emotional valence. The bridge must come from the client's experience since time does not allow creating a new one.

e. Confront all sidetracking the client may use to avoid the shift. Examine denials, alibis, excuses, sabotages, and evasions; press for the shift. You may wish to refer to the perceptual shift worksheet (see p. 80) as a guide.

Method 2. Marathon Session

In a severe crisis, spend three or four hours teaching your client cognitive methods. Take no breaks. Flood the client with countering techniques; repeat them until the client comprehends their use. The therapist should dispute the key damaging beliefs causing the crisis, concentrating on the here-and-now perceptions. Sometimes several therapists may work with one client, increasing the persuasiveness of the counters. As in other crisis intervention techniques, the therapist presents an assured, self-confident manner, to enhance the client's feelings of support. The therapist assumes control of the session and actively directs the client's responses.

Method 3. Brief Cognitive Restructuring

Prepare a series of questions for your client to answer. Keep the client focusing on the content of the questions. Directly and actively intervene to help your client develop effective responses.

- What are you feeling at this moment?
- What triggers elicit your emotions?
- What are you telling yourself at this moment that is causing you to feel upset?
- What other thoughts underlie this belief?
- If the thoughts are false, what is the key untruth?
- What evidence do you have against it?
- What are your best arguments disputing the thought?
- What practical method can you use to help convince yourself of the falseness of your thoughts?
- If the thoughts are true, what constructive steps can you take to change, avoid, or cope with the situation?

Method 4. Other Cognitively Oriented Crisis Techniques

As in other crisis intervention methods, the cognitive therapist must immediately intervene in an active, directive manner (Greenstone & Leviton,

1979, 1980, 1983; Rosenbluh, 1974). Several CRT techniques can be adapted to this style.

1. *Alternative attitudes and anti-catastrophic thinking:* Show clients less disastrous alternatives to their fears.
2. *Coping statements:* Give your crisis clients a series of self-statements that they can use to cope with the immediate crisis. For example: "Distressing but not dangerous." "Ignore trying to solve all your problems, just work on this one." "Spoil yourself right now." "This is not a question of sickness or guilt; it is a matter of finding a solution." "I will solve this just as I have solved the other crises in my life."
3. *Label shift:* Change negative labels like "bad," "sick," "nervous breakdown," "going crazy" to neutral ones like "mistaken," "upset," "confused."
4. *Rational beliefs:* Direct much of your intervention towards helping clients form rational judgments of the crisis rather than correcting irrational ones.
5. *Objectifying:* Help clients separate their emotions connected to the crisis from the objective assessment of the crisis.
6. *Here and now:* Concentrate on present perceptions rather than their historical roots.
7. *Covert assertion:* Most clients behave passively in crisis. Teach them how to solve their problems assertively, by practicing assertive coping images.
8. *Paradoxical methods:* In crisis situations avoid the use of paradoxical, or complicated techniques. Clients are already confused and such techniques may bewilder them more. Clients need procedures that are direct, simple, and easy to remember.

Comment

Crisis intervention aims at solving the immediate problem, not removing all maladaptive cognitions and behaviors. The therapist should work only with those perceptions that are exacerbating the present situation. Later, after the crisis is resolved, the therapist can work on the fundamental core beliefs which laid the groundwork for the crisis.

Further Information

For more general crisis intervention techniques see the work of Greenstone and Leviton, 1979, 1980, 1983; Lindemann, 1944; and Rosenbluh, 1974.

IMAGES TECHNIQUES

Principles

Images are used in all aspects of cognitive restructuring; in fact, about a third of the techniques listed in this book use some form of imagery. Techniques such as conditioning and perceptual shifting are based primarily on images and visualization. On the other hand, many techniques, such as countering and logical analysis, modify the *language* of clients far more than their *images*.

Virtually all linguistic techniques can be adapted into image visualization procedures. For many patients, the best approach is to interweave linguistic and imaging techniques, as the combination produces more powerful changes than one approach alone. However, if the therapist discovers that a client is especially adept at visualization, or if the client seems especially responsive to image modification, the therapist may wish to emphasize the image work.

Method

1. To complete the first three steps of CRT, find the client's core metaphysical beliefs, objectively analyze their truth or falseness, and develop a series of counters or rational replacement beliefs (Mc Mullin & Giles, 1981). Although these three steps can use visualization successfully, we have found that language generally is a more comprehensive and flexible tool than visualization in the initial stages of CRT—largely because of the problems clients encounter in visualizing their beliefs. It is difficult, for example, to imagine visual images to accompany a belief such as, "I feel I have no purpose in life." Thus, we recommend the use of linguistic techniques in these first three steps, for the sake of simplicity and efficiency.

2. Determine the imagining capacity of clients by using one of the scales developed by Lazarus (1977, 1982). These scales help determine the client's overall visualization ability and pinpoint areas in need of improvement. They examine the client's ability to create images of self vs. others; past, present, and future; pleasant and unpleasant; and a range of other areas.

3. If clients score low on their visualization capacity, you may wish to employ the image-building techniques described by Lazarus (1982).
4. Select specific images to help your clients shift from irrational perceptions to rational ones. Since images do not involve language, clients can often shift their perceptions more rapidly and completely using visual images rather than semantics. You can use many different types of images to create these perceptual shifts. Following is a list of some of the major types.

- Coping images—in which clients imagine themselves successfully handling difficult situations—are used to correct passive, avoidant thinking. ("Picture asking your boss for a raise.")
- Relaxing images, including nature scenes and sensual visualizations, are used to counter fear-producing, anxious thoughts. These are frequently used as part of cognitive desensitization.
- Mastery images, in which clients imagine themselves completing tasks perfectly, can be paired against irrational thoughts of failure and helplessness. ("Imagine having a successful, happy marriage.")
- Small detail coping images, which focus on specifics, help clients who feel overwhelmed by complex problems. With this method, clients break major problems into a series of minor problems and imagine themselves surmounting each of these smaller difficulties. For instance, a client might break the problem of buying a car into 20 small tasks and imagine successfully completing each consecutive task, beginning with buying *Consumer Reports New Car Guide* and ending with the successful purchase of the ideal vehicle.
- Modeling images may be used if a client has trouble envisioning the component steps in resolving a problem or mastering a skill. In this technique, the client pictures imitating a model who excels in a given task. For instance, the client might analyze and then visualize the forehand stroke of John McEnroe or the debating skill of William F. Buckley
- Noxious images are used in aversive, escape, and avoidant conditioning to counter negative behaviors. ("Picture your smoking causing your kids to get emphysema.")
- Idealized images are used when clients can't think of their final goals. ("Ten years from now, where do you want to be living, and with whom? What do you want to be doing?")
- Rewarding images, often used in operant cognitive restructuring therapy, reinforce realistic thinking. ("What good things could happen to you if you finish the project?")
- Leveling images reduce the negative effects of aversive, fearful visualizations. ("Picture your boss in a duck costume, quacking.")

- Reconceptualizing images changes the interpretation of events. ("Imagine that your wife wasn't angry at you, but had had a bad day at work.")
- Negative vs. positive images — visualizing a negative situation against a positive background, as in higher order conditioning, can change the emotional valence of the situation. ("Imagine being criticized by an antagonist, while sitting in a tropical lagoon on a warm summer day.")
- Corrective images undo mistakes the clients made in the past. ("Picture how you would do it if you had it to do all over again.")
- Generalized corrective images have the client correct all past incidences of a specific type. For example, a passive client might imagine having been assertive every time in his life he had backed away from a problem.
- Future perspective imaging has clients look back to the present situation from some future time, thereby clarifying their values. ("Imagine you are 85 looking back at your life. What do you wish you had done differently?")
- Blowup images teach clients to cope with the worst possible consequences of an event. ("What is the worst thing that could possibly happen as a result of losing your job? What would you do about it?")
- Visualization of low probability images requires that clients picture all the terrible events that could happen to them, so that they learn to give up trying to control everything. Paradoxical techniques often employ these images. ("What terrible things could happen to you while reading the Sunday funnies? While taking a bath? While lying in your bed?")
- Assertive response images may be contrasted with images of passive, aggressive and passive-aggressive responses, so that the client can see the consequences of each response. ("Imagine asking for your money back passively, aggressively, and assertively.")
- Ultimate consequences images have clients visualize a troublesome situation a week, month, or year after the event to determine the lasting consequences. ("If you kill yourself, how sad do you imagine your girlfriend will be eight years from now?")
- Empathy images teach clients to perceive the world from another's internal frame of reference. ("How does the person you hurt feel about you?")
- Cathartic images allow the client to imagine expressing previously unexpressed emotions like anger, love, jealousy, or sadness. ("Imagine yelling back at your boyfriend.")
- Zero reaction images have clients visualize receiving only neutral consequences in phobic situations. These images are often used in extinction procedures. ("Imagine getting up in front of the whole congregation and then walking out. Picture nobody noticing or caring.")

- Fanciful images solve problems in imagination that cannot be solved in reality. ("Picture your dead grandmother before you now. What do you say to her? How does she answer?")
- Preventive images are used to prepare clients to cope with problems to be encountered in the future, such as death, rejection, physical problems, poverty, etc.
- Negative reinforcing images involve the clients' imagining a fearful action which removes them from an even more fearful situation (e.g., holding a snake keeps a person from being criticized by his peers).
- Security images give clients a feeling of safety in threatening situations. ("When you are on the plane, imagine your mother is holding you in your warm, pink blanket.")
- Satiated images, used in covert flooding procedures, repeat the same visualization over and over again until the client gets tired of imagining it. ("Imagine, for the next two weeks, that your wife makes love to every man you see.")
- Alternative images are used when clients must decide among different courses of action. ("Visualize what your life would be like living in New York for the next year vs. what it would be like living in Denver.")
- Negative consequences images show the aversive results of something the client may see as positive. ("Imagine, after you became famous, being trapped in your house, unable to go anywhere without being plagued by autograph hounds.")
- Resisting temptation images turn appealing objects into aversive objects. ("Imagine your cigarette is dried buffalo chips.")

5. Have clients practice visualization until selected images become vivid.
6. After clients finish practicing their images, reintroduce the language component by asking them to summarize changes in their belief systems. ("Now that you have shifted your emotions by using these images, what are your conclusions? What irrational thoughts were you thinking before? What rational beliefs do you have now?")

Example

As implied above, specific images are paired with specific irrational beliefs to bring about cognitive changes. Below are some of the visualizations we have used to correct various client irrationalities.

Core belief: People must always love me or I will be miserable.
Corrective images: Progressive coping images. Provide clients with coping images which show them (a) being loved by everyone, (b) being loved by

everyone in their environment except for one person, (c) being loved by most people, (d) being loved by half the people they know, (e) being loved by only a few people in their environment, (f) being loved by only one person. Describe these images in such a way that clients successfully cope with the decreasing number of people who love them.

———

Core belief: Making mistakes is terrible.
Corrective images: Noxious images may be used with this thought. Clients pair the aversive images with trying to be perfect all the time. ("Imagine the suicidal boredom perfection would bring.")

———

Core belief: It's terrible when things go wrong.
Corrective images: Leveling and zero reaction images. Have clients picture nothing at all happening when something goes wrong.

———

Core belief: My emotions can't be controlled.
Corrective images: Rewarding images. Teach the client to imagine all the positive consequences of having their emotions free and spontaneous.

———

Core belief: Self-discipline is too hard to achieve.
Corrective images: Mastery images. Clients picture excellent self-discipline in a variety of situations.

———

Core belief: I must always depend on others.
Corrective images: Idealized images. Clients visualize scenes of freedom, independence, and being untethered.

———

Core belief: My bad childhood must make my adult life miserable.
Corrective images: Modeling images. Clients imagine a whole series of people who have been happy and successful despite having had a horrible childhood.

———

Core belief: I believe there is a right, correct, perfect solution for my problems and all I have to do is find it.

Corrective images: Small detail coping images. Have clients imagine the necessary but small steps they must take to solve each specific problem.

———

Core belief: I am an exceptional person (a prince in disguise or Clark Kent looking for a phone booth). I require special privileges and favors; therefore, I shouldn't have to live within the limits and restrictions of ordinary mortals.

Corrective images: Empathy images. "If you were someone else, would you wish to know yourself? Would you like you?"

———

Comment

Some cognitive therapies, such as RET, seem to be primarily linguistic in emphasis; others, such as Leuner's (1969) guided affective imagery, are mostly visual. In cognitive restructuring we have found the combination far more effective than either one alone.

Further Information

The literature on images is extensive. The reader should refer to the major works of Kosslyn (1980), Lazarus (1977, 1982), Richardson (1969), Sheikh (1983a, 1983b), Singer (1974, 1976) and Singer and Pope (1978).

———

HANDLING CLIENT SABOTAGE

Principles

Many clients attempt to sabotage their own therapeutic progress. Such cases are far from being in the majority, but there are more of them than beginning counselors might anticipate. Our aim here is to alert, but not to alarm, professionals who are relatively inexperienced. The worst scenario I can imagine is one in which a beginning therapist eyes all of his or her clients suspiciously, even pugilistically, ready to spring upon anyone who shows the slightest sign of resistance.

Three key points should be emphasized here. First, not all clients come into therapy for the expected reasons. For some, the therapist is merely a potential ally who will, it is hoped, support the client's view in an ongoing argument between the client and significant others. Some clients enter therapy in search of the companionship a counselor might offer. Some enter therapy to "try it out," to see what it feels like. For others, therapy is a form of "conspicuous consumption," much like owning an expensive home or car that one can boast about at social gatherings. Still others view therapy as a challenge, a contest between themselves and the trained counselor. They might or might not have won many such contests in the other arenas of their lives, but they will be determined to win this one. Whenever the client has such a covert agenda, the professional faces a particular challenge.

Second, even illegitimate reasons for entering therapy can be façades. It is important not to immediately dismiss a client who does not appear to have a sincere need for assistance. The time invested in an initial session or two, if it is properly managed, might reveal both to the therapist and client that there is a greater need for services than the client had previously recognized or acknowledged.

Third, resistant behaviors result from feelings, which begin with thoughts. Hence, sabotages are themselves, in essence, forms of mistaken beliefs. They represent an outer hull of damaging perceptions that must be treated before addressing inner sources of client discomfort. Within the cognitive restructuring framework, sabotages should be handled in the same manner as other sources of clients' negative emotions. The beliefs are labeled, analyzed, and then subjected to therapeutic intervention.

Sabotages are distinguished from other types of client problems only in that they are treated *first*, for until they have been neutralized or replaced, little if any progress will be made in alleviating other client discomforts.

There are various types of sabotages:

- *Secondary Gain:* Environmental reinforcements anchor the beliefs. ("It is easier not to change.")
- *Social Support:* "People wouldn't like me if I changed."
- *Value Contradiction:* Not changing attitudes are attached to a higher value in client's hierarchy. ("It would be wrong to change.")
- *Internal Consistency:* The belief is tied to so many other thoughts in the client's cognitive system that changing one would cause many others to change. ("I would have to change too many other things.")
- *Defense:* "It would be dangerous to change."
- *Competitive:* "I won't let anybody tell me what to do."

- *Dependency:* "If I change I won't be able to see you anymore."
- *Magic Cure:* "I shouldn't have to work hard to change. It should happen quickly without a great deal of effort."
- *Motivation:* "I don't believe that I have to replace these thoughts. I can be happy while thinking the same way."
- *Denial:* "I understand everything you are telling me." "I will never understand anything you are telling me."
- *Behavioral Sabotages:* Clients may be sabotaging when they don't do their homework, come to appointments late, skip sessions, argue against every principle presented, do no work in sessions but call constantly during off hours, don't pay their fees, keep on complaining about not being cured, jump from one therapist to another every time they reach an arduous phase of counseling, complain about all the therapists they have seen before, or see the counselor only in crisis, discontinuing the minute the crisis is over.

All the cognitive techniques can be used for sabotage beliefs as well as other irrational thoughts. But some procedures seem particularly effective in this area.

Method 1. Counter Sabotage

After you and your clients have developed a list of counters to an irrational thought, ask clients to write down any sabotages or arguments against the counters that automatically occur to them. Next have them analyze these sabotages and dispute and challenge them before they attack the irrational thought (Loudis, 1979).

Example

Irrational Thought: "I can't let people know who I am. I need to hide behind a social mask to protect myself."

Counter: "If I don't show who I am no one can ever get close to me. I will always be alone."

Sabotage: "But they may reject me."

Counter: "They are rejecting me now because I am hiding behind a cardboard mockup of myself."

Sabotage: "Better they don't know me, then dislike me."
Counter: "Better to give people a chance to like or dislike me than to assure their rejection by playing hide and seek with myself."

———

The counter sabotage process is continued until clients can no longer think of any sabotages to their counters.

Method 2. Preventing Sabotages

It is far better to undercut sabotages before clients resort to them. Once these attitudes are revealed, clients have a certain tendency to defend them against attack, thus protracting the therapeutic process.

If it appears to you that a client is likely to sabotage therapy, in an early counseling session have your client make a list of all the ways a person could keep counseling from working. Ask him or her to identify what particular method he or she would use. Then discuss why the sabotage would keep the client from reaching his/her therapeutic goals.

This technique is usually introduced as follows:

> One of the things I have noticed after counseling clients for 20 years is that most clients have mixed feelings about therapy. Part of them wants to improve things in their life and for this reason they come to therapy. But another part of them resists changing or worries about risking getting into a worse state than they are in now. It's like they have two tape-recorded voices in their brain, one shouting "Grow, change, be better," while the other shouts, "Be careful! You may get worse; let it be."
>
> I have also found that most clients have difficulty telling their therapist about these conflicting feelings, so they usually don't. Instead they subtly sabotage the therapy, and often try to convince themselves that they aren't doing do.
>
> I am going to give you some ways others have attempted to sabotage counseling. I would like you to add some more. If you were going to sabotage but you didn't want me to know it, what methods would you use?

Sabotaging may be more ubiquitous than most therapists think, because when I present the concept, every client seems to know exactly what I am talking about.

Method 3. Monitoring Progress

To undercut the sabotage of "I am not getting any better" or "I am never going to improve," keep an accurate record of the baseline measurements of a client's symptoms. Periodically, update it to show the client positive changes.

Method 4. Impact Survey

This technique permits the therapist to determine the possible source of future sabotages.

Using the future perspective imaging technique (p. 274), have clients imagine that they have removed all their irrational beliefs. Then ask them to survey what negative things could still occur even though they no longer had the beliefs.

Method 5. Finding Payoffs

List the client's sabotages separately. Hypothesize what positive or negative reinforcers (payoffs) are connected to them. Discuss these payoffs with your clients and help them discover other methods of getting them. Help them discriminate between useful payoffs and destructive ones.

USE OF ALTERED STATES

Principles

Basic physiology has a lot to do with how well clients understand and respond to various therapeutic techniques. Some research has shown that clients who are physically taut, with tense muscles and high levels of brain activity as a result of their processing a variety of stimuli simultaneously, are much less responsive to therapy than those who are not functioning under those conditions. Relaxation, hypnosis, and meditation can ease muscle tensions and diminish brain activity levels, enabling clients to narrow their focus to the task at hand.

There is some evidence—though it is far from being conclusive—that Alpha states (8-12 Hz) and Theta states (4-7 Hz) improve clients' capacity to absorb information because clients are able to receive inputs uncritically and with fewer competing stimuli (Goleman, 1977; Groff, 1975, 1980). Our own experience suggests that invoking altered mental states is merely an adjunct technique; permanent or lasting changes are seldom effected solely by this method. This particular adjunct works best in supplementing conditioning and perceptual shifting techniques, but is less effective with other procedures.

Types of Altered State Inductions

CRT uses the following methods to produce relaxed states.

1. Biofeedback (Steiner & Dince, 1981)
2. The client breathes from the diaphragm and inhales slowly through the nose, holds his or her breath, and then exhales a little air at a time. Yawning and stretching accompanying slow rhythmic breathing generate additional results.
3. The counselor may play nature tapes to induce relaxation. These tapes are recordings of the natural sounds of an ocean, a country stream, meadows, and other environmental sonances. (They may be purchased from The Nature Company, Berkeley, California.)
4. Separately, or along with the nature tapes, therapists may read environmental scripts which describe the sensations of being in a natural setting, such as a beach or a mountain cabin. (Kroger and Fezler (1976) have some excellent scripts.)
5. Relaxation can be heightened if the therapist repeats phrases like, "My legs are getting heavy and warm. I am calm and relaxed. All my muscles are loose, limp and slack." These comments will produce a meditative state if they are repeated for 20 minutes.
6. Standard relaxation instructions (Benson, 1975, 1985; Jacobson, 1974; White & Fadiman, 1976).
7. Standard hypnotic inductions (Clark & Jackson, 1983; Crasilneck & Hall, 1975; Hilgard, 1977).
8. White Noise (we recommend Marsonal 1200 Sound Conditioner which can be purchased from The Sharper Image, San Francisco).
9. Pink Noise (Tapes can be purchased from Behavioral Medicine, 7503 Marin Dr., Denver, Colorado.)

Use of Reduced Brain Wave States

1. Relaxed states can be used with all CRT techniques.
2. But they are most effective with the following:
   a. They help clients unmask the core irrational beliefs connected to their

emotional problems. In a relaxed state clients often focus better on their automatic thoughts.
b. Relaxed states reinforce clients' positive cognitive changes.
c. They give clients the necessary distance to gauge their beliefs objectively.
d. Through memory regression, relaxation states enable clients to identify the historical roots of core beliefs.
e. They improve the effectiveness of many of the techniques presented in this book. Most specifically: *countering techniques* — guided countering, practicing counters; *perceptual shifting techniques* — cognitive focusing, conceptual shifting, transposing beliefs; *conditioning techniques* — covert reinforcement, cognitive aversive, cognitive desensitization, cognitive flooding, cognitive escape conditioning; *paradoxical methods* — teach thyself, forced catastrophes, obtaining goals, self flimflam. *adjuncts* — images techniques.

Comments

Our use of Theta or Alpha states shows contradictory results. We have found the learning of cognitive methods to be state-dependent. If client's problems occur in one state, then accessing that state to change cognitions seems practical. If not, then the creation of Alpha or Theta states has diminished efficiency. With certain clients they can be helpful, but we cannot clinically support the hoopla and exaggerated claims for curative effects of these states.

The reader should be aware of the distinction between relaxation, which has been positively demonstrated to help clients, and Alpha and Theta altered states, which have not. They are correlated but not necessarily causally related. See Beyerstein, 1985.

Further Information

The battle between the proponents and opponents of altered states rages on. On the pro side are books written mostly for the lay public; see Brown, 1974; Stearn, 1976; Zaffuto, 1974. Against are more technical works; see Beatty and Legewie, 1977; Beyerstein, 1985; Orne and Paskewitz, 1973; Plotkin, 1979; Simkins, 1982.

The most famous therapist using altered states is Milton Erickson. See Erickson and Rossi, 1981; Havens, 1985; Lankton and Lankton, 1983; Rossi, 1980; Rossi and Ryan, 1985.

HISTORICAL PERSPECTIVES

Principles

Before 1977, cognitive restructuring therapists tended to concern themselves only with their clients' *present* irrational beliefs, making little attempt to understand the historical evolution of mistaken sentiment. The prevailing feeling seemed to be that too great a focus on the past might obscure the central target—solving today's problems. Reconstructing the history of a misperception also required more time than many clients, eager for *immediate* relief, seemed willing to tolerate.

But time and experience have shown that many clients cannot discard current irrationalities without detaching them from their historical roots. Damaging beliefs do not spring up overnight, and the longer they are preserved the more difficult they are to neutralize or replace. Resynthesizing the historical roots of these misperceptions has proven to be a successful remedial strategy for most clients. Hence, today's CRT therapist is much more likely to incorporate this adjunct technique along with other strategies presented in this book.

Three historical perspective techniques are offered in the following pages. We have used these methods for a decade and have always found them to be powerful therapeutic aids, especially in treating misperceptions that have been preserved by clients for many years.

Method 1. Critical Life Events

Past critical life events often forge misperceptions. Clients have stored these irrationalities in their memories, and they often need to correct the earlier mistakes to shift the present ones.

1. Relax the client.
2. Compile lists of the critical events that occurred during the client's life. You may generate the record by listening to the client's history and jotting down the key events, but generally it is better to use a more structured system. As homework, ask the client to collect four lists: daily, adult,

adolescent, and child. The lists recount key events linked to the client's symptoms. For example, if the client is anxious, then she writes four lists of the key anxiety attacks she has had in her life. The daily list includes the worst anxiety she has during each day. The adult list contains the ten worst anxieties as adults. The adolescent and childhood lists encompass earlier traumas.

3. Sometimes we find it more appropriate to substitute more specific lists for general ones. When working with delayed stress syndrome among Vietnam veterans we employ three lists: pre-Vietnam critical events, during combat events, and post-Vietnam events.

4. Suggest that your client describe these events in detail.

5. After discussion with your client, ascertain if the critical events have fabricated beliefs which still cause problems in the present.

6. Also discuss how the client's emotions and behaviors have altered because of the beliefs formed at the time of the critical events.

7. Then, help you client reinterpret the old events with new, more rational beliefs. Have her scrutinize the events with the advantage of distance and time, so she can rectify earlier mistaken perception with adult reasoning.

8. You may wish to use corrective, coping imagery at this point, so that your client can revise the event by imagining that she had thought and acted reasonably.

9. Review all major critical events; detect the belief and have the client imagine correcting the situation. Then and only then, work on present irrationalities.

Method 2. Earliest Recollections

Many therapies attribute great significance to earliest memories. Adler (1964), Binder and Smokler (1980), Mosak (1958, 1969), and Olson (1979) use earliest recollections as an important ingredient in their therapies.

Cognitive restructuring uses clients' earliest memories to identify core damaging beliefs, but without a psychodynamic theoretical framework. Frequently earliest memories identify lifelong beliefs. The themes probably didn't originate with the events, for usually only a whole series of experiences can do that. But the events often unveil the existence of the belief during early stages of clients' lives.

1. Have the client imagine the current situation where anxiety or another emotion occurs. Take some time on this. Help the client to use all his senses to make the scene vivid. When the scene is clear, ask the client to focus on the core belief, gestalt, or theme.

2. Instruct your client to focus on the first or earliest recollection he has of thinking a belief. Concentrate on the initial situation when the fear or other emotion developed. Again have him imagine the scene and visualize it clearly. It is helpful if your client's says the false belief to himself in his earlier voice (child or adolescent).

3. Ask the client, "What was erroneous in your interpretation of this event? How did you misperceive it? What did you say to yourself then that was untrue? Why was your interpretation mistaken? Who, or what experiences, taught you this misperception?"

4. Discuss with your client how he is misjudging the present situation in the same way he misjudged the earlier one.

5. Correct the earliest mistaken belief. Have the client imagine redoing the situation by thinking a rational, realistic thought instead of what he first believed. Ask him to imagine how he would have felt and how he would have acted differently if he had thought rationally.

6. Finally, get your client to picture his present difficulty differently. Correct the present mistaken belief just as the earlier one was corrected.

Method 3. Chronological Beliefs

Thoughts transform over time and have their own developmental history, just as organisms change physically. The power behind a present belief is assessed by tracing its development from the past. Thoughts have a vertical depth. Cognitive trees have long roots, for beliefs stretch back from the present into the distance past. To illustrate, a present perception of inferiority is diagrammed chronologically:

- *Present:* "I am inferior as a husband, father and employer."
- *Recent past:* "I am not a terrific boyfriend or worker."
- *Adolescent:* "I am a lousy student, and girls don't like me."
- *Young adolescent:* "I stink at sports and other guys are a lot tougher than me."
- *Late childhood:* "I am a bad boy. My brother is better."
- *Early childhood:* "Mommy and daddy don't like me."

In this case the client's present inferiority feelings are represented in the past. His earlier mistaken beliefs contribute to his present irrationality.

1. Develop longitudinal cognitive maps for your client's beliefs. Pick out each thought and trace its origins—how it has transformed into other beliefs, and how its representation has changed during different stages of the client's life.

2. What other thoughts, emotions, behaviors, or additional environmental triggers have become linked with the theme as it developed? How has the misperception spread from one zone of a client's life to another?
3. Have your clients imagine what their life would have been like if they had perceived correctly. Ask them to imagine their history differently based on a rational perceptive.

Example

Mark was sent to me by another cognitive behavioral therapist. He was suffering from agoraphobia, had seen several different therapists over five years, and had made some progress. He was capable of traveling most places and performing most activities without undo fear. However, in one area he hadn't mastered his fear—he still couldn't fly on airplanes. He had attended special classes on fear of flying run by a major airline; he had completed desensitization therapy on agoraphobia, and had even received private *in vivo* practice from a psychiatrist who owned his own plane. All to no avail. He still hadn't flown.

We did a complete analysis of the thoughts he had about flying and found them to be typical for an agoraphobic. Mark didn't fear the plane crashing, but he was afraid of getting panicky on it. He felt that he would be trapped in the plane while panicking, and that he wouldn't be able to escape.

His core belief was not our original discovery. Previous cognitive therapists had identified it. But former attempts at disputing it had not worked. No one previously identified or challenged the historical roots of the belief; thus they were still intact. We decided to change these roots in order to shift his contemporary belief.

Mark worked hard and energetically searched for the historical forerunners to his present irrational thought. We found the environmental trigger for these formative irrationalities.

- Age 2 to 6
  Trigger: Overprotected by mother.
  Irrational belief: Life is dangerous and I need someone to protect me. I can't handle this world by myself.
- Age 6 to 12
  Trigger: Spoiled
  Irrational belief: Life should be as easy as it once was.
  Irrational belief: I shouldn't have to feel pain.
- Age 12 to 16
  Trigger: Rejected by peers because he acted spoiled.
  Irrational belief: It's horrible if everybody doesn't like me.

Irrational belief: If I am perfect I will be liked.
Irrational belief: I need to control everything to be perfect.

Trigger 2: Saw a fellow student vomit in a classroom and observed that all his classmates rejected the student.
Irrational belief: People will reject me unless I control everything physical going on inside my body.

Trigger 3: Panicked about getting sick in a car during a cross-country trip. Started to fear panic itself.
Irrational belief: Now I must control everything psychological going on in my body so that people don't reject me.

Trigger 4: Thinking about flying.
Irrational belief: I won't be able to control my fear in a plane, and I won't be able to escape.

Comment

Many therapies explore the historical routes of present-day problems. CRT differs, however, because of its emphasis on the history of clients' irrational beliefs. We do not assume that it is necessary or useful to synthesize these histories with abstruse notions like ego states, psychosexual stages of development, fixation, regression, or cathexis.

Further Information

Guidano and Liotti's comprehensive work (1983) explores the historical roots of irrational beliefs.

ENVIRONMENTAL PRACTICE

Principles

Environmental practice is a technique that reinforces therapeutic gain. It does so by providing clients with an opportunity to practice cognitive shifts in real-life situations. Hence, clients are urged to engage in a feared behavior to prove that no harm actually befalls them. Subsequent testing under the same conditions, while practicing cognitive techniques, helps clients realize that what has worked covertly will also work *in vivo*.

Environmental practice is not always necessary. Some clients who can imagine themselves coping under adverse conditions don't actually have to create those conditions and then subject themselves physically to them in order to become comfortable with a new, rational belief. Some of our clients eliminate their anxieties totally by covert, cognitive means, without any environmental practice. But for most clients environmental practice is a valuable last step for all cognitive techniques, as the following discussion illustrates.

Method

1. List the core beliefs connected to your client's problems.
2. Teach all aspects of covert, countering, perceptual shifting, or other cognitive techniques with these beliefs.
3. After discussing it with your client develop a conclusive environmental test of the beliefs. For example, you could test the thought, "I could go crazy if I travel far from home" (the agoraphobic's fear), by suggesting your client travel six miles, then seven, then 15, etc. Develop a test for each irrational thought.
4. The client then actually performs the tests and records the results.

Example

John was a young man who entered therapy to remove his compulsive behaviors. Every day he performed 40 or 50 meaningless rituals to reduce anxiety. He had seen a rational emotive therapist and a behaviorist, but the frequency of his rituals was not reduced.

I felt that a combination of the two approaches would work, although singly they had not. Since environmental practice combines cognitive and behavioral methods, he agreed to try it.

We first identified what he said to himself before the rituals and found many beliefs.

- If I don't do the rituals, some catastrophic thing will happen.
- Rituals protect me from danger.
- I must have people like and respect me.
- I must always be in control. I cannot let myself feel something that I don't control.
- I have the power to make myself feel anything I want. Rituals exercise this power.
- If I give up the power, I will be in great danger.

We then used disputing, counterconditioning and perceptual shifting procedures to change his beliefs. He first practiced all the cognitive techniques covertly. We taped the sessions, and he practiced the techniques at home several times a week.

We then decided to try the techniques *in vivo*. The first environmental practice used a single-subject experimental design. He conducted a study with himself to compare the effects of doing the ritual versus doing a cognitive technique.

He did the experiment for five weeks. We used an individual time series design. (See "Experimental Treatment" in Chapter 7).

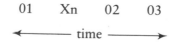

$$01 \quad Xn \quad 02 \quad 03$$

$$\longleftarrow \quad \text{time} \quad \longrightarrow$$

with 0's = Self-rating of anxiety level on a 1–10 scale.
with 01 = his tension level immediately before he engaged in the ritual.
with 02 = his anxiety immediately after he either did the ritual or did some alternative treatment (X's).
with 03 = his anxiety 15 minutes later.

The independent variable (Xn) stands for:

X-1. Doing the ritual.
X-2. Not doing the ritual.
X-3. Substituting relaxation for the ritual.
X-4. Finding the thoughts causing the anxiety preceding the ritual.

X-5. Objectively analyzing the truth or falseness of the thoughts.
X-6. Contradicting, challenging, and disputing his thoughts.
X-7. Switching to another ritual.
X-8. Finding the environmental trigger preceding the anxiety and ritual.
X-9. Imagining a relaxing scene.
X-10. Changing the visual components of the ritual.
X-11. Doing something behaviorally assertive in the situations.
X-12. Countering his fears when he doesn't do ritual.

Since John averaged 40 rituals a day before treatment, I told him to pick four or five times each day when he would record his anxiety and try to interrupt the ritual by doing something else. Table 7 shows which interruptions (Xn) helped most.

Table 5
Mean Self-ratings of Anxiety (10-0) During
Different Time Periods (O's), in Different
Experimental Conditions (X's). N = 175 trials.

01	XN	02	03	mean change (anxiety reduction)
3.75	1	0	0	− 3.75
4.17	2	2.5	0	− 1.67
3.67	3	1.83	0	− 1.79
3.75	4 to 6	1.02	0	− 2.73
3.50	8	1.05	0	− 2.45
3.00	10	1.00	0	− 2.00
4.00	11	.71	0	− 3.29
3.00	12	1.00	0	− 2.00

The study shows several things: (a) His rituals reduced he anxiety more effectively than any other technique. That is why he was obsessive. (b) Whether he did the ritual or not, his anxiety left after 15 minutes, usually in a minute or two. (c) Besides doing the ritual, identifying and countering his thoughts reduced his anxiety the most (4 to 6 SUDS); finding the environmental triggers (8), and doing something assertive in the situation (11) also helped.

After the study we decided to try environmental practice. He was told to use his most effective intervention techniques to reduce the rituals; the procedure would take 85 days. Each day he was allotted a certain number of times he could engage in ritualistic behavior. He could not do rituals if he had fulfilled his daily allotment. When he closed in to his daily limit he was told to counter his thoughts, find the environmental CS's and do something assertive instead of doing a ritual. He would monitor his practice with a hand counter. The following is a record of his environmental practice.

Day	Rituals Allowed	Rituals Used
1	40	26
2	39	23
3	38	34
4	37	26
5	36	30
6	35	22
7	34	21
8	33	28
7	32	17
8	31	17
9	30	14
10	29	13
11	28	19
12	27	19
13	26	14
14	25	23
15	24	17
16	23	15
17	22	16
18	21	21
19	20	14
20	19	15

The ritual behavior gradually reduced. This reduction continued.

31	9	10
32	8	9
33	7	8
34	6	8
35	5	6

At this point he was going over his daily limit so we shifted the approach. Each week he was allotted a maximum but decreasing number of rituals. If he went over his allotment one day he had to take it from the next day's allotment. Finally, on day 70, he began to do no rituals.

70	2	0
71	2	1
72	2	2
73	2	0
74	1	0

75	1	1
76	1	0
77	1	0
78	1	0

We continued the practice until he consistently didn't do the rituals.

Comment

As the last step in CRT, we almost always have clients practice techniques in the real-life situations. Without this procedure, most clients feel they haven't really completed their work.

Further Information

Several authors have debated the necessity of environmental practice of cognitive techniques. See Bandura, 1977a, 1977b, 1982, 1984; Bandura et al., 1982.

Other authors suggest that a combination of cognitive and behavioral techniques is superior to either one alone. See D' Zurilla and Goldfried, 1971; Wilson et al., 1983; and Wolpe et al., 1985.

7

CRT Tools

Having and using the proper tools is a mark of the experienced craftman. This chapter highlights several tools—actually special techniques—which are more concerned with helping therapists monitor and confirm the effectiveness of their techniques than with responding to client needs.

CRT was originally envisioned as a 15–20-session therapy, and this clearly represents a substantial investment of time and resources for both clients and therapists. For many clients, the length of time during which they are receiving the guidance and support of a counselor could undermine their confidence that any progress is being made or even *can* be made. Therapists should be able to determine readily whether they have made the proper techniques for particular clients. The more efficiently they can meet the needs of their clients, the more clients they can help.

We have found several techniques helpful to us in such critical areas of practice as:

1. Deciding which techniques seem to be most beneficial to which clients. See our discussion in "Experimental Treatment."
2. Monitoring a client's progress under a particular treatment. Not only is this information important in confirming our original selection of a particular technique, but it also provides us with a means of providing clients with motivating and carefully substantiated feedback on their progress. Such feedback is especially helpful in cases in which treatment persists over a long period of time. "Monitoring Client Progress" introduces an approach that we have found to be helpful in this regard.

3. Confirming that we have followed the standard CRT procedures and not omitted some important elements. In "Major Components of CRT: A Checklist," we provide a useful means by which therapists can double-check to insure that they have covered the key aspects of CRT.
4. The final tool, "Optimizing Human Performance," offers suggestions as to how counselors might expand cognitive techniques into nonclinical areas such as management, organizational development, skill improvement, and goal attainment.

EXPERIMENTAL TREATMENT

Principles

Which treatment should each client receive? The question is important. This handbook provides an arsenal of techniques to draw upon, and in most instances the choice is not a matter of selecting the right *one*—three or four might be equally suitable, at least as starting points, for a particular client's condition. We don't want to waste our client's time and resources on a procedure that might require weeks of sessions and offer little hope of relieving the client's discomfort.

At the same time, we don't want to become petrified at the thought that we might mismatch client and treatment. The best decisions of the most experienced therapists are always marked, to some degree, by an element of guesswork.

The most important foci, during the early exploratory sessions with a client, should be upon:

1. Getting as much background information as possible on a client, in part to confirm whether this person has a legitimate need for services.
2. Instilling cognitive principles within the client.
3. Gaining an understanding of the nature and source of the client's discomfort. Avoid being too hasty in making a diagnosis. When you think you have the problem pinpointed, take a little time to confirm your suspicion before you embark upon a definite course of action. And don't overlook the fact that, in many clients, there are multiple problem conditions that must be identified and analyzed. In such cases it will likely be necessary for you to decide which condition should be treated *first*, in addition to deciding which techniques are most appropriate for the full range of problems that you will be addressing.

Therapists should take care, during these initial sessions, to set their clients' expectations at the proper level. Clients should understand that long-standing problems will not be cured overnight, but that you have a commitment to help them find lasting relief as quickly as possible. They should understand that your success in that regard will depend largely upon the extent to which they are willing to cooperate with you. And they should also understand that you will probably attempt a variety of techniques in order to discover which ones work best for them. By acknowledging at the outset that a given technique might *not* work as well as you and your client would prefer, you relieve yourself of the pressure to have to make a perfect treatment choice.

Your commitment to efficiency in the selection of a suitable treatment is very important. In our experience, one of the best ways to fulfill that commitment is by conducting an individual experiment with each client in order to ascertain which among a likely range of techniques might be most suitable.

This approach might seem a little radical to some, but it really isn't. Most of what goes on in counseling involves a high degree of informal experimentation. With this technique we have simply formalized the approach somewhat by conducting a structured experiment with our clients, using many of the same procedures employed by research psychologists. The purpose of this procedure, however, is not to prove or disprove scientific principles, but to expedite the process of finding the most suitable treatment for a given client.

Method

1. Develop a list of the client's basic irrational beliefs.
2. Record the key situations where the client gets upset. Have the client describe them in enough detail so that they can be formed into visual images.
3. Elaborate a companion list of the rational and most useful perceptions in opposition to the irrational beliefs.
4. Compile a series of cognitive techniques which, based on your experience, have a good probability of helping the client.
5. Design a single-subject research design to measure the effects of the treatment. A multiple baseline time-series design may be most useful. For instance:

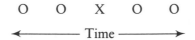

$$O \qquad O \qquad X \qquad O \qquad O$$

$$\longleftarrow \text{Time} \longrightarrow$$

with O = observational period where the client response is measured (dependent variable). Have the client picture one of the upsetting scenes until it is clearly in mind. Then measure his emotional response to the scene either by using his rating on a 1–100 scale or by using various biofeedback measures. The responses to the scenes are recorded before and after the treatment variable is introduced. X = specific treatment variable (independent variable). Introduce the treatment variable, record how long the clients take to complete it, and monitor whether it is done correctly.

6. Make a record sheet for the client so that he can conduct the experiment at home using a tape of the techniques made during the counseling sessions. At home he randomly alternates the techniques, carefully recording the differential results.
7. After some data have been collected, the therapist should notice which techniques are showing the most effective changes. The therapist should continue the experiment by modifying the successful procedures to make them even more helpful.

Example

A woman client was sent to me from another cognitive behavioral therapist because she suffered from a rather classic case of agoraphobia. Although she had never become housebound, she had all the other symptoms. She had been helped by previous cognitive treatment with the other therapist, but her agoraphobia remained.

Since the other cognitive therapist had tried some cognitive techniques without success, we decided to use an experimental treatment approach so we could determine, rather than just guess, as to what was effective and what was not.

We used the following research design:

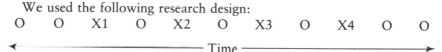

O   O   X1   O   X2   O   X3   O   X4   O   O

$\longleftarrow$ —————————— Time ————————— $\longrightarrow$

with O = client subjective SUDs readings, and a GSR differential from a five-minute base reading. The responses were recorded after the client indicated a particular visualization was clearly in mind. The image was a specific anxious scene where she was sitting in a small conference room with all her bosses, and they were waiting for her to respond to a question.
with X1 = a countering technique—assertive countering
with X2 = a perceptual shifting technique—transposing
with X3 = a paradoxical technique—reductio ad absurdum
with X4 = another countering approach—probing counters.

She practiced the different treatments at home for one month but in different order. For instance:

X1	X2	X3	X4
X4	X3	X2	X1
X3	X1	X4	X2
X2	X4	X1	X3

In every case she recorded her level of emotional anxiety (SUDs) before and after the X.

The key perception which she identified as causing all of her fear was—"I must not lose control over myself." All the techniques she used were different ways to counter or shift this perception.

All the techniques helped her to some extent. Some days transposing was most useful because it reminded her that she had anticipated losing control a thousand times in the last three years, but her memory showed her it hadn't happened even once. Other times assertive countering got her angry at the irrational thought; reductio ad absurdum demonstrated that the worst result of losing control would be better than all her fear now. But based upon her own data, the most effective technique in shifting her perception was Probing Counters. She came up with a list of questions and wrote them on index cards. Her practice was simply reading the questions and then thinking of the answers. After practicing the technique for several weeks, she started to realize that her belief was impossible and based on quasi-mysticism. Worse than that, it was silly.

To the belief "I must not lose control over myself," she asked the following questions:

- How can I own something (control) that I don't have?
- What is the "I" that is supposed to be controlling myself?
- What is the "self" that is being controlled by the "I"?
- How is this mystical "I" able to control this mystical "self"?
- Why is this "must" there? Is it a necessity?
- Why would it be so terrible to "lose control"?

Comment

After using the experimental approach with over 50 clients, we have determined that no one technique seems best for all clients. The probing technique worked best for the aforementioned client, but was ineffective for others. And so it is for most of the techniques we have used. Therapists who routinize their techniques for all clients insure that their success in treatment will be hit or miss.

Further Information

For research design, see the classic work by Campbell and Stanley (1963) and Cook and Campbell (1979). Information about individual case experiments can be found in Kazdin (1980, 1982) and Kratochwill (1978).

———

MONITORING CLIENT PROGRESS

Principles

Both therapists and clients need to know as soon as possible whether a particular treatment is progressing well. The therapist's commitment to client monitoring should be explained at the outset of the relationship. In our experience, clients appreciate knowing that serious consideration will be given to monitoring their progress, and are willing to give therapists the kind of feedback they require for monitoring purposes.

As has been suggested in "Experimental Treatment," CRT is like a mini time-series design with an "N" of one. It is necessary for the therapist to monitor the dependent, independent, and control variables to determine treatment effectiveness, and to make changes in treatment procedures where appropriate in order to improve the efficacy of those procedures. Therapy, then, becomes a closed loop, consisting of treatment, client response, evaluation, correction of treatment (if necessary), and then starting again with treatment.

Client monitoring procedures should be as unobtrusive as possible, so that they do not disrupt or needlessly complicate the treatment procedures. In our experience, the following strategy seems ideally suited for getting the feedback needed in the most efficient manner possible.

Method

1. Get SUD's level (Wolpe, 1973) on target emotion before and after therapeutic session, and before and after the introduction of a particular therapeutic technique.
2. Use client's subjective rating to determine the strength of counters, perceptual shifting, conditioning, or other CRT procedures.

3. Before each counseling session rate the strength of master beliefs. Continue to measure client changes on core beliefs periodically throughout the duration of the counseling.

4. For in vivo practice that involve client's exercises, the therapist can estimate the strength of the client's assertiveness by using the following formula.

$$(1 \text{ to } 10) \times (0 \text{ to } 3) = \text{strength of assertiveness}$$

> with 1–10 measuring how difficult the activity was for the client to perform. The level is rated before the activity.
> with 0 to 3 measuring how assertively the client performed the activity. 0 = not performing it, and 3 = doing it perfectly.

5. Periodically, as a homework assignment, you may consider giving a quiz to your clients to determine how much they understand from the previous therapeutic sessions.

6. Clients are supplied manuals which review some of the major principles discussed in the therapeutic sessions. (Mc Mullin and Casey, 1975; McMullin, Assafi, and Chapman, 1978). There are different manuals for different types of client populations: parenting, elderly, children, adults, and different kinds of clinical problems—alcoholism, phobias, depression, drug abuse, abusive behavior, etc.

7. Clients can give a verbal or written summary of their last session to determine how much they recall.

8. Have the clients pinpoint the key negative emotions they had for one week, at the beginning of therapy. Record their frequency, intensity and duration. Throughout therapy, occasionally check on these pinpoints to ascertain the effectiveness of your intervention.

9. For many of the CRT techniques, there are homework report sheets which help the counselor determine how well the techniques have been mastered. They have been noted throughout this text.

10. Biofeedback is used extensively in CRT counseling. Migraine headaches, tension, and anxiety as well as other autonomic functions have been monitored and treated using GSR, EMG, heart rate, blood pressure, and body temperature readings (Bakal & Kaganov, 1977; Basmajian, 1979; Schwartz, 1973).

In CRT biofeedback has been used to assess the autonomic effects of the irrational thoughts, counters, perceptual shifting, counter conditioning and image techniques. There are several methods.

a. *Experimental CRT:* Develop a hierarchy of client's beliefs with their accompanying situations and record a baseline reading of the client's autonomic responses while imagining these situations. Using the previously discussed 01 X1 02 X2 03 04 research design, measure the autonomic changes of different CRT techniques (X's). Continue refining the X's to the point of maximum effect by constant observation of biofeedback changes.

b. *Biofeedback desensitization:* Get the client's relaxed baseline reading; it takes at least five minutes. Record the responses the client has while imagining the core irrational beliefs with their accompanying scenes. Using the client as the control system in the feedback loop, have the client reduce autonomic responses to the irrational thoughts by monitoring tension level. Continue with the biofeedback readings while thinking the irrational thoughts, until the readings do not vary from the relaxed baseline.

c. *Second order biofeedback desensitization:* Employ the same procedures as in the above (b), but have clients associate biofeedback reduction with an external conditioned stimulus, such as saying the word "calm," imagining a relaxing image, or thinking a realistic thought like, "It is not dangerous." The CS2 can then be used to produce the same autonomic reduction without the presence of the biofeedback equipment.

Comment

Biofeedback, in our experience, is not the royal road to accurately determining the strength of the client's dependent variable. Many clients do not show recordable sympathetic nervous system responses or catabolic functions to conditioned stimuli. In addition, biofeedback devices often don't sufficiently screen out autonomic responses from gross musculature or other movements and interference.

Further Information

For more information about the positive and negative uses of biofeedback see Beatty and Legewie, 1977; Plotkin, 1979; and Simkins, 1982.

MAJOR COMPONENTS OF CRT: A CHECKLIST

Principles

The checklist is a convenient method to determine if the necessary components for CRT have been established. Since there are many more aspects to cognitive restructuring therapy than can be encompassed within this handbook, the checklist provides a landscape view of the therapy. Hence, it is a useful reference tool for periodic review by both beginning practitioners and experienced therapists who might need an occasional overview of the full breadth of this brand of therapy.

CRT Checklist

Note: Some of these items are more important than others within the total context of CRT therapy.

1. Do your clients believe that thoughts cause emotions, or do they still think situations elicit feelings? There is no point in continuing a cognitive therapy if your clients are still believing that physical events are causing their anxieties or depressions.
2. Can they distinguish between situations, thoughts, and emotions or do they confuse the three? Remember, situations are environmental variables outside the organism, thoughts are frontal lobe processing, and emotions are subcortical feeling responses.
3. Have your clients found the core beliefs linked to their emotional responses? If the beliefs you have worked on are irrelevant to the client's feelings, then changing them will not remove the emotion. The first step in cognitive counseling of all types is to clearly identify the most basic belief which is causing the client problems. The beliefs the client is aware of are usually only the surface thoughts, and the therapist often needs to dig for five or six sessions before the core is uncovered. See my earlier book for help on this step (Mc Mullin & Giles, 1981).
4. Do the clients see the negative effects of their beliefs on their lives? Or do they think their thoughts are irrelevant to what they feel and how they act?

5. Have clients acquired distance from their own thinking so that they can perceive thoughts objectively?
6. Can the clients discern the interrelationship between one thought and another? Do they see that their fear in a grocery store is fundamentally the same as their fear in a restaurant, elevator, or conference room? Can they draw a cognitive map of these relationships?
7. Do they understand the need to analyze the truth or falseness of their beliefs, or do they think that feeling something strongly establishes its validity?
8. Can they successfully analyze statements and make decisions as to their truth or falseness?
9. Have they made a commitment that if a thought is logically false, it is useful to change it?
10. Have they practiced disputing the least emotionally upsetting beliefs first, so that the strongest irrationalities are not confronted before clients develop the ability to change them?
11. Can your clients counter their beliefs? Have they developed sufficient arguments against their thoughts? Are their counters just words, or do they have some believability?
12. In counterconditioning, have they practiced the techniques enough? (Some beliefs may take a year or more of practice.) Unfortunately, many clients believe in magic and think that one afternoon of disputing will make up for 15 years of believing the irrationality.
13. If you use a visualization or imagery technique, does your client have sufficient visualization capacity to picture scenes clearly? You can use some of the scales described in the "Images Techniques" in Chapter 6 to assess this capacity.
14. Have clients practiced the techniques over a period of time, or do they only use them only when they are in crisis?
15. Do they use the procedures mechanically or have they shown they understand the underlying concept?
16. Have they modified your procedures so much that they have destroyed the active therapeutic element? We encourage client creativity when using our techniques, but you need to make sure that the client doesn't change the technique so much that it becomes ineffective.
17. Do your clients recognize that therapists don't have the power to change beliefs, and that only they have that power? Do they accept the counseling relationship as more of a teacher-student rather than doctor-patient one? Or are they waiting for you to cure them?
18. Are the clients' perception of therapeutic efficacy so low that they expect therapy to fail? The work on self-efficacy is rather strong on this point.

If clients expect to fail, they will often do subtle things that will help their prediction come true.

19. Do they think that another approach or another therapist would help them more? If so, they may not put any effort into your therapy, since they feel it is second best. Suggest they try the other approach first and then return to you if it proves ineffective.

20. Do clients do their homework, or do they only work in your therapeutic sessions? One hour engaged in the right direction does not clear away 112 hours of working in the wrong direction.

21. Are your techniques ineffectual because the client is sabotaging counseling? (See "Handling Client Sabotage" in Chapter 6).

22. Are there too many noncognitive factors interfering with your techniques? Your clients' central problems may be cognitive, but in order for them to effectively work on them, they need to have the time and freedom from constant crisis to effectively change their negative perceptions. Clients with severe marital problems, those who are physically ill, and those who are not sure of where their next meal is going to come from are hardly in the right frame of reference to work on their psychological soundness. In such situations it is better to mitigate the crisis before you attempt therapy.

————

OPTIMIZING HUMAN PERFORMANCE

Principles

The previous sections of this handbook have presented a variety of techniques and procedures for disengaging clients from damaging beliefs that have evolved over their histories, so that they can live fuller lives today. The primary goal of the therapy is to help clients cope *today*, but there is more to life than the present. To live fully, one must also consider the future. Human performance is optimized when clients are relieved of present-day limitations on their ability to cope—even if those limitations are self-imposed—and when they are able to effectively focus their talents and energies upon goals that are appropriate, meaningful, and important to them.

Hence, our primary focus thus far has been upon removing negative emotions, irrational thoughts, and nonadaptive behavior. But CRT can be used at a second level for nontherapeutic concerns. These two levels can be distinguished by referring to the first as "treatment," and the second as the "optimal performance." Table 6 summarizes the major differences between these two levels.

As the table demonstrates, CRT for optimal performance focuses on the future rather than the past, is goal-oriented (core life values) rather than remedial, and attempts to create positive emotions (promotive thoughts) rather than merely removing negative ones. Two new concepts, "core life value" and "promotive thoughts," need further definition.

Core Life Values

We hypothesize that most people formulate a meaning for their lives, a central purpose, a core life goal. It is their basic *raison d'être*, the way they make sense out of their existence. While most people have never consciously articulated this value, their behavior often demonstrates their choice. Questions about what they want to accomplish in life can make the value explicit. The value is usually accompanied by satellite values which relate directly to it, and which actually represent the specific means by which the goal is to be achieved. Hence, one's core value might be to become the fastest runner one is capable of being, and a satellite value would be to practice running a certain number of laps in decreasing time periods every week.

Table 6
Comparison of Treatment vs Optimal Performance

CRT FOR TREATMENT −	0	CRT FOR OPTIMAL PERFORMANCE +
avoidance behavior	nondirectional	behavior aimed at core life value
focus on removing pain	focus on maintenance	focus on goals
irrational thought	rational thought	promotive thought
past	present	future
negative emotions	lack of negative emotions	positive emotions
remedial	normal	optimal
reactive	neutral	proactive
movement from	no movement	movement toward

Core life values might change several times over the course of a lifetime, which is fine. Change is inevitable in life, and once a goal has been achieved, it is only healthy to move on to yet another motivating goal. These values serve as a kind of roadmap to life, which people use it to create specific goals, to measure their worthwhileness, and to judge their accomplishments.

Promotive Thoughts

These are the cognitions people use to achieve their core life value. They produce the most beneficial emotions and the optimal behavior. They are the cognitive means which lead people to their chosen ends. In the case of our runner, for example, a promotive thought might be: "I know that I am an exceptional runner, and that I am capable of becoming even more exceptional." Promotive thoughts are those beliefs, self-statements, or perceptions which will most likely help clients to realize their core life values.

Core life values and promotive thoughts are necessary to move people towards optimal performance; removing all irrational beliefs is simply not sufficient. Imagine an athlete whose performance is reduced because he fears large crowds. By using the techniques already included in this handbook—countering, conditioning, and perceptual shifting—his fears could be eliminated. But is removing unrealistic thinking all that he needs to perform up to his maximum physical potential? Does rational thinking alone lead people to their core life value? Mahoney (1979) and others have demonstrated that top athletes not only think rationally but also think promotively. They think in ways that maximize their athletic skill, so that they can reach their core goal.

In our experience, CRT for optimal performance can best be used with groups, including all of the members of a family, all of the players of an athletic team, groups of business managers, educators, students, or any other assembly in which all of the individual members share a common goal of optimizing their collective performance. Hence, many CRT therapists will find the method discussed here useful in reaching beyond their offices to render valued service to a much broader client base.

All the techniques listed in this handbook can be modified to help people reach optimal performance, and get closer to obtaining their core value.

Method

1. The first step in developing promotive thinking is to help individuals identify their core life values (see Table 7). What people want to accomplish in life in general will direct and clarify what specific goals they should create. Without identifying the central value, situationally specific goals

Table 7
Identifying Core Life Values

What do you really want from life?

Take ten minutes to answer these questions. How do you see your lifetime goal right now? What is your core value? Stay general and abstract, but take the time to re-view personal, family, social, career, financial, community, and spiritual values. Make your list all-inclusive. Try to list as many ideas as you can in the time period. Record whatever comes into your head.

How would you like to spend the next five years?

Take five minutes to answer the above question; then take another two minutes to include whatever you may have missed the first time.

If I knew now that I would be struck dead by lightning six months from today, how would I live until then?

Assume that you have attended to all of the legal and financial matters relating to your death. Concern yourself only with how you would live these last six months.

have no base and no relevancy. Goals and plans need to be attached to a core life purpose to have meaning, substance and believability. The counselor's first task is to help the person tie goals and promotive thoughts to an overall guiding life principle. Unless the core value is clearly iden-tified, then individual goals cannot be formed. The core value is subjec-tive and general while the goals are more objective and specific.

There are many methods to identify the core life value. In this handbook two sections—"Philosophical Shifts" and "Hierarchy of Values Bridges" in Chapter 2—discuss some procedures, but essentially the counselor must help the individual to answer the existential question: "What do you want to accomplish with your life?"

2. The next step is to help the individual set specific goals based upon the core life value. The counselor helps the individual set goals and facilitates the identification of the desired peak performance for any situation.

3. With the individual's help, the counselor identifies the optimal emotional state and the specific behavioral components for each goal.

4. Next the counselor carefully develops a list of the key promotive cognitions (self-talk, self-efficacy, self-concept, evaluations, self-instructions, perceptual schemata) that may carry the individual's emotions and behaviors towards the optimal performance.

5. The promotive thoughts are screened for accuracy and utility. They must be rational and based upon objective reality.

6. After the list has been compiled, the counselor can use any of the techniques presented in this handbook to help the individual develop promotive thoughts in a variety of life situations.

7. The client then practices the thoughts in real-life situations.

Example 1

Note that more than one promotive thought can be associated with a particular core life value, but that each such thought must relate directly to that value.

Core life value: I want to live in a supportive helpful environment, surrounded by family and friends.

Goal: To encourage and sustain others.

Desired emotion and behavior: Empathy toward others. (Or, in other words, treating others the way I want to be treated will secure for me the kind of environment I want to live in.)

Promotive thought 1: People are of equal value to me.

Promotive thought 2: Listening to others enables me to better understand them, to learn from them and share in their lives.

Example 2

Core life value: I want to contribute to humanity and to have this contribution last even when I am gone.

Goal: Finish my book

Desired emotion and behavior: Endurance and perseverance

Promotive thought: Completing the book is like walking in a jungle trying to get to the other side. There are thousands of distractions and things that try to push me off the path. My aim is to continue to walk no matter how strong the distractions or how numerous the things occur to throw me off balance. If I get off the track I want to get back on as quickly as possible.

Example 3

The Frazer family came to counseling because the two children were arguing and fighting, and the parents were feeling a lack of support from each other in their efforts to quell the unrest. The parents thought that all of their family problems might be rooted in some sort of severe marital problem. After an initial discussion with the members of this family, we all agreed that their problems did not really require family therapy, but that they needed some help in functioning as a family unit.

The first step was to help the family develop a common value that they would all agree to, and that would help the family act optimally. One session on values clarification established a common family value. They all agreed that what they wanted was an atmosphere of warmth and mutual caring, where all family members could grow and develop without trampling individuality.

The next step was to set specific goals to help all family members reach their core family value. They developed the following:

1. Spend more time together as a family.
2. Reinforce each other's individuality.

To reach these goals they decided to practice the following specific behaviors.

1. Have a family meeting each week to review goals and to make plans for the next week.
2. Engage in one major family activity a week that all members would enjoy.
3. Each parent would spend 1½ hours a week alone with each child.
4. The parents would spend Friday morning together without the children where they would discuss common plans.

One of the most important aspects of the sessions with the Frazer family was to help the parents develop the most useful cognitions to reach their core family goal. Initially each parent felt the other was selfish and unwilling to work for a common purpose. But after the values clarification session, both realized that they wanted the same things, but had different ways of obtaining it. The husband felt he could best support the family by earning a lot of money, while the wife felt she had the total responsibility to care for the children. The promotive belief that helped them the most was the recognition that both were supporting the growth of the family, even though they had different ways of doing it.

Comment

The key to using CRT to promote optimal goal attainment is to be sure that the individual does not need remedial help first. If the individual has severe emotional problems, then therapy is called for and should be undertaken before helping the person reach life goals.

Further Information

Stephen Chapman, director of the Center for Human Resource Development, created the main concepts presented in this section.

Herzberg (1968) supports the importance of internal motivations on job attitude and performance, and pursing a core life value would be one of the greatest motivators.

A classic study gives evidence that the individual's cognitions (promotive thoughts) actually create positive physiological changes. The study shows that placebos produce endogenous opiate-like substance (endorphins) that reduce pain (Levine et al., 1978.)

Benson (1985) reviews some evidence about the positive physical messages elicited by changed perceptions.

Some popular works have emphasized similar concepts presented here. See Garfield (1984) and Samuels and Samuels (1975).

Appendix:
Summary of Research

Although written for therapists rather than theoreticians or researchers, this handbook makes frequent reference to research underpinnings of the therapy. Two sections in Chapter 7, "Experimental Treatment" and "Monitoring Client Progress," describe the single-case time-series design used to measure the effectiveness of all techniques. In addition, each section both refers the reader to some major research literature and also describes actual case examples where the therapeutic procedure were used.

But other protocols have been used to establish validity. From the first CRT group, inaugurated in 1973 with eight clients in a mental health center, pre and post tests were administered to ascertain whether therapy helped ameliorate the clients' symptoms. Since that occasion all clients (individual and group) have been given evaluative tests to demonstrate treatment efficacy.

The following tables summarize some of the data assembled over these years. They should be regarded as descriptive rather than inferential.

Group Treatment

The subjects of group therapy were clients who had volunteered for therapy at a large urban mental health center. The center's mental health intake workers made the initial diagnosis, rated the clients' characteristics on state forms in use at the time and referred clients to treatment modalities. The therapists running CRT groups were generally not involved in the initial evaluations. Client subjects were randomly assigned to group cognitive restructuring therapy by the intake workers.

Group treatment was semi-didactic and consisted of 10 sessions lasting two hours, meeting once a week. Each group had an average attendance of 17.5 clients. Two therapists would run the groups and there would be four facilitators (who were usually professionals who wished to learn the CRT approach). Presentations utilized slide projectors, overhead projectors, and a blackboard; homework sheets and a client manual— *Talk Sense to Yourself* (Mc Mullin, 1975)—were handed out to each client. The previous book (Casey & Mc Mullin, 1976) describes the treatment more completely.

Table 1
Subject Characteristics of Group Treatment

Variable	Percentage
Diagnostic Assessment (*DSM-II*)	
Depressive neurosis (300.4)	24%
Anxiety neurosis (300.0)	17%
Mixed anxiety and depression including adjustment reaction (307.3)	17%
Marital and social maladjustment (316.0–1)	10%
Antisocial personality (301.81)	10%
Alcohol addiction (303.2)	7%
Passive-aggressive personality (301.84)	5%
Inadequate personality (301.82)	5%
Psychotic (295- and 296-)	3%
Occupational maladjustment (316.2)	2%
Severity Level	
Mild	37%
Moderate	38%
Severe	25%
Length of Symptoms	
One month or less	3%
Two to six months	20%
Six months to one year	17%
More than one year	60%
Previous Therapy	
Gestalt, Cathartic, Experiential	19%
Psychodynamic	17%
Hospital in patient treatment	14%
None	12%
Marital	10%
Medication only	10%
Behavioral	7%
Transactional analysis	6%
Alcoholic	5%

(*continued*)

Table 1
(*Continued*)

Variable	Percentage
Educational Level	
Less than high school	3%
High school	43%
Some college	27%
College degree	20%
Professional degree	7%
Age	
21–30	20%
31–40	46%
41–50	27%
51 +	7%
Marital Status	
Married	50%
Single	10%
Divorced	40%
Sex	
Male	33%
Female	67%

Interpretation: The chart demonstrates that the CRT subjects were typical of the clients seen in a mid-western urban mental health center in the middle seventies. Clients were suffering from anxiety and depression at a moderate severity level; had their symptoms for more than a year; had extensive previous treatment; were in their thirties; one-half of them were single or divorced; and two-thirds were women.

Individual Treatment

Individual treatment averaged 15 sessions which lasted for an hour. The same techniques were used as in the groups but were less formally presented, and more individual attention to problem beliefs was possible. The therapist was the author, who also did intake analysis. All clients were seen as outpatients at the mental health center and the Counseling Research Institute.

Table 2
Subject Characteristics of Individual Treatment

Variable	Percentage
Diagnostic Assessment (*DSM-III*)	
Dysthymic Disorder (300.40)	27%
Anxiety Reaction	
Agoraphobia with panic (300.21)	12%
Social phobia (300.23)	8%
Dependent personality (301.60)	23%
Marital problems (V61.10)	23%
Social phobia (300.20)	9%
Antisocial personality disorder (301.70)	8%
Severity Level	
Mild	35%
Moderate	25%
Severe	40%
Length of Symptoms	
One month or less	0%
Six months or less	5%
Six months to one year	25%
One to two years	15%
Two to three years	15%
Three to four years	15%
Four or more years	25%
Previous Therapy	
Gestalt, cathartic, experiential	13%
Psychodynamic	44%
Hospital inpatient treatment	6%
None	4%
Marital	11%
Medication only	0%
Behavioral	19%
Transactional analysis	0%
Alcoholic	3%
Educational Level	
Less than high school	0%
High school	13%
Some college	33%
College degree	40%
Professional degree	14%
Age	
21–30	50%
31–40	31%
41–50	7%
51 +	12%
Marital Status	
Married	33%
Single	39%
Divorced	28%
Sex	
Male	33%
Female	67%

Interpretation: Compared to group subjects, individual clients were younger, higher educated, had their symptoms far longer, and had more often tried analytic therapy before CRT. Many of these differences can be attributed to the variance of clientele seeking therapy from a mental health center as opposed to a private agency.

Procedures

Subjects were given test before therapy and at various times after therapy was completed (identified in each of the following studies). Tests were either standard published tests—Minnesota Multiphasic Personality Inventory (MMPI), Spielberger's State Trait Anxiety Inventory (Spielberger, 1966), the Social Introversion scale from the MMPI, Zung Self-Rating Depression Scale (Zung, 1965), or three tests that were normalized locally: Wolpe's assertiveness questionnaire (Wolpe, 1969), the Mc Mullin irrational thought questionnaire and Wolpe's Fear Inventory (Wolpe, 1969). Other tests were used at different times for different populations.

Therapists included the author and other professional psychologists, psychiatric social workers, mental health workers, and psychiatric nurses (N = 24) who conducted the therapy at different times during the research period. The majority of the therapists had eight or more years experience in conducting therapy with the exception of study where beginning therapists were used. All therapists were trained by the author.

Study 1

One of the earliest studies evaluated the effectiveness of group CRT treatment (see Table 3).

Table 3
Mean Percentile Changes of CRT Group Treatment on Six Outcome Measures

	N	Pre	Post	t scores
State anxiety (Spielberger)	45	78.8	39.8	5.13**
Trait anxiety (Spielberger)	44	89.6	46.0	4.66**
Irrational thoughts (Mc Mullin)	44	91.1	44.3	10.09**
Assertiveness (Wolpe)	39	29.9	51.6	3.93**
Depression (Zung)	35	62.0	43.1	5.26**
Social introversion (MMPI Si scale)	17	74.3	44.3	3.03*

* = p < .10
** = p < .001

Note: Different N's because not all groups received all tests. Post-tests were administered immediately after completion of therapy.

Interpretation: Clients showed significant changes on all measures in the positive direction except for reduction of social introversion.

Study 2

Pre and post therapy means of later groups showed similar changes.

Table 4
Table of Pre and Most Means CRT Group Treatments

	N	X pre	S.D.	X post	S.D.	within t
State anxiety	54	49.65	12.33	36.44	11.94	6.289*
Trait anxiety	51	52.02	11.43	39.20	10.92	8.197*
Assertiveness	59	15.02	5.15	18.76	4.38	4.798*
Irrational thoughts	60	86.26	13.48	66.10	12.26	9.970*
Depression	36	44.78	9.13	36.11	9.33	6.620*
Social Introversion	19	17.84	5.70	12.63	6.63	5.940*

* = sig. < .001

Study 3

We discovered that clients approached or exceeded the general population scores on many scales after treatment.

Table 5
Comparison of Pre and Follow-up Test Scores with Normal Population Scores for Group CRT Treatments

	N	X pre	S.D.	X post	S.D.	% change
State anxiety	68	49.34	12.22	37.63	12.37	24%
(normal population)	m			40.01	7.85	
	f			39.39	8.62	
Trait anxiety	66	52.14	11.37	40.23	10.75	23%
(normal population)	m			38.07	8.20	
	f			38.22	8.20	
Assertiveness	73	15.10	5.08	18.52	4.39	23%
(normal population)	m			19.45	3.34	
	f			18.52	5.20	
Irrational thoughts	74	86.83	13.85	67.61	13.34	22%
(normal population)	m + f			68.00	11.00	

* = p < .001

Note: Follow-up tests were administered one and a half to three and a half months after the completion of therapy.

Interpretation: CRT clients showed significant, positive changes in all categories. Average follow-up scores compare favorably with the average score form a "normal" population.

Study 4

A study was conducted to determine whether clients had to practice their cognitive change *in vivo* to ensure that the cognitions would shift (see "Environmental Practice" in Chapter 6). Groups combining assertive training and CRT were formed and these groups were compared with CRT without the assertion component. Both types of groups met for ten weeks, with each session lasting two hours. About five groups of both types were compared.

Table 6

Comparison of CRT Without Assertion Component
and CRT With Assertion

	N	X pre	S.D.	X post	S.D.	% change
CRT Groups						
State anxiety	68	49.34	12.22	37.63	12.37	24%*
CRT + Assertion Groups						
State anxiety	40	42.73	10.40	32.63	7.56	24%*
CRT Groups						
Trait anxiety	66	52.14	11.37	40.23	10.75	23%*
CRT + Assertion Groups						
Trait anxiety	35	44.97	9.27	37.31	7.79	17%*
CRT Groups						
Assertiveness	73	15.10	5.08	18.52	4.39	23%*
CRT + Assertion Groups						
Assertiveness	49	14.36	4.58	21.12	3.97	47%*
CRT Groups						
Irrational beliefs	74	86.03	13.05	67.61	13.34	22%*
CRT + Assertion Groups						
Irrational beliefs	49	82.00	12.10	68.12	13.32	17%*

* = p < .001

Interpretation: Both modalities significantly increased clients' assertiveness. Clients in the combined groups showing a greater increase in assertion. There were no differences between the two groups in reduction of state anxiety, and only slight differences in irrational thoughts and trait anxiety (favoring the noncombined groups). Both groups significantly reduced clients' symptoms.

Study 5

CRT groups were also compared with standard Anxiety Management Training Groups (AMT). The AMT groups were generally smaller (N = 6), but lasted ten weeks. They consisted of teaching full relaxation procedures while clients imagined threatening scenes.

Table 7

Comparison of Outcome Measures of CRT Groups vs. Anxiety Management Training Groups

	N	X pre	S.D.	X post	S.D.	% change
CRT Groups						
State anxiety	68	49.34	12.22	37.63	12.37	24%***
AMT Groups						
State anxiety	23	46.13	12.49	42.22	12.86	8% #
CRT Groups						
Trait anxiety	66	52.14	11.37	40.23	10.75	23%***
AMT Groups						
Trait anxiety	21	50.52	12.80	48.71	13.73	3% 0

*** = $p < .001$
\# = $p < .10$
0 = no significant difference

Interpretation: CRT groups reduced clients' anxiety to a significantly greater extent than the AMT groups.

Study 6

An exploratory study was undertaken to determine whether beginning therapists could successfully run group CRT treatment. Beginning therapists were defined as those counselors who had one year or less therapeutic experience after completing their academic coursework. Groups run by novices were compared with those run by the author and other more experienced counselors (10 + years of experience).

Table 8
Expert-Run vs. Nonexpert-Run CRT Groups

	N	X pre	S.D.	X post	S.D.	significant diff. between groups
State anxiety						
Expert run	28	48.64	11.99	34.86	10.69	
Novice run	40	49.82	12.51	39.58	13.20	p<.20
Trait anxiety						
Expert run	26	53.77	11.96	37.39	8.45	
Novice run	40	51.08	11.00	42.08	11.75	p<.10
Irrational thoughts						
Expert run	30	88.33	15.17	64.87	11.83	not
Novice run	44	85.81	12.96	69.48	14.11	signif.
Assertiveness						
Expert run	30	15.23	5.42	19.47	3.91	
Novice run	43	15.00	4.88	17.86	4.63	p<.20

Interpretation: Novice-run groups tend to show less changes then expert-run groups, but CRT as a technique, whether employed by novices or expert therapists, significantly reduces client symptoms.

Study 7

Individual and group clients generated hierarchies of the ten most feared situations. They rated these scenes on a SUD's scale (0 to 100) after vividly imagining being in the situations. Before therapy the mean rating of all ten scenes was 50.5. After therapy their mean rating was 10.36.

Study 8

Individual and group clients were told to record the frequency, intensity, and duration of their target symptoms (fear, depression, anger, or guilt) for one week at three times: before therapy (baseline), immediately after therapy (post), and one year later (follow-up). The strength of their symptoms were judged by the clients on a SUD's scale (1–10). Table 9 is a copy of the card they used.

Table 9

Index Card Used to Record Client Target Emotion

Target Emotion: _____

DAY	STIMULI	STRENGTH 1–10	LENGTH hrs
Mon			
Tue			
Wed			
Thu			
Fri			
Sat			
Sun			

Table 10

Mean Frequency, Intensity and Duration of Target Emotion

	mean f for one week	mean intensity	mean duration
Before Therapy	7.98	7.17	4¾ hrs
After Therapy	6.90	2.84	1½ hrs
One Year Follow-up	2.46	3.89	1½ hrs

Interpretation: Although the frequency of the target emotion did not significantly decrease immediately after therapy, there was a major reduction in the intensity and duration of the emotion. For example, the typical client suffering from anxiety still felt scared seven times a week, but instead of rating the feeling moderate to severe (6.9 out of 10), it was now judged to be mild (2.8), and instead of its lasting four and three-quarters hours, it now lasted only an hour and a half. After a year, the frequency of the target symptom reduced greatly (two and a half times) while the duration remained the same. The intensity raised slightly, but this result may be misleading since over 50% of the clients reported one or no symptoms per week, while all clients reported above one symptom immediately after therapy.

Study 9

The dropout rate for a mental health center is notoriously high. The mental health center kept extensive records of all clients who had dropped out of treatment. A dropout was defined as any client who attended the first therapy session, but did not attend the last two sessions. The rate does not indicate treatment failure, since many clients may have missed the last two meetings because they moved, were ill, couldn't get a babysitter, etc. Dropouts can not be equated with therapeutic failure, for as a sample study revealed, 75% of the clients recorded as dropouts were very satisfied with the treatment they received, while only 25% were dissatisfied. Thus if the dropout rate listed below is 40%, then probably only 10% were dissatisfied.

Table 11 records the dropout rate of CRT group treatment vs. the other treatment modalities used in the mental health center.

Table 11

Treatment Dropout Rates for All Mental Health Center Clients

When dropouts occurred	% = dropouts/ total enrollment
Between initial phone call and intake appointment	28.6%
Between intake appointment and first therapy session	41.5%
Individual Therapy	18.0%
General Groups (Includes the following) Medication Clinic Crisus Group Young Adult Eclectic Group Marital Group Operant Marital Group Family Group Kids Group Parents Group	38.0%
Long Term Groups (Includes the following) Partial Care Transactional Analysis General Adult Mixed Adult Group Social Relearning Group	66.0%
CRT Groups	26.0%

Interpretation: The CRT groups had the lowest drop out rate of any groups in the mental health center. Only the individual therapy rate was lower.

Study 10

The effectiveness of individual CRT therapy was analyzed on several measures. Clients were seen for an average of 15 sessions in outpatient treatment. The author was the therapist in all cases. No clients dropped out of treatment. (N = 30).

Table 12

Mean Percentile Changes on Multiple Measures for Individual CRT Treatment

	N	Pre Test %	Follow-up %	% Changes
State anxiety	30	87.75	27.75	−54.00
Assertiveness	30	36.33	74.41	+38.08
Irrational thoughts	30	73.26	28.08	−45.20
Depression (Zung)	7	58.75 SDS	28.00 SDS	−30.75 SDS
MMPI (K added and converted to %iles from T scores)				
Hs	30	69.1	53.1	−16.0
D	30	94.3	67.0	−27.3
Hy	30	83.4	76.4	−07.0
Pd	30	94.2	86.6	−07.6*
Mf (female)	23	22.4	31.2	+08.8
Mf (male)	7	94.5	86.4	−08.1
Pa	30	89.2	73.2	−16.0
Pt	30	90.3	57.5	−32.8
Sc	30	89.2	71.2	−18.0
Ma	30	61.8	61.4	−00.4*
Si	30	76.7	33.7	−43.0

*The summation of the mean percentile scales for these scores can be somewhat misleading since client scoring extremely low on Pd or Ma would have benefited from higher scores while those with very high scores would have benefited with lower readings.

Note: Follow-up tests were administered from two months to one year after the termination of therapy.

Interpretation: All test data show changes in positive direction, even (in some cases) a year after termination. Most notable were decreases in state anxiety, irrational thinking, depression, generalized anxiety, and social introversion. In addition, there were appropriate increases in assertiveness and extroversion.

Study 11

Professional therapists must not only validate the effectiveness of their therapeutic procedures, but ensure that their clients have been satisfied with the treatment they received. A client satisfaction survey was conducted with 36

CRT individual and group clients randomly selected from a far larger pool of clients. The survey was administered either one year or a year and a half after termination or dropout. Mental health center personnel not connected with the counseling did the survey. The following continuums record the sum of their answers (X).

Table 13
One-Year Follow-up Survey on Client Satisfaction

1. The services I received in counseling were:

5	X	4	3	2	1
very satisfactory		satisfactory	neutral	unsatisfactory	very unsatisfactory

2. I feel the problem that I sought counseling for is:

5	X	4	3	2	1
much better		better	same	worse	much worse

3. Have you gone to another therapist since you finished CRT for the same or a similar problem?

	No	Yes
	95%	5%

4. Overall do you feel CRT was helpful in alieviating your problems?

5	X	4	3	2	1
very much		much	a little	not at all	damaging

5. Compared to other counseling you may have had, do you feel CRT was:

5	X	4	3	2	1
much better		better	the same	worse	much worse

6. Do you use the techniques you learned in CRT on a regular basis?

	Yes	No
	90%	10%

Interpretation: We tried to ensure the interviewers, who were not therapists, did nothing to lead the clients to favorable answers. They were instructed to say "The more honest your answers are, the better the counseling will become in this center. Please answer as candidly as you can. Your answers are confidential and the therapist you worked with will only see the group data and will not know your individual responses."

Study 12

Individual and group data were reviewed to determine if a prediction scale could be developed identifying which clients would be most likely to succeed in CRT therapy. The most successful clients were selected (based on post tests improvement, client satisfaction, reduction of target emotions and the opinion of the clients' therapists (N = 39)), and compared to a like group of the least successful clients (N = 31). Clients scoring between the two extremes (the large majority), were eliminated from further calculations.

By comparing the two groups on their pretests and intake data, the following prediction chart was developed. It was used later during initial intake sessions to determine whether clients should be referred to CRT therapy.

Table 14
Prediction Chart for Success in CRT Treatment

% ile	Trait Anxiety	Irrational Thoughts	Depression	Assertiveness	Client Defensiveness
100	−2	−2	−3	−2	−4
90	−1	0	−1	−1	−3
80	+3	+1	0	0	−2
70	+2	+1	+2	0	−1
60	+1	+2	+1	+1	0
50	+1	0	+1	+1	+1
40	0	0	+2	+2	+2
30	0	0	+1	−1	0
20	0	−1	0	−1	0
10	0	−2	0	−3	0
0					

Note: The percentile ratings are based on clinical norms rather than general population norms. Thus an anxiety rating of 73% means the client rated higher than 73% of other clients who had applied for treatment.

Interpretation: The chart is based on the following clinical and research observations. Very high levels of trait anxiety, irrational thoughts and depression were poor predictors of therapeutic success because clients were either too upset or too confused to concentrate on important aspects of the therapy. Slightly above average levels, however, served as motivators. Defensiveness was a major negative factor at any level, while assertion had a bipolar effect; too high levels often turned into aggression and oppositional behavior, while too low levels kept clients from being able to confront their own irrational thoughts. Low-medium levels on assertiveness were the best predictors.

Study 13

A study was done to determine whether a hypnotic component blended with CRT (see "Use of Altered States" in Chapter 6) would significantly help depressed clients more than CRT alone. Two institutions—Counseling Research Institute of Colorado and the Behavioral Services Center of New Jersey—conducted the experiment with a total of 78 psychiatrically depressed client. Dependent variables were MMPI-D (depression) scales, IP Index and MMPI-E (ego strength) scales.

Table 15
Means and Standard Deviations of Pre-Post Tests Comparing CRT With Hypnosis to CRT Without

	CRT Alone (Colorado)		CRT with Hypnosis (New Jersey)	
	X	SD	X	SD
IP Index Pretest	3.80	1.21	5.16	2.77
IP Index Posttest	2.37	1.45	2.68	1.75
MMPI-D Scale* Pretest	71.19	15.50	74.75	12.80
MMPI-D Scale* Posttest	56.25	13.27	57.27	13.51
MMPI-E Scale* Pretest	51.94	10.02	44.00	11.59
MMPI-E Scale* Posttest	62.00	9.42	52.73	11.67

*T Scores

Interpretation: Multivariate analysis of covariance indicated that both groups significantly ($p < .001$) reduced clients' depression and increased clients' ego strength. There was no evidence that the addition of hypnosis improved CRT.

Study 14

The final study was the most recently undertaken. MMPI's were given before counseling and on the average of four months following. I was the therapist and averaged 18 individual sessions per client. (The number of sessions increased by three because of the addition of the historical treatment component. See "Historical Perspectives" in Chapter 6.) (N = 16.)

Table 16
Pre and Follow-up MMPI Percentile Scores
Individual CRT

	pre	post	change
MMPI (K added and converted to %iles from T scores)			
Hs	76.9	53.5	−23.4
D	96.0	63.8	−32.2
Hy	89.9	78.8	−11.1
Pd	95.3	87.3	−08.0*
Mf (female)	20.4	30.8	+10.4
Mf (male)	97.4	87.5	−09.9
Pa	92.1	74.2	−17.9
Pt	93.6	64.3	−29.3
Sc	91.7	71.5	−20.2
Ma	53.6	56.8	+03.2*
Si	81.9	39.0	−42.9

*The summation of the mean percentile scales for these scores can be somewhat misleading since clients scoring extremely low on Pd or Ma would have benefited from higher scores while those with very high scores would have benefited with lower readings.

Interpretation: Most notable decreases were in anxiety, depression, and social introversion, which approached the population average.

Bibliography

Adler, A. (1964). *The individual psychology of Alfred Adler: A systematic presentation in selections from his writings*. New York: Harper & Row.

Anderson, J. (1980). *Cognitive psychology and its implications*. San Francisco: Freeman.

Angell, J. (1904). *Psychology: An introductory study of the structures and functions of human consciousness*. New York: Holt.

Arnold, M. (1960). *Emotion and personality* (Vols. 1–2). New York: Columbia University Press.

Aronson, E. (1980). *The social animal*. San Francisco: Freeman.

Ascher, L., & Cautela, J. (1972). Covert negative reinforcement: An experimental test. *Journal of Behavior Therapy and Experimental Psychiatry, 3*, 1–5.

Ascher, L., & Cautela, J. (1974). An experimental study of covert extinction. *Journal of Behavior Therapy and Experimental Psychiatry, 5*, 233–238.

Attneave, F. (1968). Triangles as ambiguous figures. *The American Journal of Psychology, 81*, 447–453.

Aubut, L., & Ladouceur, R. (1978). Modification of self-esteem by covert positive reinforcement. *Psychological Reports, 42*, 1305–1306.

Ayer, A. *Language, truth and logic*. (1952). New York: Dover Publications, Inc.

Azrin, N., Hutchinson, R., & Hake, D. (1967). Attack, avoidance, and escape reactions to aversive shock. *Journal of the Experimental Analysis of Behavior, 10*, 131–148.

Bajtelsmit, J., & Gershman, L. (1976). Covert positive reinforcement: Efficacy and conceptualization. *Journal of Behavior Therapy and Experimental Psychiatry, 7*, 207–212.

Bakal, D., & Kaganov, J. (1977). Muscle contraction and migraine headache: Psychophysiologic comparison. *Headache, 17*, 208–214.

Bakker, T. (1982). *Run to the roar*. Harrison, AR: New Leaf Press.

Bandler, R., & Grinder, J. (1979). *Frogs into princes*. Moab, UT: Real People Press.

Bandura, A. (1977a). *Social learning theory*. Englewood Cliffs, NJ: Prentice-Hall.

Bandura, A. (1977b). Self-efficacy: Toward a unifying theory of behavior change. *Psychological Review, 84*, 191–215.

Bandura, A. (1978). Reflections on self efficacy. In S. Rachman (Ed.), *Advances in behaviour research and therapy* (Vol. 1). Oxford: Pergamon Press.

Bandura, A. (1982). Self-efficacy mechanism in human agency. *American Psychologist, 37*, 122–147.

Bandura, A. (1984). Recycling misconceptions of perceived self-efficacy. *Cognitive Therapy and Research, 8*, 231–255.

Bandura, A., Adams, N., Hardy, A., & Howells, G. (1980). Tests of the generality of self-efficacy theory. *Cognitive Therapy and Research, 4,* 39–66.

Bandura, A., & Barab, P. (1973). Process governing disinhibitory effects through symbolic modeling. *Journal of Abnormal Psychology, 82,* 1–9.

Bandura, A., Reese, L., & Adams, N. (1982). Microanalysis of actions and fear arousal as a function of differential levels of perceived self-efficacy. *Journal of Personality and Social Psychology, 43,* 5–21.

Bandura, A., & Schunk, D. H. (1981). Cultivating competence, self-efficacy, and intrinsic interest through proximal self-motivation. *Journal of Personality and Social Psychology, 41,* 586–598.

Barlow, D., Agras, W., Leitenberg, H., Callahan, E., & Moore, R. (1972). The contribution of therapeutic instructions to covert sensitization. *Behavior Research and Therapy, 10,* 411–415.

Barlow, D., Leitenberg, H., & Agras, W. (1969). Experimental control of sexual deviation through manipulation of the noxious scene in covert sensitization. *Journal of Abnormal Psychology, 74,* 596–601.

Barlow, D., Reynolds, E., & Agras, W. (1973). Gender identity change in a transsexual. *Archives of General Psychiatry, 28,* 569–576.

Basmajian, J. (Ed.) (1979). *Biofeedback: Principles and practice for clinicians.* Baltimore, MD: Williams & Wilkins.

Beatty, J., & Legewie, H. (Eds.) (1977). *Biofeedback and behavior.* New York: Plenum Press.

Beck, A. (1967). *Depression: Clinical, experimental, and theoretical aspects.* New York: Hoeber.

Beck, A. (1975). *Depression: Causes and treatment.* Philadelphia, PA: University of Pennsylvania Press.

Beck, A. (1976). *Cognitive therapy and the emotional disorders.* New York: New American Library.

Beck, A., Rush, A., Shaw, B., & Emery, G. (1979). *Cognitive therapy of depression.* New York: Guilford Press.

Benson, H. (1975). *The relaxation response.* New York: Morrow.

Benson, H. (1985). *Beyond the relaxation response.* New York: Berkeley Books.

Berne, E. (1961). *Transactional analysis in psychotherapy: A systematic individual and social psychiatry.* New York: Grove Press.

Berne, E. (1964). *Games people play; The psychology of human relationships.* New York: Grove Press.

Beyerstein, B. (1985). The myth of alpha consciousness. *The Skeptical Inquirer, 10,* Fall.

Biederman, I., Glass, A., & Stacy, E. (1973). Searching for objects in real world scenes. *Journal of Experimental Psychology, 97,* 22–27.

Binder, J., & Smokler, I. (1980). Early memories: A technical aid to focusing in time-limited dynamic psychotherapy. *Psychotherapy: Theory, Research and Practice, 17,* 52–62.

Binder, V., Binder, A., & Rimland, B., (Eds.) (1976). *Modern therapies.* Englewood Cliffs, NJ: Prentice-Hall.

Bistline, J., Jaremko, M., & Sobleman, S. (1980). The relative contributions of covert reinforcement and cognitive restructuring to test anxiety reduction. *Journal of Clinical Psychology, 36,* 723–728.

Bloom, L., Houston, B., Holmes, D., & Burish, T. (1977). The effectiveness of attentional diversion and situation redefinition for reducing stress due to a noambiguous threat. *Journal of Research in Personality, 11,* 83–94.

Bond, L., & Rosen, J. (Eds.) (1980). *Primary prevention of psychopathology: Competence and coping during adulthood.* Hanover, NH: University Press of New England.

Boring, E. (1930). A new ambiguous figure. *American Journal of Psychology, 42,* 444.

Brehm, J. (1966). *A theory of psychological reactance.* New York: Academic Press.

Brehm, J., Stires, L., Sensenig, J., & Shaban, J. (1966). The attractiveness of an eliminated choice alternative. *Journal of Experimental Social Psychology, 2,* 301–313.

Brown, B. (1974). *New mind, new body.* New York: Harper & Row.

Brown, C. W., & Ghiselli, E. (1955). *Scientific method in psychology.* New York: McGraw-Hill.

Brownell, K., Hayes, S., & Barlow, D. (1977). Patterns of appropriate and deviant sexual arousal: The behavioral treatment of multiple sexual deviation. *Journal of Consulting and Clinical Psychology, 45,* 1144–1155.

Bruner, J., Goodnow, J., & Austin, G. (1956). *A study of thinking.* New York: Wiley.

Brunn, A., & Hedberg, A. (1974). Covert positive reinforcement as a treatment procedure for obesity. *Journal of Community Psychology, 2,* 117–119.

Bucher, B., & Fabricatore, J. (1970). Covert positive reinforcement as a treatment procedure for obesity. *Behavior Therapy, 1,* 382–385.

Buchwald, A. (1977). *I am not a crook.* New York: Fawcett.

Bugelski, B. (1970). Words and things and images. *American Psychologist, 25,* 1002–1012.

Bulfinch's mythology: The age of fable; the age of chivalry; legends of charlemagne. New York: Thomas Y. Crowell.

Cameron, N. (1963). *Personality development and psychopathology: A dynamic approach.* Boston: Houghton Mifflin Company.

Campbell, D., & Stanley, J. (1963). *Experimental and quasi-experimental designs for research.* Chicago: Rand-McNally.

Caplan, G. (1964). *Principles of preventative psychiatry.* New York: Basic Books.

Carr, H. (1925). *Psychology: A study of mental activity.* New York: Longman.

Casey, B., & Mc Mullin, R. (1976). *Cognitive restructuring therapy package.* Lakewood, CO: Counseling Research Institute.

Cautela, J. (1966). Treatment of compulsive behavior by covert sensitization. *Psychological Record, 16,* 33–41.

Cautela, J. (1967). Covert sensitization. *Psychological Record, 20,* 459–468.

Cautela, J. (1970). Covert reinforcement. *Behavior Therapy, 1,* 33–50.

Cautela, J. (1971a). Covert extinction. *Behavior Therapy, 2,* 192–200.

Cautela, J. (1971b). Covert conditioning. In A. Jacobs, & L. Sachs (Eds.). *The psychology of private events: Perspectives on covert reponse systems.* New York: Academic Press.

Cautela, J., & Wisocki, P. (1969). The use of imagery in the modification of attitudes toward the elderly: A preliminary report. *The Journal of Psychology, 73,* 193–199.

Chapman, A., & Foot, H. (Eds.) (1976). *Humour and laughter: Theory, research and applications.* London: Wiley.

Chapman, A., & Foot, H. (Eds.) (1977). *It's a funny thing, humour.* Oxford: Pergamon Press.

Clark, J., & Jackson, J. (1983). *Hypnosis and behavior therapy.* New York: Springer.

Coan, R. (1974). *The optimal personality.* New York: Columbia University Press.

Coleman, P. (1982). A comparison of coverant self-management techniques. *Dissertation Abstracts International, 42,* 3396B.

Cook, T., & Campbell, D. (1979). *Quasi-experimentation: Design and analysis issues for field settings.* Chicago: Rand-McNally.

Cooke, S. (1975). An experimental study of the effectiveness of coverant conditioning in alleviating neurotic depression in college students. *Dissertation Abstracts International, 35,* 3574.

Corsini, R. (1957). *Methods of group psychotherapy.* New York: McGraw-Hill.

Corsini, R. (Ed.) (1981). *Handbook of innovative psychotherapies.* New York: Wiley.

Corsini, R., & Ozaki, B. (Eds.) (1984). *Encyclopedia of psychology* (Vols. 1–4). New York: Wiley.

Crasilneck, H., & Hall, J. (1975). *Clinical hypnosis: Principles and applications.* New York: Grune & Stratton.

Crooke, W. (1926). *Religion and folklore of Northern India.* Oxford: Oxford University Press.

Dallenbach, K. (1951). A puzzle-picture with a new principle of concealment. *American Journal of Psychology, 64,* 431–433.

Dalyell, J. (1835). *The darker superstitions of Scotland.* Glasgow.

Davis, K., & Moore, W. (1945). Some principles of stratification. *American Sociological Review, 10,* 242–249.

Dennis, R., & Moldof, E. (Eds.) (1977). *Becoming human* (Vols. 1–2). Chicago: The Great Books Foundation.

Dennis, R., & Moldof, E. (Eds.) (1978). *The individual and society* (Vols. 1–2). Chicago: The Great Books Foundation.

de Villiers, P. (1974). The law of effect and avoidance: A quantitative relation between response rate and shock frequency reduction. *Journal of the Experimental Analysis of Behavior, 21*, 223–235.

Dewey, J. (1886). *Psychology.* New York: Harper.

Dilts, R., Grinder, J., Bandler, R., DeLozier, J., & Cameron-Bandler, L. (1979). *Neuro-linguistic programming I.* Cupertino, CA: Meta.

Duhl, B. (1983). *From the inside out and other metaphors.* New York: Brunner/Mazel.

Dunlap, K. (1932). *Habits: Their making and unmaking.* New York: Liveright.

D'Zurilla, T., & Goldfried, M. (1971). Problem solving and behavior modification. *Journal of Abnormal Psychology, 78,* 107–126.

Ellis, A. (1962). *Reason and emotion in psychotherapy.* New York: Lyle Stuart.

Ellis, A. (1971). *Growth through reason: Verbatim cases in rational-emotive therapy.* Hollywood, CA: Wilshire Books.

Ellis, A. (1973). *Humanistic psychotherapy: The rational-emotive approach.* New York: Julian Press.

Ellis, A. (1974). *Techniques for Disputing Irrational beliefs (DIB'S).* New York: Institute for Rational Living, Inc.

Ellis, A. (1975). The rational-emotive approach to sex therapy. *Counseling Psychologist, 5,* 14–22.

Ellis, A. (1985). *Overcoming resistance: Rational-emotive therapy with difficult clients.* New York: Springer.

Ellis, A. (1986). Personal communication.

Ellis, A., & Abrahms, E. (1978). *Brief psychotherapy in medical and health practice.* New York: Springer.

Ellis, A., & Bernard, M. (1985). *Clinical applications in rational emotive therapy.* New York: Springer.

Ellis, A., & Grieger, R. (Eds.) (1977). *Handbook of rational-emotive therapy.* New York: Springer.

Ellis, A., & Harper, R. (1961). *A guide to rational living.* Hollywood, CA: Wilshire Books.

Ellis, A., & Harper, R. (1971). *A guide to successful marriage.* Hollywood, CA: Wilshire Books.

Ellis, A., & Harper, R. (1975). *A new guide to rational living* (2nd ed.). Hollywood, CA: Wilshire Books.

Ellis, A., & Whiteley, J. (Eds.) (1979). *Theoretical and empirical foundations of rational-emotive therapy.* Monterey, CA: Brooks/Cole.

Ellis, A., Wolfe, J. & Moseley, S. (1966). *How to raise an emotionally healthy, happy child.* Hollywood, CA: Wilshire Books.

Ellis, W. (1939). *A source book of gestalt psychology.* New York: Harcourt, Brace and Co.

Engum, E., Miller, F., & Meredith, R. (1980). An analysis of three parameters of covert positive reinforcement. *Journal of Clinical Psychology, 36,* 301–309.

Epstein, L., & Hersen, M. (1974). A multiple baseline analysis of coverant control. *Journal of Behavior Therapy and Experimental Psychiatry, 5,* 7–12.

Erickson, M. (1982). *My voice will go with you: The teaching tales of Milton H. Erickson M.D.* (S. Rosen, ed.). New York: Norton.

Erickson, M., & Rossi, E. (1981). *Experiencing hypnosis: Therapeutic approaches to altered states.* New York: Irvington.

Escher, M. (1971). *The graphic work of M.C. Escher.* New York: Ballantine Books.

Fagan, M., & Shepherd, I. (1970). *Gestalt therapy now.* Palo Alto, CA: Science & Behavior Books.

Farrelley, F., & Brandsma, J. (1974). *Provocative therapy.* Cupertino, CA: Meta.

Fearnside, W., & Holther, W. (1959). *Fallacy: The counterfeit of argument.* Englewood Cliffs, NJ: Prentice-Hall.

Feder, B., & Ronall, R. (Eds.) (1980). *Beyond the hot seat: Gestalt approaches to group*. New York: Brunner/Mazel.

Feirstein, B. (1983). *Real men don't eat quiche*. New York: Pocket Books.

Fernberger, S. (1950). An early example of a "hidden-figure" picture. *American Journal of Psychology, 63*, 448–449.

Festinger, L. (1957). *A theory of cognitive dissonance*. Stanford, CA: Stanford University Press.

Festinger, L. (1964). *Conflict, decision, and dissonance*. Stanford, CA: Stanford University Press.

Fishbein, M., & Ajzen, I. (1975). *Belief, attitude, intention, and behavior*. Reading, MA: Addison-Wesley.

Fisher, G. (1968). Ambiguity of form: Old and new. *Perception and Psychophysics, 3*, 189–192.

Flannery, R. (1972). A laboratory analogue of two covert reinforcement procedures. *Journal of Behavior Therapy & Experimental Psychiatry, 3*, 171–177.

Flemming, D. (1967). Attitude: The history of a concept. *Perspectives in American history, 1*, 287–365.

Flew, A. (1952). *Logic and language* (First series). Oxford: Basil Blackwell.

Flew, A. (1953). *Logic and language* (Second series). Oxford: Basil Blackwell.

Flew, A. (1956). *Essays in conceptual analysis*. London: Macmillan and Company, Ltd.

Foree, D., & Lo Lordo, V. (1975). Stimulus-reinforcer interactions in the pigeon: The role of electric shock and the avoidance contingency. *Journal of Experimental Psychology: Animal Behavior Processes, 104*, 39–46.

Frankel, A. (1970). Treatment of a multisymptomatic phobic by a self-directed, self-reinforced imagery technique: A case study. *Journal of Abnormal Psychology, 76*, 496–499.

Frankl, V. (1959). *From deathcamp to existentialism*. Boston: Beacon Press.

Frankl, V. (1960). Paradoxical intention: A logotherapeutic technique. *American Journal of Psychotherapy, 14*, 520–535.

Frankl, V. (1972). The feeling of meaninglessness: A challenge to psychotherapy. *American Journal of Psychoanalysis, 32*, 85–89.

Frankl, V. (1977). *The doctor and the soul: From psychotherapy to logotherapy*. New York: Knopf.

Frankl, V. (1978). *Psychotherapy and existentialism*. New York: Simon & Schuster.

Frankl, V. (1980). *Man's search for meaning: An introduction to logotherapy*. New York: Simon & Schuster.

Freud, S. (1933). New introductory lectures on psychoanalysis. *The Standard Edition of the Complete Psychological Works* (Vol. xxii), J Strachey (Trans. and Ed.). New York: Norton.

Freund, P. (1965). *Myths of creation*. New York: Washington Square Press.

Fromm, E. (1973). *The anatomy of human destructiveness*. New York. Holt, Rinehart & Winston.

Garcia, J., & Koelling, R. (1966). The relation of cue to consequence in avoidance learning. *Psychonomic Science, 4*, 123 124.

Gardner, M. (1957). *Fads and fallacies*. New York: Dover Publications.

Gardner, M. (1978). *Aha! Insight*. New York: Scientific American, Inc.

Gardner, M. (1981). *Science: Good, bad and bogus*. Buffalo, NY: Prometheus Books.

Gardner, R. (1971). A test of coverant control therapy to reduce cigarette smoking: A comparative study of the effectiveness of two different strategies with a direct test of the effectiveness of contingency management. *Dissertation Abstracts International, 32*, 3001B.

Garfield, C. (1984). *Peak performance*. New York: Warner Books.

Gendlin, E. (1962). *Experiencing and the creation of meaning: A philosophical and psychological approach to the subjective*. New York: The Free Press of Glencoe.

Gendlin, E. (1964). A theory of personality change. In P. Worchel & D. Byrne (Eds.), *Personality change*. New York: Wiley.

Gendlin, E. (1967). Focusing ability in psychotherapy, personality and creativity. In J. Shlien (Ed.), *Research in psychotherapy*, Vol. 3. Washington, DC: American Psychological Association.

Gendlin, E. (1969). Focusing. *Psychotherapy: Theory, Research, and Practice, 6*, 4–15.

Gendlin, E. (1981). *Focusing*. New York: Everest House.

Gendlin, E., Beebe, J., Cassues, J., Klein, M., & Oberlander, M. (1968). Focusing ability in psychotherapy, personality and creativity. *Research in Psychotherapy, 3,* 217–241.

Genovese, F. (1979). The use of covert operants (coverants) as the commitment training component in a self-control of study habits paradigm for high school students. *Dissertation Abstracts International, 40,* 1332B.

Gibson, J. (1950). *The perception of the visual world.* Boston: Houghton Mifflin.

Gibson, J. (1966). *The senses considered as perceptual systems.* Boston: Houghton Mifflin.

Giles, T. (1979). Some principles of intervention in the absence of therapeutic alliance. *Transactional Analysis Journal, 9,* 294–296.

Goffman, E. (1961). *Encounters.* Indianapolis: Bobbs Merrill.

Goffman, E. (1971). *The presentation of self in everyday life.* New York: Basic Books.

Goffman, E. (1980). *Forms of talk.* Philadelphia: University of Pennsylvania Press.

Goldfried, M. (1971). Systematic desensitization as training in self-control. *Journal of Consulting and Clinical Psychology, 37,* 228–234.

Goldfried, M. (1977). Behavioral assessment in perspective. In J. Cone and R. Hawkins (Eds.), *Behavioral assessment.* New York: Brunner/Mazel, 1977.

Goleman, D. (1977). *The varieties of the meditative experience.* New York: Dutton.

Gordon, D. (1978). *Therapeutic metaphors.* Cupertino, CA: Meta.

Gotestam, K., & Melin, L. (1974). Covert extinction of amphetamine addiction. *Behavior Therapy, 5,* 90–92.

Gottschaldt, K. (1939). Gestalt factors and repetition. In W. Ellis (Ed.), *A source book of gestalt psychology.* New York: Harcourt, Brace and Co.

Greenberg, I. (Ed.) (1974). *Psychodrama: theory and therapy.* New York: Behavioral Publications.

Greenburg, D. (1964). *How to be a Jewish mother.* Los Angeles: Price/Stern/Sloan, Inc.

Greeno, J. (1978). Notes on problem-solving abilities. In W. Estes (Ed.), *Handbook of learning and cognitive processes.* Hillsdale, NJ: Lawrence Erlbaum Associates.

Greenstone, J., & Leviton, S. (1979). *The crisis intervener's handbook,* (Vol. 1.). Dallas: Crisis Management Workshops.

Greenstone, J., & Leviton, S. (1980). *The crisis intervener's handbook* (Vol. 2.). Dallas: Rothschild.

Greenstone, J., & Leviton, S. (1983). *Crisis intervention: A handbook for interveners.* Dubuque, IA: Kendall-Hunt.

Gregory, R. (1977). *Eye and brain: The psychology of seeing.* New York: World University Library.

Grinder, J., & Bandler, R. (1975). *The structure of magic, I.* Palo Alto: Science and Behavior Books.

Grinder, J., & Bandler, R. (1982). *Reframing: Neuro-linguistic programming and the transformation of meaning.* Moab, UT: Real People Press.

Grof, S. (1975). *Realms of the human unconscious: Observations from LSD research.* New York: Viking Press.

Grof, S. (1980). Realms of the human unconscious: Observations from LSD research. In R. Walsh & F. Vaughan (Eds.), *Beyond ego: Transpersonal dimensions in psychology.* Los Angeles: Tarcher.

Guidano, V., & Liotti, G. (1983). *Cognitive processes and emotional disorders: A structural approach to psychotherapy.* New York: Guilford Press.

Haley, J. (1973). *Uncommon therapy.* New York: Norton.

Hartmann, G. (1935). *Gestalt psychology.* New York: Ronald.

Hauck, P. (1967). *The rational management of children.* New York: Libra Publishers.

Havens, R. (Ed.) (1985). *The wisdom of Milton H. Erickson.* New York: Irvington.

Hayes, J. (1982). *Problem solving techniques.* Philadelphia: Franklin Institute Press.

Hayes, S., Brownell, K., & Barlow, D. (1978). The use of self-administered covert sensitization in the treatment of exhibitionism and sadism. *Behavior Therapy, 9,* 283–289.

Haygood, R., & Bourne, L. (1965). Attribute and rule learning aspects of conceptual behavior. *Psychological Review, 72,* 175–195.

Herrnstein, R. (1969). Method and theory in the study of avoidance. *Psychological Review, 76,* 49–69.

Herzberg, F. (1968). One more time: How do you motivate employees? *Harvard Business Review, 46,* 53–62.

Hilgard, E. (1977). *Divided consciousness: Multiple controls in human thought and action.* New York: Wiley.

Hineline, P., & Rachlin, H. (1969). Escape and avoidance of shock by pigeons pecking a key. *Journal of the Experimental Analysis of Behavior, 12,* 533–538.

Hobson, A., & McCarley, R. (1977). The brain as a dream state generator: An activation-synthesis hypothesis of the dream process. *American Journal of Psychiatry, 134*:12, 1335–1348.

Holmes, D. (1968). Dimensions of projection. *Psychological Bulletin, 69,* 248–268.

Holmes, D. (1972). Aggression, displacement, and guilt. *Journal of Personality and Social Psychology, 22,* 296–301.

Holmes, D. (1974). Investigations of repression: Differential recall of material experimentally or naturally associated with ego threat. *Psychological Bulletin, 81,* 632–653.

Holmes, D. (1978). Projection as a defense mechanism. *Psychological Bulletin, 85,* 677–688.

Holmes, D. (1981). Existence of classical projection and the stress-reducing function of attributive projection: A reply to Sherwood. *Psychological Bulletin, 90,* 460–466.

Homme, L. (1965). Perspectives in psychology: XXIV control of coverants, the operants of the mind. *The Psychological Record, 15,* 501–511.

Hopfield, J. (1982, Sept.). Brain, computer, and memory. *Engineering & Science.*

Horan, J., Baker, S., Hoffman, A., & Shute, R. (1975). Weight loss through variations in the coverant control paradigm. *Journal of Consulting and Clinical Psychology, 43,* 68–72.

Horan, J., & Johnson, R. (1971). Coverant conditioning through a self-management application of the premack principle: Its effect on weight reduction. *Journal of Behavior Therapy and Experimental Psychiatry, 2,* 243–249.

Houston, B. (1973). Viability of coping strategies, denial, and response to stress. *Journal of Personality, 41,* 50–58.

Houston, B., & Holmes, D. (1970). Effectiveness of avoidant thinking and reappraisal in coping with threat involving temporal uncertainty. *Journal of Personality and Social Psychology, 30,* 382–388.

Hovland, C., & Janis, I. (1959). *Personality and persuasibility.* New Haven: Yale University Press.

Hull, C. (1943). *Principles of behavior.* New York: Appleton-Century-Crofts.

Ingram, R., & Goldstein, B. (1978). Role of expectancy factors in behavioral self-control therapies: An experimental inquiry. *Psychological Reports, 42,* 535–542.

Jacobson, E. (1974). *Progressive relaxation.* Chicago: University of Chicago Press.

Jacobson, N., & Margolin, G. (1979). *Marital therapy: Strategies based on social learning and behavioral exchange principles.* New York: Brunner/Mazel.

Jahoda, M. (1958). *Current concepts of positive mental health.* New York: Basic Books.

James, W. (1890). *The principles of psychology.* New York: Holt.

James, W. (1907). *Pragmatism: A new name for some old ways of thinking.* New York: Longman Green.

Joffe, J., & Albee, G. (1981). *Prevention through political action and social change. The primacy prevention of psychopathology* (Vol. 5). Hanover, NH: University Press of New England.

Johnson, D. (1972). *A systematic introduction to the psychology of thinking.* New York: Harper and Row.

Jourard, S., & Landsman, T. (1980). *Healthy personality: An approach from the viewpoint of humanistic psychology.* New York: Macmillan.

Kahneman, D., et al. (1982). *Judgment under uncertainty: Heuristics and biases.* Cambridge, England: Cambridge University Press.

Kamin, L. (1956). Effects of termination of the CS and avoidance of the US on avoidance learning. *Journal of Comparative and Physiological Psychology, 49,* 420–424.

Kamin, L., Brimer, C., & Black, A. (1963). Conditioned suppression as a monitor of fear of the CS in the course of avoidance training. *Journal of Comparative and Physiological Psychology, 56,* 497–501.

Kazdin, A. (1980). *Research design in clinical psychology.* New York: Harper & Row.

Kazdin, A. (1982). *Single-case research designs: Methods for clinical and applied settings.* New York: Oxford University Press.

Kazdin, A., & Smith, G. (1979). Covert conditioning: A review and evaluation. *Advances in Behavior Research and Therapy, 2,* 57–98.

Kelleher, R. (1966). Conditioned reinforcement in second order schedules. *Journal of the Experimental Analysis of Behavior, 9,* 475–485.

Kent, M., & Rolf, J. (Eds.) (1979). *Primary prevention of psychopathology: Promoting social competence in children* (Vol. 4.). Hanover, NH: University Press of New England.

Keutzer, C. (1968). Behavior modification of smoking: The experimental investigation of diverse techniques. *Behavior Research and Therapy, 6,* 137–157.

Klinger, E. (1980). Therapy and the flow of thought. In J. Shorr, G. Sobel, P. Robin, & J. Connella (Eds.), *Imagery: Its many dimensions and applications.* New York: Plenum.

Koffka, K. (1935). *Principles of gestalt psychology.* New York: Harcourt, Brace.

Köhler, W. (1947). *Gestalt psychology: An introduction to the new concepts in modern psychology.* New York: Liveright.

Korchin, S. (1976). *Modern clinical psychology.* New York: Basic Books.

Kosslyn, S. (1980). *Image and mind.* Cambridge, MA: Harvard University Press.

Kosslyn, S., & Pomerantz, J. (1977). Imagery, propositions, and the form of internal representations. *Cognitive Psychology, 9,* 52–76.

Kratochwill, T. (Ed.) (1978). *Single-subject research: Strategies for evaluating change.* New York: Academic Press.

Kroger, W., & Fezler, W. (1976). *Hypnosis and behavior modification: Imagery conditioning.* Philadelphia: Lippincott.

Krop, H., Calhoon, B., & Verrier, R. (1971). Modification of the "self-concept" of emotionally disturbed children by covert reinforcement. *Behavior Therapy, 2,* 201–204.

Kuhn, T. (1977). Objectivity, value judgment, and theory choice. In T. Kuhn (Ed.), *The essential tension: Selected studies in scientific tradition and change.* Chicago: University of Chicago Press.

Ladouceur, R. (1974). An experimental test of the learning paradigm of covert positive reinforcement in deconditioning anxiety. *Journal of Behavior Therapy and Experimental Psychiatry, 5,* 3–6.

Ladouceur, R. (1977). Rationale of covert reinforcement: Additional evidence. *Psychological Reports, 41,* 547–550.

Lakoff, G. (1985). *Women, fire and dangerous things.* Chicago: University of Chicago Press.

Lankton, S., & Lankton, C. (1983). *The answer within: A clinical framework of Ericksonian hypnotherapy.* New York: Brunner/Mazel.

Lazarus, A. (1971). *Behavior therapy and beyond.* New York: McGraw-Hill.

Lazarus, A. (1977). *In the mind's eye: The power of imagery for personal enrichment.* New York: Rawson.

Lazarus, A. (1981). *The practice of multimodal therapy.* New York: McGraw-Hill.

Lazarus, A. (1982). *Personal enrichment through imagery* (cassette recording). New York: BMA Audio Cassettes/Guilford Publications.

Lazarus, A., Kanner, A., & Folkman, S. (1980). Emotions: A cognitive phenomenological analysis. In R. Plutchik & H. Kellerman (Eds.), *Theory of emotions.* New York: Academic Press.

Leuner, H. (1969). Guided affective imagery (GAI): A method of intensive psychotherapy. *American Journal of Psychotherapy, 23,* 4–22.

Levine, J., Gordon, N., & Fields, H. (1978). The mechanism of placebo analgesia. *The Lancet, 2,* 654–657.

Lin, N. (1973). *The study of human communication.* New York: Bobbs-Merrill.

Lindemann, E. (1944). Symptomatology and management of acute grief. *American Journal of Psychiatry, 101*, 141–148.

Litchtenstein, E., & Keutzer, C. (1969). Experimental investigation of diverse techniques to modify smoking: A follow-up report. *Behaviour Research and Therapy, 7*, 139–140.

Loudis, L. (1979). Personal communication.

Low, A. (1952). *Mental health through will-training.* Boston: Christopher.

Macdonald, M. (1954). *Philosphy and analysis.* Oxford: Basil Blackwell.

Mach, E. (1959). *The analysis of sensations and the relation of the physical to the psychical.* Mineola, NY: Dover Publications.

Mac Phail, E. (1968). Avoidance responding in pigeons. *Journal of the Experimental Analysis of Behavior, 11*, 625–632.

Mahoney, M. (1971). The self-management of covert behavior: A case study. *Behavior Therapy, 2*, 575–578.

Mahoney, M. (1979). Cognitive skills and athletic performance. In Kendall, P. & Hollon, S. *Cognitive-behavioral interventions: Theory, research, and procedures.* New York: Academic Press.

Mahoney, M., & Arnkoff, D. (1978). Cognitive and self-control therapies. In S. Garfield & A. Bergin (Eds.), *Handbook of psychotherapy and behavior change.* New York: Wiley.

Mahoney, M., & Thoresen, C. (1974). *Self-control: Power to the person.* Monterey, CA: Brooks-Cole.

Mahoney, M., Thoresen, C., & Danaher, B. (1972). Covert behavior modification: An experimental analogue. *Journal of Behavior Therapy and Experimental Psychiatry, 3*, 7–14.

Mana: A South Pacific Journal of Language and Literature. (1980 to present). Suva, Fiji: South Pacific Creative Arts Society, Mana Publications.

Marshall, W., Gauthier, J., & Gordon, A. (1979). The current status of flooding therapy. In M. Hersen, R. Eisler, & P. Miller (Eds.), *Progress in behavior modification, 7*, New York: Academic Press.

Martin, L. (1914). Ueber die Abhangigkeit visueller Vorstellungsbilder vom Denken, *Zsch. f. Psychol., 70*, 214.

Maslow, A. (1971). *The farther reaches of human nature.* New York: Viking.

Maultsby, M. (1971). Rational emotive imagery. *Rational Living, 6*, 22–26.

Maultsby, M. (1976). *Help yourself to happiness through rational self-counseling.* Boston: Esplanade Institute for Rational Living.

Maultsby, M. (1984). *Rational behavior therapy.* Englewood Cliffs, NJ: Prentice-Hall.

Maultsby, M., & Ellis, A. (1974). *Techniques for using rational-emotive imagery (REI).* New York: Institute for Rational Living.

Mc Mullin, R. (1972). Effects of counselor focusing on client self-experiencing under low attitudinal conditions. *Journal of Counseling Psychology, 19:4*, 282–285.

Mc Mullin, R., Assafi, I., & Chapman, S. (1978). *Straight talk to parents: Cognitive restructuring for families.* Brookvale, Australia: F. S. Symes (dis.), and Lakewood, CO: Counseling Research Institute.

Mc Mullin, R., & Casey, B., (1975). *Talk sense to yourself: A guide to cognitive restructuring therapy.* New York: Institute for Rational Emotive Therapy (dis.), and Lakewood, CO: Counseling Research Institute.

Mc Mullin, R., Casey, B., & Navas, J. (trans.) (1975). *Hablese con sentido a si mismo.* San Juan, Puerto Rico: Centro Caribeno de Estudios Postgraduados.

Mc Mullin, R., & Giles, T. (1981). *Cognitive-behavior therapy: A restructuring approach.* New York: Grune & Stratton.

Meichenbaum, D. (1975). A self-instructional approach to stress management: A proposal for stress inoculation training. In I. Sarason & C. Spielberger (Eds.), *Stress and anxiety* (Vol. 2.). New York: Wiley.

Meichenbaum, D. (1977). *Cognitive-behavior modification: An integrative approach.* New York: Plenum.

Miller, L. (1962). *Counseling leads*. Boulder, CO: Pruett Press.
Miller, N., & Campbell, D. (1959). Recency and primacy in persuasion as a function of the timing of speeches and measurement. *Journal of Abnormal and Social Psychology, 59*, 1–9.
Moreno, J., & Zeleny, L. (1958). Role theory and sociodrama. In J. Roucek (Ed.). *Contemporary sociology*. New York: Philosophical Library.
Mosak, H. (1958). Early recollections as a projective technique. *Journal of Projective Techniques, 22*, 302–311.
Mosak, H. (1969). Early recollections: Evaluation of some recent research. *Journal of Individual Psychology, 25*, 56–63.
Mowrer, O., & Lamoreaux, R. (1946). Fear as an intervening variable in avoidance conditioning. *Journal of Comparative Psychology, 369*, 29–50.
Munitz, M. (1981). *Contemporary analytic philosophy*. New York: Macmillan.
Nagel, E. (Ed.) (1950). *John Stuart Mill's philosophy of scientific method*. New York: Hafner.
Nelson, R., Hay, L., & Hay, W. (1977). Cue versus consequence functions of high-probability behaviors in the modification of self-monitored study coverants and study time. *Psychological Record, 3*, 589–599.
Newell, A., & Simon, H. (1972). *Human problem solving*. Englewood Cliffs, NJ: Prentice-Hall.
Newhall, S. (1952). Hidden cow puzzle-picture. *American Journal of Psychology, 65*, 110.
Nisbett, R. & Ross, L. (1980). *Human inference: Strategies and shortcomings of social judgment*. Englewood Cliffs, NJ: Prentice-Hall.
Olson, H. (1979). *Early recollections: Their use in diagnosis and psychotherapy*. Springfield, IL: Thomas.
Orne, M., & Paskewitz, D. (1973). Visual effects on alpha feedback training. *Science, 181*, 361–363.
Palmer, S. (1978). The effects of contextual scenes on the identification of objects. *Memory and Cognition, 3*, 519–526.
Pavlov, I. (1928). *Lectures on conditioned reflexes*. New York: International Publishers.
Pavlov, I. (1960). *Conditioned reflexes*. New York: Dover.
Perls, F. (1969a). *Gestalt therapy verbatim*. Lafayette, CA: Real People Press.
Perls, F. (1969b). *In and out the garbage pail*. Lafayette, CA: Real People Press.
Perls, F. (1973). *The Gestalt approach*. Palo Alto, CA: Science & Behavior Books.
Petty, R., & Cacioppo, J. (1981). *Attitudes and persuasion: Classic and contemporary approaches*. Dubuque, IA: Brown.
Piaget, J. (1954). *The construction of reality in the child*. New York: Basic Books.
Piaget, J. (1963). *The origins of intelligence in children*. New York: Norton.
Piaget, J. (1970). *Structuralism*. New York: Harper & Row.
Piaget, J. (1973). *The child and reality: Problems of genetic psychology*. New York: Grossman.
Plotkin, W. (1979). The alpha experience revisited: Biofeedback in the transformation of psychological state. *Psychological Bulletin, 86*, 1132–1148.
Plutchik, R. (1980). *Emotions: A psychoevolutionary synthesis*. New York: Harper & Row.
Polster, E., & Polster, M. (1973). *Gestalt therapy integrated: Contours of theory and practice*. New York: Brunner/Mazel.
Pomerantz, J., Soyer, L., & Stoever, R. (1977). Perception of wholes and their component parts: Some configural superiority effects. *Journal of Experimental Psychology: Human Perception and Performance, 3*, 422–435.
Popper, K. (1959). *The logic of scientific discovery*. New York: Basic Books.
Porter, P. (1954). Another puzzle-picture. *American Journal of Psychology, 67*, 550–551.
Premack, D. (1965). Reinforcement theory. In D. Levine (Ed.) *Nebraska Symposium on Motivation*. Lincoln, NB: University of Nebraska Press.
Progoff, I. (1977). *At a journal workshop*. New York: Dialogue House Library.
Quine, W., & Ullian, J. (1978). *The web of belief* (2nd Ed.). New York: Random House.
Rabkin, J. (1974). Public attitudes toward mental illness. A review of the literature. *Schizophrenia Bulletin, 10*, 9–33.

Radnitzky, G. (1970). *Contemporary schools of metascience*. Goteborg, Sweden: Akademi forlaget.

Randi, J. (1982). *Flim-flam: Psychics, ESP, unicorns and other delusions*. Buffalo, NY: Prometheus Books.

Ray, W., & Ravizza, R. (1981). *Methods toward a science of behavior and experience*. Belmont, CA: Wadsworth.

Reed, A. (1978). *Aboriginal myths: Tales of the dreamtime*. Frenchs Forest, NSW, Australia: A. H. Reed.

Rescorla, R. (1967). Pavlovian conditioning and its proper control procedures. *Psychological Review, 74*, 71–80.

Rescorla, R. (1969). Pavlovian conditioned inhibition. *Psychological Bulletin, 72*, 77–94.

Reynolds, D. (1976). *Morita psychotherapy*. Berkeley, CA: University of California Press.

Reynolds, D. (1981). Morita therapy. In R. Corsini (Ed.), *Handbook of innovative psychotherapies*. New York: Wiley.

Richardson, A. (1967). Mental practice: A review and discussion (Part 1 & 2). *Research Quarterly, 38*, 95–107; 263–273.

Richardson, A. (1969). *Mental imagery*. New York: Springer.

Richie, B. (1951). Can reinforcement theory account for avoidance? *Psychological Review, 58*, 382–386.

Rizley, R., & Rescorla, R. (1972). Associations in higher order conditioning and sensory preconditioning. *Journal of Comparative and Physiological Psychology, 81*, 1–11.

Rogers, C. R. (1951). *Client-centered therapy: Its current practice, implications, and therapy*. Boston: Houghton Mifflin.

Rogers, C. R. (1959). A theory of therapy, personality, and interpersonal relationships, as developed in the client-centered framework. In S. Koch (Ed.), *Psychology: A study of a science: Vol. 3. Formulations of the person and the social context*. New York: McGraw-Hill.

Rokeach, M. (1964). *The three Christs of Ypsilanti: A psychological study*. New York: Knopf.

Rokeach, M. (1968). *Beliefs, attitudes, and values*. San Francisco: Jossey-Bass.

Rokeach, M. (1973). *The nature of human values*. New York: Free Press/Macmillan.

Rokeach, M. (Ed.) (1979). *Understanding human values: Individual and societal*. New York: Free Press/Macmillan.

Rosenbluh, E. (1974). *Techniques of crisis intervention*. New York: Behavioral Science Services.

Rossi, E. (Ed.) (1980). *The collected papers of Milton H. Erickson on hypnosis* (Vols. 1–4). New York: Irvington.

Rossi, E., & Ryan, M. (Eds.) (1985). *Life reframing in hypnosis: The seminars, workshops and lectures of Milton H. Erickson*. New York: Irvington.

Ryle, G. (1957). *The revolution in philosophy*. London: Macmillan & Co.

Samuels, M., & Samuels, N. (1975). *Seeing with the mind's eye: The history, techniques and uses of visualization*. New York: Random House.

Sargant, W. (1959). *Battle for the Mind: A physiology of conversion and brainwashing*. New York: Harper and Row.

Schachter, S. (1966). The interaction of cognitive and physiological determinants in emotional state. In C. D. Spielberger (Ed.), *Anxiety and behavior*. New York: Academic Press.

Schachter, S., & Singer, J. (1962). Cognitive, social and physiological determinants of emotional state. *Psychological Review, 69*, 379–399.

Schwartz, B. (1978). *Psychology of learning and behavior*. New York: Norton.

Schwartz, G. (1973). Biofeedback as therapy: Some theoretical and practical issues. *American Psychologist, 28*, 666–673.

Scott, D., & Leonard, C. (1978). Modification of pain threshold by the covert reinforcement procedure and a cognitive strategy. *The Psychological Record, 28*, 49–57.

Scott, D., & Rosenstiel, A. (1975). Covert positive reinforcement studies: Review, critique and guidelines. *Psychotherapy: Theory, Research and Practice, 12*, 374–384.

Seligman, M., & Johnson, J. (1973). A cognitive theory of avoidance learning. In F. Mc Guigan & D. Lumsden (Eds.). *Contemporary approaches to conditioning and learning.* Washington, DC: Winston-Wiley.

Sheikh, A. (Ed.) (1983a). *Imagery: Current theory, research and application.* New York: Wiley.

Sheikh, A. (Ed.) (1983b). *Imagination and healing.* New York: Baywood.

Sheikh, A., & Shaffer, J. (Eds.) (1979). *The potential of fantasy and imagination.* New York: Brandon House.

Shorr, J. (1972). *Psycho-imagination therapy: The integration of phenomenology and imagination.* New York: Intercontinental.

Shorr, J. (1974). *Psychotherapy through imagery.* New York: Intercontinental.

Sidman, M. (1953). Two temporal parameters of the maintenance of avoidance behavior in the white rat. *Journal of Comparative and Physiological Psychology, 46,* 253–261.

Sidman, M. (1966). Avoidance behavior. In W. Honig (Ed.), *Operant behavior: Areas of research and application.* New York: Appleton-Century-Crofts.

Simkins, L. (1982). Biofeedback: Clinically valid or oversold. *Psychological Record, 32,* 3–17.

Simon, J. (1978). *Basic research methods in social science.* New York: Random House.

Singer, J. (1974). *Imagery and daydream methods in psychotherapy and behavior modification.* New York: Academic Press.

Singer, J. (1976). *Daydreaming and fantasy.* London: Allen & Unwin.

Singer, J., & Pope, K. (Eds.) (1978). *The power of human imagination.* New York: Plenum.

Skinner, B. F. (1953). *Science and human behavior.* New York: Free Press.

Skinner, B. F. (1972). *Beyond freedom and dignity.* New York: Bantam Books.

Skinner, B. F. (1974). *About behaviorism.* New York: Knopf.

Smith, M., Bruner, J., & White, R. (1956). *Opinions and personality.* New York: Wiley.

Sober-Ain, L., & Kidd, R. (1984). Fostering changes in self-blame: Belief about causality. *Cognitive Theory and Research, 8,* 121–138.

Sokolov, E. (1963). *Perception and the conditioned reflex.* New York: Macmillan.

Solomon, R. (1964). Punishment. *American Psychologist, 19,* 239–253.

Solomon, R., & Wynne, L. (1954). Traumatic avoidance learning: The principles of anxiety conservation and partial irreversibility. *Psychological Review, 61,* 353–385.

Solomon, R., & Wynne, L. (1956). Traumatic avoidance learning: Acquisition in normal dogs. *Psychological Monographs, 67,* Whole No. 354.

Spielberger, C. (Ed.) (1966). *Anxiety and behavior.* New York: Academic Press.

Sprague de Camp, L. (1983). *The fringe of the unknown.* Buffalo, NY: Prometheus Books.

Stampfl, T., & Levis, D. (1967). Essentials of implosive therapy: A learning theory-based psychodynamic behavioral therapy. *Journal of Abnormal Psychology, 72,* 496–503.

Stearn, J. (1976). *The power of alpha thinking: Miracle of the mind.* New York: Signet.

Steiner, S., & Dince, W. (1981). Biofeedback efficacy studies: A critique of critiques. *Biofeedback and Self-Regulation, 6,* 275–287.

Stubbs, D., & Cohen, S. (1972). Second order schedules: Comparison of different procedures for scheduling paired and non-paired brief stimuli. *Journal of the Experimental Analysis of Behavior, 18,* 403–413.

Suinn, R., & Richardson, F. (1971). Anxiety management training: A nonspecific behavior therapy program for anxiety control. *Behavior Therapy, 2,* 498–510.

Suppe, F. (Ed.) (1974). *The structure of scientific theories.* Urbana, IL: University of Illinois Press.

Szasz, T. (1960). The myth of mental illness. *American Psychologist, 15,* 113–118.

Szasz, T. (1970a). *Ideology and insanity: Essays on the psychiatric dehumanization of man.* Garden City, NY: Anchor Books.

Szasz, T. (1970b). *The manufacture of madness.* New York: Harper & Row.

Szasz, T. (1978). *The myth of psychotherapy.* Garden City, NY: Doubleday.

Taylor, F. (1949). *A short history of science and scientific thought.* New York: Norton.

Taylor, J. (1962). *The behavioral basis of perception.* New Haven: Yale University Press.

Taylor, S., & Fiske, S. (1975). Point of view: Perception of causality. *Journal of Personality and Social Psychology, 32,* 439–445.

Teasdale, J. (1978). Self-efficacy: Toward a unifying theory of behavior change? *Advances in Behaviour Research and Therapy, 1*, 211–215.

Todd, F. (1972). Coverant control of self-evaluative responses in the treatment of depression: A new use for an old principle. *Behavior Therapy, 3*, 91–94.

Torrey, E. (1972). *The mind game: Witchdoctors and psychiatrists.* New York: Bantam Books.

Toulmin, S. (1967). The evolutionary development of natural science. *American Scientist, 55*, 456–471.

Trabasso, T., & Bower, G. (1968). *Attention in learning: Theory and research.* New York: Wiley.

Turkat, I., & Adams, H. (1982). Covert positive reinforcement and pain modification: A test of efficacy and theory. *Journal of Psychosomatic Research, 26*, 191–201.

Turner, L., & Solomon, R. (1962). Human traumatic avoidance learning: Theory and experiments on the operant-respondent distinction and failure to learn. *Psychological Monographs, 76*, Whole No. 559.

Ullmann, L., & Krasner, L. (1975). *A psychological approach to abnormal behavior.* Englewood Cliffs, NJ: Prentice-Hall.

Urmson, J. (1950). *Philosophical analysis.* Oxford: Clarendon Press.

Vasta, R. (1975). Coverant control of self-evaluations through temporal cueing. *Journal of Behavior Therapy and Experimental Psychiatry, 7*, 35–37.

Vinacke, W. (1974). *The psychology of thinking.* New York: McGraw-Hill.

Warner, W. et al. (1949). *Social class in America.* Chicago: Science Research Associates.

Watkins, J. (1976). Ego states and the problem of responsibility: A psychological analysis of the Patty Hearst case. *Journal of Psychiatry and Law,* Winter, 471–489.

Watkins, J. (1978). Ego states and the problem of responsibility II. The case of Patricia W. *Journal of Psychiatry and Law,* Winter, 519–535.

Watkins, J., & Watkins, H. (1980). Ego states and hidden observers. *Journal of Altered States of Consciousness, 5*, 3–18.

Watkins, J., & Watkins, H. (1981). Ego-state therapy. In R. Corsini (Ed.), *Handbook of innovative psychotherapies.* New York: Wiley.

Watson, P., & Johnson-Laird, P. (1972). *Psychology of reasoning: Structure and content.* Cambridge, MA: Harvard University Press.

Watzlawick, P., Bavelas, J. B., & Jackson, D. (1967). *Pragmatics of human communication.* New York: Norton.

Weeks, G., & L'Abate, L. (1982). *Paradoxical psychotherapy: Theory and practice with individuals, couples and families.* New York: Brunner/Mazel.

Weimer, W. (1979). *Notes on the methodology of scientific research.* Hillsdale, NJ: Erlbaum.

Weiss, J., Glazer, H., Pohorecky, L., Brick, J., & Miller, N. (1975). Effects of chronic exposure to stressors on avoidance-escape behavior and on brain norepinephrine. *Psychosomatic Medicine, 37*, 522–534.

Wertheimer, M. (1945). *Productive thinking.* New York: Harper & Row.

Wever, E. (1927). Figure and ground in the visual perception of form. *American Journal of Psychology, 38*, 196.

White, J., & Fadiman, J. (1976). *Relax.* New York: Confucian Press.

Wicklund, R., & Brehm, J. (1976). *Perspectives on cognitive dissonance.* Hillsdale, NJ: Erlbaum.

Wilson, J. *Thinking with concepts.* (1963). London: Cambridge University Press.

Wilson, J. (1967). *Language and the pursuit of truth.* London: Cambridge University Press.

Wilson, P., Goldin, J., & Charbonneau-Powis, M. (1983). Comparative efficacy of behavioral and cognitive treatments of depression. *Cognitive Therapy and Research, 7*, 111–124.

Wittgenstein, L. (1953). *Philosophical investigations.* Oxford: Basil Blackwell.

Wolpe, J. (1958). *Psychotherapy by reciprocal inhibition.* Stanford, CA: Stanford University Press.

Wolpe, J. (1969). *The practice of behavior therapy.* New York: Pergamon Press.

Wolpe, J. (1973). *The practice of behavior therapy* (2nd ed.). New York: Pergamon Press.

Wolpe, J. (1978). Cognition and causation in human behavior and its therapy. *American Psychologist, 33*, 437–446.

Wolpe, J. (1981a). The dichotomy between classical conditioned and cognitively learned anxiety. *Behavioral Therapy and Experimental Psychiatry, 12,* 35–42.

Wolpe, J. (1981b). Perception as a function of conditioning. *The Pavlovian Journal of Biological Science, 16,* 70–76.

Wolpe, J., Lande, S., McNally, R., & Schotte, D. (1985). Differentiation between classically conditioned and cognitively based neurotic fears: Two pilot studies. *Journal of Behavioral Therapy and Experimental Psychiatry, 16,* 287–293.

Wolpe, J., & Lazarus, A. (1967). *Behavior therapy techniques.* London: Pergamon Press.

Wolpe, J., Salter, A., & Reyna, L. (Eds.) (1964). *The conditioning therapies: The challenge in psychotherapy.* New York: Holt, Rinehart & Winston.

Woodworth, R. (1958). *Dynamics of behavior.* New York: Holt, Rinehart & Winston.

Young, J. (1954). *The Prose Edda of Snorri Sturluson: Tales from Norse Mythology.* Berkeley, CA: University of California Press.

Zaffuto, A. (1974). *Alpha-genics: How to use your brain waves to improve your life.* New York: Warner Paperback.

Zimmer-Hart, C., & Rescorla, R. (1974). Extinction of Pavlovian conditioned inhibition. *Journal of Comparative and Physiological Psychology, 86,* 837–845.

Zung, W. (1965). A self-rating depression scale. *Archives of General Psychiatry, 12,* 63–70.

Author Index

Subject Index

349